KEY TO THE BIBLE - III

Record of the Fulfillment: The New Testament

KEY TO THE

BIBLE

WILFRID J. HARRINGTON, OP

VOL. III

RECORD OF THE FULFILLMENT
THE NEW TESTAMENT

ALBA · HOUSE   alba house   NEW · YORK

SOCIETY OF ST. PAUL, 2187 VICTORY BLVD., STATEN ISLAND, NEW YORK 10314

Nihil Obstat:
Rev. Bernard O'Riley, O.P.
Rev. Augustine Rock, O.P.
Censores Deputati

Imprimatur:
† Most Rev. John P. Cody, D.D.
Archbishop of Chicago
May 25, 1966

The Nihil Obstat and Imprimatur are
a declaration that a book or pamphlet is considered
to be free from doctrinal or moral error. It it is not implied
that those who have granted the Nihil Obstat and
Imprimatur agree with the contents,
opinions or statements expressed.

Designed, printed and bound in the United States of
America by the Fathers and Brothers of the
Society of St. Paul, 2187 Victory Boulevard,
Staten Island, New York 10314, as part of their
communications apostolate.

Library of Congress Catalogue Number 74-27606

© Copyright 1975 by the Society of St. Paul

ABBREVIATIONS USED FOR
THE BOOKS OF THE BIBLE

Gn.: Genesis
Ex.: Exodus
Lv.: Leviticus
Nm.: Numbers
Dt.: Deuteronomy
Jos.: Joshua
Jgs.: Judges
Ru.: Ruth
1,2 Sm.: 1,2 Samuel
1,2 Kgs.: 1,2 Kings
1,2 Chr.: 1,2 Chronicles
Ez.: Ezra
Neh.: Nehemiah
Tb.: Tobit
Jdt.: Judith
Est.: Esther
Jb.: Job
Ps.: Psalms
Prv.: Proverbs
Qoh.: Qoheleth (Ecclesiastes)
Ct.: Canticle of Canticles

Wis.: Wisdom
Sir.: Sirach (Ecclesiasticus)
Is.: Isaiah
Jer.: Jeremiah
Lam.: Lamentations
Bar.: Baruch
Ezek.: Ezekiel
Dn.: Daniel
Hos.: Hosea
Jl.: Joel
Am.: Amos
Obad.: Obadiah
Jon.: Jonah
Mi.: Micah
Na.: Nahum
Hb.: Habakkuk
Zeph.: Zephaniah
Hag.: Haggai
Zech.: Zechariah
Mal.: Malachi
1,2 Mc.: 1,2 Maccabees
Mt.: Matthew

Mk.: Mark
Lk.: Luke
Jn.: John
Acts: Acts
Rm.: Romans
1,2 Cor.: 1,2 Corinthians
Gal.: Galatians
Eph.: Ephesians
Phil.: Philippians
Col.: Colossians
1,2 Thes.: 1,2 Thessalonians
1,2 Tm.: 1,2 Timothy
Ti.: Titus
Phm.: Philemon
Heb.: Hebrews
Jas.: James
1,2 Pt.: 1,2 Peter
1,2,3 Jn.: 1,2,3 John
Jude: Jude
Ap.: Apocalypse (Revelation)

WORKS OF REFERENCE

Atlante Biblico: Atlante Storico della Bibbia
BJ: *Bible de Jérusalem*
(BJ): A separate fascicle of the *Bible de Jérusalem*
BW: *Bibeltheologisches Wörterbuch*
CBQ: *Catholic Biblical Quarterly*
DBS: *Dictionnaire de la Bible* (Supplement)
IB: *Introduction à la Bible*
PBC, *Instr.: Instruction on the Historical Truth of the Gospels*
PCB: *Peake's Commentary on the Bible*
VTB: *Vocabulaire de Théologie Biblique*

\Preface

I have taken advantage of this abridged, paperback edition of my larger Introduction to the Bible (1) to revise the work and bring it up to date. Because the *Record of the Fulfillment* is so much longer than either of the other two volumes, it had to be drastically worked over in order to meet the paperback requirements. But this has proved a distinct advantage. It has demanded such a radical re-writing that *Key to the Bible* III is, in large measure, a new book. Thus, Chapters I to IV, the formation of the synoptic gospels and the introductions to the individual gospels, are entirely new — and so is the treatment of the Fourth Gospel. Elsewhere, there has been a change of stance. So, for instance, I have opted firmly for the non-Pauline authorship not only of the Pastorals but of Ephesians and Colossians also. These and other fresh options follow on an increasing familiarity with the New Testament over the past decade.

One has been led to believe that the earlier three-volume Introduction has served a useful purpose. It is to be hoped that, in its revised and more accessible format, it will continue to be of help.

W. J. H.

[1] *Record of Revelation: The Bible; Record of the Promise: The Old Testament; Record of the Fulfillment: The New Testament,* (Chicago: The Priory Press 1965, 1966).

Table of Contents

Abbreviations Used in this Book   v

Preface   vii

ONE: *The Formation of the Synoptic Gospels*   1
  1. THE WORDS AND WORKS OF JESUS   2
    1) *The Sayings*   2
    2) *The Narratives*   3
  2. THE APOSTOLIC TRADITION   5
    1) *The Preaching*   5
    2) *Form Criticism of the Synoptic Gospels*   6
    3) *Pre-Synoptic Literary Units*   10
    4) *Fact and Interpretation in the Tradition* 12
    5) *Demythologising the Gospel*   14
  3. THE EVANGELISTS   15
    1) *Redaction Criticism*   15
    2) *The Synoptic Problem*   21

TWO: *The Gospel of St. Mark*   27
  1. AUTHORSHIP, DESTINATION AND DATE   27
  2. THE STYLE OF ST. MARK   28
  3. THE PLAN   31
  4. THE PURPOSE OF MARK   32
  5. THE MESSIANIC SECRET   35

THREE: *The Gospel of St. Matthew*   37
  1. AUTHORSHIP, DESTINATION AND DATE   37

2. THE PLAN   38
3. THE STRUCTURE   38
4. MATTHEW'S MILIEU   40
5. THE COMMUNITY OR CHURCH IN MATTHEW   41
6. THE SERMON ON THE MOUNT   43
7. THE GREAT COMMISSION, Mt. 28:18-20   45

FOUR: *The Gospel of St. Luke*   48
1. AUTHORSHIP, DESTINATION AND DATE   48
2. THE PLAN   48
3. THE MINISTER OF THE WORD   49
4. THE PURPOSE   51
5. THE MESSAGE OF LUKE   52

FIVE: *The Acts of the Apostles*   58
1. AUTHOR AND DATE   58
2. PURPOSE AND SCOPE   58
3. THE PLAN   61
4. THE SOURCES   61
5. HISTORICITY   64
6. THE DOCTRINE   65
1) *The Kerygma*   65
2) *The Holy Spirit*   68

SIX: *The Pauline Epistles*   71
1. THE NEW TESTAMENT EPISTLES   71
1) *Letter and Epistle*   71
2) *The Language and Style of Paul* 72
2. 1,2 THESSALONIANS   72
1) *1 Thessalonians*   72
2) *2 Thessalonians*   74
3. THE MAJOR EPISTLES   76
1) *Galatians*   76
2) *1 Corinthians*   79
3) *2 Corinthians*   84
4) *Romans*   89
4. THE CAPTIVITY EPISTLES   99
1) *Philippians*   99
2) *Philemon*   102
3) *Colossians*   104
4) *Ephesians*   109

5. THE PASTORAL EPISTLES   118
   1) *Common Characteristics of the Epistles*   118
   2) *Authorship*   119
   3) *1 Timothy*   122
   4) *Titus*   125
   5) *2 Timothy*   127
6. HEBREWS   130
   1) *Authorship, Origin and Date*   131
   2) *Structure*   132

SEVEN: *The Catholic Epistles*   139
  1. JAMES   139
  2. 1 PETER   143
  3. JUDE   149
  4. 2 PETER   151

EIGHT: *The Johannine Writings*   154
  1. THE FOURTH GOSPEL   154
  2. THE THREE EPISTLES OF JOHN   169
  3. THE APOCALYPSE OF JOHN   175

Bibliography   193

ONE

The Formation of the Synoptic Gospels

THE WORDS AND WORKS OF JESUS

THE APOSTOLIC TRADITION

THE EVANGELISTS

The Greek word for gospel is *euangelion* whence the Latin *evangelium*. (Our 'gospel' is from the early English god spell – 'good news'). In the early Church *euangelion* signified, not a book dealing with the words and works of Christ, but the good news of messianic salvation, the message of salvation. The word was already found in the Septuagint (the Greek translation of the Old Testament). For example, we read in Isaiah: 'How beautiful upon the muntains are the feet of him who brings *good tidings* of good' (52:7). The word is the same, but in the Old Testament the good news is of future salvation, whereas the gospel is the good news of a salvation that has been achieved.

The gospel may be the good news that Jesus himself preached (e.g. Mk. 1:15; Mt. 11:5; Lk. 4:18), or it may be the apostolic preaching about Christ and the salvation that is found in him (e.g. Acts 5:42; Rm. 1:1 f.). Both come to the same thing because it is a question of Christ and of his works and words. We should note that it is a matter of *preaching*, not of the written word, and Christian ministers are called 'evangelists' (Acts 21:8; Eph. 4:11; 2 Tm. 4:5). We must realize that in the New Testament itself the word 'gospel' means the preaching of Christ and the 'evangelist' is a preacher.

But words often change and, frequently, a word that has quite a broad meaning acquires a precise, technical sense. So it was that in the second century A.D. *euangelion* came to designate the written account of the life and teaching of our Lord, and it was at the same time, too, that the authors of the gospels were named evangelists. We should keep in mind that our very special meaning for 'gospel' and 'evangelist' is not quite that of the New Testament it-self.

When, in the second century, *euangelion* came to mean the written gospel, these writings were still regarded as filling a missionary need and served the same purpose as the spoken word: to waken and strengthen faith (cf. Jn. 20:31). Similarly, the evangelist too is a preacher and behind him stands the whole teaching authority of a living Church; of that Church he is a spokesman. His work is kerygmatic: to herald Jesus Christ, his works and words. And because this is so, an evangelist has, necessarily, a care for the historical and a certain biographical interest: the good news that he preaches is all concerned with a person who lived and moved among men and taught them, a man who died at a given time and place and rose from the dead. A gospel, after all, is a recital of the historical narrative of the suffering, death and resurrection of Jesus Christ, prefaced by an account of his ministry. The person of Jesus, seen and interpreted in the light of the resurrection, is the very center of salvation history and the presentation of his words and deeds, seen in that light, is necessarily theological. The evangelist does not intend to write a biography of Jesus; his intention remains, fundamentally, kerygmatic and theological.

1. THE WORDS AND WORKS OF JESUS
1) The Sayings

We shall see that the gospels are not biographies of Jesus. They do purport, however, to present his teaching, and they do put before us certain stages and events of his earthly career. But, if we are to attain to the words and deeds of Jesus, we can do so only by working backward from the third and second stages of the tradition (the apostolic tradition and the evangelists). For the moment we simply presuppose the work of the evangelists and of the apostles and indicate how we may reach the very kernel of the gospel.

When we turn to the sayings of Jesus we find that, on the whole, the same sayings are recorded by the three evangelists — although Mark has notably less of them than Matthew and Luke. But rarely do we find that any saying occurs in identical form in any two gospels. Generally, the differences are insignificant, but frequently enough they are more far-reaching. We must see the problem in proper perspective. It would be unreasonable to have the words of Jesus always recorded in just the same way. Indeed, it is impossible to have any of his sayings *exactly* as they came from his lips, for the good reason that he spoke Aramaic while our gospels are written in Greek. However, an Aramaic substratum is sometimes discernible and can be a valuable pointer to sayings of his that still retain the form and cast he gave them. But, even here, one must reckon with the possibility that the Aramaic coloring may reflect the earliest preaching tradition.

A fascinating field of study is provided by the parables. It would seem that, in the parables we indeed have hope not only of discerning the authentic teaching of Jesus but of hearing that teaching in his own words. In fact, however, the parables have been worked over by the Church and the evangelists. The circumstances of the early Church were not those of the ministry of Jesus, hence, if his parables were to suit later needs, they had to be adapted to some extent. Although the parables have two settings – their original setting in the ministry of Jesus and their later setting in the life of the primitive Church – (and even, it may be, a further setting in the special place given them by an evangelist) we can, in some cases, recover the original form with some measure of success.[1]

2) The Narratives

We learn from the early chapters of Acts that, after Pentecost, Peter was the principal witness of Christ. In his preaching he traced the main lines of the life of Jesus, always after a definite pattern (cf. Acts 1:21 f.; 2:22-24; 10:37-41). This order is basic to the first three gospels: (1) Preparation and Baptism in Judaea; (2) Ministry in Galilee; (3) Journey from Galilee to Jerusalem; (4) in Jerusalem: Passion, Death and Resurrection. It is important to realize from the beginning that in the process of presenting the good news according to this fourfold division and within this framework the life and ministry of Jesus have been considerably simplified. The original plan was devised with missionary interests in view. There had to be agreement on the selection of the events of Jesus' life – and of points from his teaching; an inevitable result was simplification, schematization.

We find that in the presentation of our Savior's life, the death and resurrection are central and that this event – for it is one event – was first considered. But on a broader view it was seen that Jesus was preceded by one who had come to prepare the way for him – something had to be said about John the Baptist; he was the first herald of the good news, but when Christ appeared his task was finished. The baptism of Jesus, not only in fact but very conveniently too, brought him and John together and dramatically introduced the public ministry. This is indeed the beginning of the gospel.[2] After this Jesus carried out his mission in Galilee. Accounts of his journeys and of his miracles were grouped with records of typical preaching of his, and even with isolated sayings. The journey of Jesus to his death is all the more dramatic when it is presented as his only entry into Jerusalem.

The framework is conventional but there is no falsification of historical facts because, in this respect, the intention is not primarily historical. We are not being presented with a biography of Jesus and there is no real interest in chronology. Yet the plan does correspond to a historical and theological reality. Jesus was at first very favorably received by the people but his humble and spiritual messianism disappointed their hopes and enthusiasm waned. Already, too, the bitter opposition of the ruling classes was evident. Then he withdrew from Galilee to devote himself to the formation of a little group of faithful disciples. He won their unconditional support after Peter's confession of faith at Caesarea Philippi. That was a decisive turning-point: the road now led to Jerusalem. In the face of mounting opposition the drama of the Passion was played out, but seeming failure was turned into triumph by the Resurrection.

This is the reality, at once theological and historical, which lies behind the plan of the apostolic preaching. It is not concerned with giving a detailed biography of Jesus – this is a modern preoccupation. But it has given the essentials, there is no falsification. From the first three gospels it would appear that the public ministry lasted less than a year; that is no more than an impression – it is nowhere asserted that such was the case. One might come to that conclusion because one did not understand the outlook and intentions of those who drew up the tradition. The object was to show the ministry of the Messiah from its favorable beginning in Galilee to the tragedy in Jerusalem, and the gospels do bring home to us that historical purpose.

For us moderns the time element, a detailed chronology, would be an obvious part of any such presentation. But does the duration of the ministry of Jesus really affect the purpose and the achievement of that ministry? Is not the question of chronology very secondary indeed? The converts came to believe that the Son of

God had lived and preached among men, had suffered, died, and risen from the dead. That is all they needed to know.

2. THE APOSTOLIC TRADITION

1) The Preaching

From among his disciples Jesus chose a special group as his collaborators. He had a double purpose in view in choosing these apostles as we learn from Mk. 3:14. First, he wanted them 'to be with him' in order to form them and fill them with his spirit. But his principal purpose was to make them associates in the founding of the kingdom of God on earth. In order to prepare them for this task he sent them to preach, to drive out devils and to heal the sick (Mt. 10:1). He sent them out just as the Father had sent him (10:5-40). In the eyes of men they were representatives of Jesus and, as it were, extensions of his person: whoever received them received him; whoever despised them despised him (10:40).

After the Resurrection Christ commissioned them to preach the gospel throughout the world (28:19) – that is why they had been witnesses of Jesus (Acts 1:8). They must proclaim before men the events from the baptism of John to the ascension of Jesus, and especially the crowning event of the resurrection (1:22; 2:32). On the road to Damascus Paul, too, was made a witness of the risen Christ (22:15; 26:16). The apostles, then, were witnesses of Christ, men, especially, who had seen the risen Lord. But they must attest, too, that the risen Christ is the same Jesus with whom they had lived (1:8-21). This sets the twelve apart even from the great apostle of the Gentiles and gives their apostolate a unique character (Lk. 24:48). They were witnesses filled with the Spirit (Lk. 24:49; Acts 1:8) – inspired witnesses. They formed a group, the foundation stones of the new Israel (Ap. 21:14). The Church was organized around these 'pillars' (Gal. 2:9), the chosen Spirit-enlightened witnesses and hearers of the Incarnate Word. These are the moulders of the gospel tradition.

And yet, the disciples had not expected the resurrection and we must realize that during the lifetime of Jesus they were not conscious of the full implication of his claims; the gospels do not hide from us that they did not understand him. Certain texts of John are apposite here. After the cleansing of the Temple, and again after the entry into Jerusalem on Palm Sunday, the evangelist remarks that the disciples did not grasp the full meaning of these events until after the resurrection (Jn. 2:22; 12:16; cf. 13:7; Lk.

9:45; 18:34). Similarly, Jesus had, not once but many times, fore-told his resurrection, and yet when Peter and the beloved disciple come to the empty tomb we are faced with the blunt statement: 'for as yet they did not know the scripture, that he must rise from the dead' (Jn. 20:9). They had not yet received the Holy Spirit, and it was he alone who would help them to understand the teaching of Christ (14:26; 16:13). The Easter experience was the basis of their faith. But when they did receive the Paraclete, that faith which was theirs after the resurrection, and especially after Pentecost, was centred on the life and words of their master. It is by men filled with this faith, and certain of the great truth that Jesus the Messiah is the Son of God, that the gospel tradition was formed. But this fuller perception was not found during the ministry of Jesus.

After the resurrection it was just not possible for the apostles to view Jesus as they had known him before the great Easter-event. Meeting him now as risen Lord they recognized that the master whom they had loved and served was indeed the Son of God, even though they had not been aware of it. But, apart from this psychological factor, the words and deeds of Jesus held a wealth of meaning that had to be drawn out and made available. The promised gift of the Spirit would enable the apostles to understand the true significance of what Jesus had said and done.

2) Form Criticism of the Synoptic Gospels

Immediately after the Great War, in the years between 1919 and 1922, a new approach to the synoptic gospels developed in Germany. The explanation of the relations between the gospels in terms of common literary sources had led to the Two-Source theory: Mark is the earliest of our gospels and the other two are dependent on Mk. and on a collection of sayings of the Lord designated by Q (for German *Quelle* = 'source'). But these two sources were relatively late and represented a developed stage of the tradition. Attempts to break them down into earlier written sources met with no real success. The course of the gospel tradition between its beginnings and its well-nigh final form in Mk. and Q remained shrouded in darkness. Literary criticism alone seemed powerless to pierce the gloom. The only hope lay in going back behind the written sources and studying the oral tradition. The name given to the new approach, *Formgeschichtliche Methode*, indicates a method which concentrates on the form or structure of the primitive gospel tradition; in English it has become known as Form Criticism. The method was not entirely new: it had already been applied to parts of the Old Testament, notably Genesis and Psalms, by H. Gunkel; but it is within the field of synoptic criticism that it has grown and developed. The two most influential exponents of the method, in its application to the synoptic gospels, have been Martin Dibelius and Rudolf Bultmann. Because these scholars held radical views, form criticism as such was long suspect in the eyes of many. The 1964 *Instruction* of the Biblical Commission[3] distinguished between the literary method and the 'principles of a philosophical or theological nature which are quite inadmissible and which not infrequently vitiate' it. We shall outline and criticize the principles of the form critics and then indicate the positive contribution of the method.

1. The synoptic gospels are not literary units but mosaics of varied fragments. Consequently, the evangelists are not true authors but compilers who have grouped isolated and disparate elements into a framework of their own devising. The Passion-narrative alone has a certain literary coherence. Apart from it, the synoptic gospels are not literature in a true sense but belong to the category of popular literature; or they might be discribed as 'infra-literary.'

It is true that the gospels are not biographies of Jesus; they are, essentially, collections of his words and works. It is a fact that the gospel elements are arranged in no strict chronological or geographical order. The various units of the tradition may be separated from the editorial setting in which they now find themselves and be considered apart. What follows is that the framework alone is artificial: the individual sayings of Jesus and the individual stories are traditional and authentic. It is not true to say that the evangelists are mere compilers. In a healthy reaction against the assertion that they are it is almost universally acknowledged today that the evangelists are authors, and that the gospels are personal works, each having its own plan and individual characteristics; they are far from being mosaics of disparate fragments.

2. The constituent elements of the gospel tradition are the product of the first-generation Christian communities. The faith of the first-century Christians was colored and shaped by the 'myth of Christ' that is the work of Paul; for Paul had transformed Jesus of Nazareth into the Son of God who died for the salvation of men and rose from the dead. In the light of this faith the community created the gospel; the gospel message was 'lived' by the

believers before it was written down. The demands of preaching, apologetics, and the cult gave birth, in the primitive communities, to popular narratives developed around sayings or actions (real or invented) of Jesus. This combination of creative faith and practical demands leaves room for little or nothing of real historical value in the gospels.

A cardinal postulate of form criticism is the creative power of the community: a notable part of the synoptic material is either a free creation of the community or was formed under the influence of motifs borrowed from Jewish or hellenistic milieux. In truth, a community as such is not creative, it is always an individual who produces something new. This is evident in the field of history; in the field of literature the position is even clearer — we cannot believe that the gospel parables are the work of a community.

3. Since Dibelius and Bultmann viewed the gospels as compilations of varied fragments, they set about analyzing the gospels and classifying their component parts. It is a basic assumption of form criticism that originally the tradition circulated in separate oral units which may be classified according to their forms. Many of the forms identified are really independent units, but dissection has been carried to extremes and the over-all effect of the classification is artificial. The gospel material as a whole falls into two main groups: logia (sayings of Jesus) and narrative material (stories about Jesus). Although the two critics accept this general division, they do not quite agree in subsequent classification.

The classification of the traditional material is only a first step. It is far more important to trace the origin and development of these different literary forms. For that purpose, they must be seen against the background of the primitive community, and the needs that gave rise to them, and the tendencies they represent established. In a word, their *Sitz im Leben*, the life-situation out of which they have sprung, must be determined.

4. The picture we have sketched of form criticism does not seem a promising one. Yet, we must observe that the *Instruction* of the Biblical Commission has pointed out that the exegete is free to make judicious use of the method. In the context of the document it is clear that the positive contribution of form criticism is acknowledged to be important; for when the *Instruction* goes on to list the 'three stages of tradition' by which the teaching and the life of Jesus have come down to us' it is stressing an appreciation

of the development of the gospel material that we owe, in large measure, to the form critics. We shall, then, briefly, indicate what the method has taught us.

We are now well aware of literary units within the synoptic gospels and of the frequent loose linking of these units. We no longer seek to trace a strictly logical sequence of thought throughout the gospels, or through long passages of them, but recognize that, at times, we have to take a passage sentence by sentence, for isolated sayings may have been joined by simple catchwords. It is no longer open to question that many smaller literary compositions stand behind our written gospels.

The work of the evangelists appears more complex. Often they are dealing with pre-existing units and find their scope restricted to the extent that they respect these units. On the other hand, in direct contrast to the view of the earlier form critics, the role of the evangelist in choosing, arranging, and interpreting the material is being more and more stressed: the gospels are personal works, each having its own definite stamp and character. Neither the evangelists nor the early Christians were interested in producing a biography of Jesus according to our western standards, but this does not render their work unhistorical. 'The early Christians had not, perhaps, our regard for "history" but they had regard for the "historical." The preachers of the new faith did not intend to relate *everything* about Jesus, but they were careful to relate only what was solidly founded' (P. Benoit).

We do admit that the first Christian preachers did help to shape the tradition. We also realize that there was a development of the tradition, a process that, partially at least, is still visible in the gospels. It is not only legitimate but illuminating to seek the *Sitz im Leben* of the units of the tradition. For instance, we understand the parables better when we realize that many of them have a two-fold setting: in the ministry of Jesus and in the life of the primitive Church. The community did not create the gospels but, at the same time, we must admit that the needs of the early Church did influence the selection of the sayings of the Lord and the stories about him.

The Church did not create the gospel in the sense that it invented the gospel, yet it obviously is responsible for much of it. It composed the narrative parts and the needs and interests of the Church did influence the selection of the sayings of Jesus. This creative activity is mainly concerned with the literary forms into which the traditional data were cast, but it is not limited to these. There was, too, a certain amount of interpretation and adaptation. It would be false to the words of Christ when he promised to send the Holy Spirit on his disciples if their role were limited to the mechanical passing on of his teaching: 'The Counsellor, the Holy Spirit, whom the Father will send in my name, he will teach you all things, and bring to your remembrance all that I have said to you' (Jn. 14:26; cf. 16:13). It is evident from the gospels and the early chapters of Acts that the apostles needed more than a recollection of the words of Jesus. It is only after the resurrection that they fully understood Christ, and the account of Pentecost dramatically shows how the coming of the Spirit enlightened them. Not until then were their eyes fully opened. Not until then could the gospel have taken shape.

When it has been lightened of the impossible load that it had been asked to carry the method of form criticism does show us the real influence of the early Church on the formation of the gospel tradition. It did not create that tradition, as Bultmann would have it, but it did mould the form of it and it did interpret the tradition in the light of experience — for the Church has ever been a living entity. We owe to form criticism our awareness of these facts and, to some extent, the explanation of them and we owe to it the identification of many of the literary units of the tradition.

3) Pre-Synoptic Literary Units

Thus far we have seen that the apostolic Church gave the gospel story its shape. The passion, death, and resurrection form the central part, and the other events were chosen to trace the development from the beginning of the public ministry to Calvary. But the discourses and sayings of Jesus were also selected. Very often, sayings were preserved because they solved some pressing problems or showed the way to a line of conduct.

We may distinguish three 'milieux' in which the gospel tradition was formed: the cult, the mission, and the catechesis. Acts is our principal source for identifying these milieux. Three summaries (2:42-47; 4:32-35; 5:12-16) sketch the activities of the first community. We read that the Christians 'devoted themselves to the apostles' teaching and fellowship, to the breaking of bread and the prayers' (2:42); while 'with great power the apostles gave their testimony to the resurrection of the Lord Jesus' (4:33), and 'many signs and wonders were done among the people by the hands of the apostles' (5:12). From this it appears that the essential activity of the apostles was formed by cult, catechesis, and preaching supported by miracles.

THE LITURGY   Acts 2:42 already gives us an indication of this milieu, for the 'breaking of bread' is a technical term for the celebration of the Eucharist (cf. 1 Cor. 10:16; 11:23-25). It is widely recognized that the differences between the Mt./Mk. and Lk./Paul formulas of institution (Mt. 26:26-29; Mk. 14:22-25; Lk. 22:19-20; 1 Cor. 11:23-25) are to be traced to the liturgy: Matthew and Mark have followed the formula in use in Palestine while Paul and Luke have echoed the liturgical text with which they were familiar, doubtless the one in vogue at Antioch and then in the Pauline churches. The passion-narrative very likely was shaped in the liturgical assemblies. The account of the multiplication of loaves was influenced by eucharistic concern.

THE MISSION   The missionary preaching to Jews and pagans is
PREACHING   called *kērygma*: the proclamation of the Lord, crucified, risen, and to come. The earliest résumé of the kerygma is found in 1 Cor. 15:3-5 – 'I delivered to you as of first importance what I also received, that Christ died for our sins in accordance with the scriptures, that he was buried, that he was raised on the third day in accordance with the scriptures, and that he appeared to Cephas, then to the twelve.' To preach Jesus, to proclaim that he has reconciled us with God, that he is our peace – that is the kerygma. In the mission preaching, the miracles of Jesus had an important part. They are a sign of his messianic role (cf. Lk. 7:18-23). In the approach to the Jews, the scriptural argument was stressed. Hence, the preservation of sayings that speak of the fulfillment of Scripture (e.g. Mk. 5:17 f.), of Jesus' presentation of himself as the Suffering Servant (e.g. Mk. 8:31), and of episodes that were seen as particular fulfillments (e.g. Mk. 4:14-16; 8:17; 12:17-21). To this apologetic preaching was added the memory of conflicts with the scribes and Pharisees (e.g. Mk. 2:1-3:6). The missionary activity of the early Church was addressed to both Jews and Gentiles, and kerygmatic interest has left its mark on the gospel tradition.

THE DIDACHE   The catechetical preaching to those already within the fold, to the christian community, is called *didachē*. It includes the content of the kerygma, but goes on to the further instruction of the community: moral teaching (e.g. Mt. 18:7-20), the doctrine of the sacraments (e.g. Jn. 6), and additional episodes in the life of Jesus (e.g. Mt. 1-2; Lk. 1-2). The Sermon on the Mount (Mt. 5-7: Lk. 6:20-49) is a classic example of didache: a collection of the sayings of Jesus which form an instruction addressed to Christians, one aimed at their christian formation.

These are some of the interests of the early Church, the milieux in which elements of the tradition were shaped: cult, mission, catechetics — the activities of a living community. There were, of course, other preoccupations; but all of them sprang from the impact of the new faith on men who had accepted Jesus as Lord. We can be grateful to form criticism for making us conscious of these factors, for now we are more keenly aware that our gospels have taken rise within the Church of Christ: they are the inspired and written form of the apostolic tradition.

4) Fact and Interpretation in the Tradition

Modern scholarship has made clearer how the gospels have grown: from the oral tradition through partial written accounts, to the gospels as we know them. Drawing on this rich treasure of oral tradition and written narrative, the evangelists, each in his own way, have set before us the story of Jesus. Now it is impossible to tell a story without at the same time in some way bringing out its meaning; only so can a selection be made from among the myriad details and facets of what happened. It is considered the duty of a modern historian to present not only his interpretation of events but also a full enough, 'neutral' account of the events for the reader to evaluate his interpretation. The evangelist makes no attempt to do this: he presents only the events as he — and behind him, his community — see them with the eyes of faith. And this is an authoritative view, since the inspiration of the scriptures means that their view is guided by the Spirit. Hence in order fully to seize the message of our Lord's words we must read them in the arrangement and with the emphasis indicated by the evangelist. Ordering and selection are two means by which the evangelist brings out this message. Similarly with Jesus' actions; we must attempt, not so much to push behind the evangelist's account of the 'brute' facts, as to penetrate to and absorb the meaning which the evangelist, under the guidance of the Spirit, saw in the event. The theology of the evangelists is no private interpretation but the interpretation presented to us by the first generation of Christians under the inspiration of the Spirit.

Our task of seeing events with the eyes of the evangelists is made no easier by the gap in centuries and in culture which separates us from them. The most fundamental difference is that they were steeped in biblical imagery. The English language too has been widely influenced by biblical language, but to the early Christians — especially those sprung, like Matthew's community, from Judaism — a biblical phrase would suffice to conjure up a whole context which could immediately teach the significance of an event, the fulfillment of a promise or the associations of an action. Thus what may seem to us to be pointless or merely lively details, or even wild predictions of calamity, are in fact instances of allusive language whose meaning would be immediately clear to the first audiences of the gospel, but requires on our part laborious reconstruction. Two prime examples of descriptions of happenings where such allusive language is employed as to enable the initiated reader to appreciate the full significance of the event, while leaving to the uninitiate the impression that he is reading a commonplace account of the event, are those of the Feeding of the Five Thousand and of the Messianic Entry into Jerusalem. Similarly the eschatological discourse of Mt. 24, far from being a prediction, literal fulfillment of whose terms is to be expected in the minutest detail, is intended as an assessment, couched in terms of the imagery of the prophetic writings, of the theological significance of the event. A reader innocent of this Old Testament imagery can only presume that the account purports to present him with history; as soon as this imagery is perceived and evaluated the chapter is seen to contain rather a theology of history. It is the task of the exegete to penetrate the evangelist's form of expression, superficially misleading to us as it may often be, to uncover the message which he wished to express.

The evangelists wrote for an audience of believers. The meaning and not the historicity of Jesus' words and actions were their primary concern; their historicity might be assumed. Hence penetration to the 'actual events' will assist our understanding of the gospel message only in so far as it enables us to see more clearly the light in which these 'actual events' were viewed. It is of less interest to the believer to know what the centurion meant when he acknowledged that the crucified Jesus was 'Son of God' (Mk. 15:39) than to know the meaning of this title to the inspired evangelist. It is immaterial how many men actually accompanied Jesus on his entry into Jerusalem; the evangelist is more concerned to tell us that this entry was the accomplishment of the prophecies that the Messiah would come to his city, and in function of this intention accounts them a 'very great crowd' (Mt. 21:8). He is writing in the light of the full appreciation of the significance of the actions and the person of Jesus which came only in the course of time, and after the out-pouring of the Spirit at Pentecost. This does not mean that the events described did not occur; it means only that the intention which rules the description of them is not a determination to prove that they occurred, but a desire to show their significance to the Christian.

Nor does this imply that the historical events are not important. Indeed 'the denial of the importance of historical facts would carry with it a denial of what is of the essence of the gospel, namely, that the historical order — that order within which we must live and work — has received a specific character from the entrance into it of the eternal Word of God' (C. H. Dood). The one basic fact upon which the gospel reposes is the fact of Jesus — for, in the New Testament, the self-revelation of God is centred in the life, teaching, death, resurrection and exaltation of Jesus Christ, the Son of God — and the picture of Jesus which emerges from the different texts is a remarkably consistent one. However, we need to go beyond the evangelists because, although they have given us a fourfold account of the Good News, they themselves are not the authors of the Good News. They have put the story of the Lord in writing, but that story had existed long before they wrote. Between Christ and the evangelists come the apostles and the first preachers. Thus, we return ultimately to the early Church, for it was the Church that shaped the basic gospel which was afterwards passed on to us, according to the viewpoint of each, by the evangelists. We have, then, three stages: Jesus Christ, the apostolic Church, and the evangelists. It is only when we have taken all three into account that we can really understand the gospels.

5) Demythologising the Gospel

For Rudolf Bultmann a principal task of theology is *Entmythologisierung*, the 'demythologising' of the New Testament message. He described myth as a way of thinking in which the other-wordly and divine are represented as this-worldly and human. At the same time, he would regard the primitive conception of the universe (the three-storied universe of heaven, earth, and hell) as mythical – thus indicating a confusion in his use of the term. For him mythic thought is purely and simply opposed to scientific thought and, as such, is unacceptable to modern man. He maintained that the 'mythological' language of the New Testament has to be translated into the language of modern man – in practice, into the categories of existentialist philosophy.

The term 'demythologisation' suggests a negative approach, whereas Bultmann was profoundly concerned to bring the religious value of the New Testament home to modern man. His criticism of the biblical writings is not aimed at the elimination of mythical expressions, but at their interpretation. In his view, demythologisation is a method of hermeneutics, an existentialist interpretation which seeks to manifest the intention of the myth; the myth must be translated into a statement on the meaning of human existence.

In point of fact, his notion of myth did not take cognisance of recent studies which have tended to show that myth, as symbolic expression, is an essential part of the pattern of human thought and discourse, and that it can never be entirely replaced by logical discourse.

The question is, can myth, in the sense in which the divine is represented as this-worldly be eliminated? The fact is that we can speak of God only by analogy or symbolically in categories drawn from nature or human experience. In dealing with other-worldly matters myth and symbol are an essential part of human thinking. It seems that Bultmann has not only an inadequate notion of myth but is mistaken in his view that myth is the chief obstacle to the acceptance of the christian gospel in the modern world. His thorough-going demythologisation of the gospel is unnecessary and, despite his good intentions, leads to a gross distortion of the christian message.[4]

3. THE EVANGELISTS

1) *Redaction Criticism*[5]

Where form criticism has helped to make us aware of the importance of pre-gospel tradition (often at the expense of the evangelists' role) *Redaktionsgeschichte* ('redaction-criticism') has drawn our attention to the contribution of the evangelists. Matthew, Mark, Luke, (and John) were something more than compilers who merely strung together isolated units of tradition. They were highly original theologians who, within the restricting limits of the tradition concerning Jesus, found imaginative solutions to the problems of their different churches. So great was their contribution that they have every right to be considered as authors in the full sense. To some extent, therefore, the term 'redaction criticism' is not entirely accurate. The German *Redaktion* and the French *redaction* are both rendered in English by 'editorial'. Taken literally, therefore, redaction criticism means the study of the editorial work done by the evangelists. The snag, however, is that in English usage editorial work is opposed to creative authorship. But, the term 'redaction criticism' has passed into such general usage that it is unlikely that it will be supplanted. It is fortunate that in English 'redaction' is a neologism and so carries no false connotation.

TRADITION AND REDACTION When dealing with a particular passage of any of the gospels the scholar must begin with the problem of its literary unity. This means asking the question: are all the elements in the passage well integrated with one another, so dominated by a single intention, that it must be attributed to a single author? If the answer is in the affirmative the passage is said to be a literary unity. If the answer is in the negative then a source and a redactor must be postulated.

There is a presumption in favor of literary unity in the sense that this option can be abandoned only in the face of contrary arguments. Such arguments must be based on the presence in the passage of inconsistencies which make it difficult or impossible to attribute the whole to a single hand. Very few authors, however, are totally consistent, and there can be varying degrees of inconsistency. The delicacy of the literary critic's task consists in determining the degree of inconsistency which demands the hypothesis that a passage had been retouched either by the original author at a later period, or by a second and different hand.

It is unreasonable to claim that all elements not absolutely necessary to the point being made are secondary. Elements may have been introduced by the original author in order to evoke themes ancillary to his principal intention but not necessarily related to it. This is particularly true of New Testament authors who wrote, not simply to communicate information, but to provoke a emotional response on the part of their readers. It is equally unreasonable to maintain that only explicit contradictions within a passage betray the hand of a second author. Such contradictions do in fact exist and are naturally the easiest to detect. In the majority of cases, however, the redactor is sufficiently aware of the meaning of the original to avoid introducing such blatant conflicts. Insertions are normally in the line of the original, but since the purpose of an insertion is to give a new orientation to the original text, the result is inevitably some degree or tension between the two levels.

As an illustration of the type of tension that is in question let us look at John's account of the cure of the official's son (Jn. 4:46-53):

46. At Capernaum there was an official whose son was ill. 47. When he heard that Jesus had come from Judea to Galilee, he went and *begged him to come down and heal his son, for he was at the point of death.* 48. *Jesus therefore said to him, 'Unless ye see signs and wonders ye will not believe.'* 49. *The official* said to him, 'Sir, come down before my child dies.' 50. Jesus said to him, 'Go [singular]. Your [singular] child will live.' The man *believed the word that Jesus spoke to him and* went his way. 51. And as he was going down, his servants met him and told him that his son was living. 52. So he asked them the hour when he began to mend, and they said to him, 'Yesterday at the seventh hour the fever left him.' 53. *The father knew that that was the hour when Jesus had said to him, 'Your son will live'.* And so he himself believed and all his household.

The italicised portions of this passage are the redactor's additions. The remainder is the traditional material that he received and if this is read consecutively, that is, by skipping over the italicised portions, it will be seen to be a perfectly coherent narrative of a miracle in which Jesus cures a man's son. The tensions in the existing text which betray the hand of a redactor are: (1) There are *two* requests for Jesus' intervention, one in indirect speech (v. 47) and the other in direct speech (v. 49); (2) There are *two* statements that the man believed (vv. 50 and 53) where only one is necessary; (3) in v. 48, although Jesus is speaking to a single individual, he uses the plural form 'ye' rather than the singular 'you'; (4) Moreover, Jesus' statement in v. 48 completely misrepresents the official's attitude. The fact of his coming to Jesus reveals that he believed in Jesus' miraculous power, and the only point at issue was whether Jesus would exercize this power on his son's behalf.

Only one hypothesis can explain these awkwardnesses, namely, that the redactor inserted v. 48. In order to prepare the way for this statement by Jesus the redactor had to make the official say something, so he simply reformulated in indirect speech the request in v. 49. The insertion of v. 48 reveals that the redactor was concerned with the relation of faith to miracles. This gives adequate reason to think that he was also responsible for one of the two statements concerning the official's belief. These two statements are not identical. That in v. 53 speaks of faith as occasioned by the miracle; in other words, the official did not believe until he was sure that his son was recovering; whereas that in v. 50 speaks of faith based on the word of Jesus alone. Since the statement about belief in v. 50 harmonises with the intention of the insertion in v. 48 both can be attributed to the same redactor; they are designed as a corrective of the view expressed in v. 53.

In order to see more clearly what the redactor's problem was let us read the story as he found it:

> At Capernaum there was an official whose son was ill. When he heard that Jesus had come from Judea to Galilee, he went and said to him, 'Sir, come down before my child dies.' Jesus said to him, 'Go. Your child will live.' The man went his way, and as he was going down, his servants met him and told him that his son was living. So he asked them the hour when he began to mend, and they said to him, 'Yesterday at the seventh hour the fever left him.' And so he himself believed and all his household.

In this narrative all attention is concentrated on the *miracle*. The figure of Jesus stands only in the background as the one who performed the miracle. To the question: who is Jesus? , the only answer possible on the basis of this story is: he is the miracle-worker. From the redactor's viewpoint this was a completely inadequate understanding of Jesus. Hence, he decided to modify the story in such a way that attention would be focused on the person of Jesus. Thus, he removed all the emphasis from the official's verification of the cure by making him believe immediately on hearing the word pronounced by Jesus. In this way he ensures that the miracle will not be understood as a 'wonder' but as a 'sign' pointing towards the mystery of the person of Jesus.

The above example has allowed us to see the importance of separating tradition from redaction. In this operation we are permitted to see the mind of the redactor at work, and are enabled to perceive something of what was in that mind. The example, however, has another instructive feature. It reveals the redactor's intense respect for the tradition. Even though he disagreed with the implications of the version of the miracle that had come down to him he preserved the story intact, and contented himself with making additions that would modify the reader's understanding of the event.

DIFFERENT REDACTIONAL LEVELS A factor which has not received adequate attention in discussions of the method of redaction criticism is the problem posed by different redactional levels within the gospels. In the example of the Cure of the Official's Son, which was chosen because of its simplicity and clarity, this problem did not exist, because all the redactional elements could be attributed to one hand. This is not true of many other passages of the gospels in which it is possible to distinguish two or even three redactional levels. This is particularly evident in the Passion narratives which underwent a long development before reaching their present form.

If more than one redactional level can be distinguished in a number of passages it means that the traditional material has been edited more than once. In other words, the redaction critic has to deal with more than one redactor. He cannot, therefore, assume that the last hand to retouch one passage was the last hand to re-touch any other passage. Unfortunately, however, this assumption is commonly made, and vitiates much of the work that has been done. In the interest of simplicity there is a tendency to consider that *any* redactional element can be attributed to the *last* redactor. Frequently there is an effort to give this assumption a scientific foundation by appeal to stylistic criteria. The fact that stylistic traits can be presented statistically gives this technique an air of great objectivity. However, what this means in fact is that if a word occurs 50 times in Matthew, 3 times in Mark, 10 times in Luke, 6 times in John, and 15 times in the Acts of the Apostles, it is said to be a preferred word of the evangelist Matthew and characteristic of his style. In other words, a statistic concerning a *book* (which is admittedly composite) suddenly – and mysteriously – becomes a statistic concerning the *author* of part of that work. The illegitimacy of this shift is patent. The objectivity of statistics is completely spurious unless the terms tabulated have already been assigned to different literary levels for reasons other than style.

What has just been said is intended as a criticism of the way redaction criticism is practised in many current works, and not as a condemnation of the method in itself. It is also conceived as a plea for a sounder methodology in this domain. The task is extremely difficult because of the complexity of the gospel material, but it is not impossible.

DIFFERENT
LIFE-SITUATIONS
During the period when form criticism was the dominant approach to the gospels the term *Sitz im Leben* (life-situation) came into vogue to designate the social context in which a particular passage of the gospels was located. Fundamentally this social context was constituted by the community, and more proximately it was specified by the functional needs of that community in the sphere of liturgy, catechesis, morality, and so on.

Inevitably as redaction criticism developed the question arose of its relationship to the life-situation that was so important for form criticism. The point has given rise to considerable discussion which, for the most part, has concerned itself with matters of terminology. There is little real difference among the various authors regarding the realities. Form criticism was preoccupied with finding a *typical* life-situation for individual units of tradition. In other words, it was not interested in the specific situation in which a narrative took form, because this was rightly seen to be beyond the reach of the historical method, but concentrated on the type of situation with which a particular form of narrative seemed to have a special affinity.

Redaction criticism is concerned with the theological attitudes of a *specific* individual. Hence, the life-situation that is in question can only be that of a unique individual. To this extent, therefore, there is a real difference between the life-situation envisaged by form criticism and that sought after by redaction criticism. This difference, however, should not be exaggerated to the point of saying that form criticism sought a community life-situation while redaction criticism seeks an individualistic life-situation. It has been stressed already that the redactors of the gospel tradition wrote from within a community and for a community. It is entirely legitimate to suppose that in redacting elements of the tradition (e.g. the partial collections of material discovered in Mk. 2:1-3:6; 4:1-34; 10:1-45, and so on), and later in assembling the gospels as we know them, the redactors were consciously meeting a need of their particular community at a particular point in its history. Hence, it is impossible to exclude a community dimension in the life-situation proper to redaction criticism.

Nonetheless, that life-situation is refracted through the preoccupations of a single individual. It has a life and clarity which that of form criticism lacks. If form criticism permitted us to see the community frozen in certain crucial moments of its existence, redaction criticism enables us to perceive the community adapting to the new situations which were the conditions of its life. Form criticism showed us the static conclusions reached by the community, but redaction criticism shows us the community as conscious of difficulties and in quest of solutions. Both approaches have their specific contributions to make to our total understanding of the gospels, and there is no question of choosing one in preference to the other. Redaction criticism, however, brings us into contact with a mind of the first century at work on a problem which remains perennially actual. How is fidelity to the past to be reconciled with concern for the present? When does flexibility in response to the needs of the present become infidelity to the legitimate demand of continuity with the past which is the source of our christian identity? In view of the complexity on contemporary existence, the way in which the redactors of the first century handled this problem is more important than the specific solutions they adopted. The great merit of redaction criticism is to have brought this home to us.

2) The Synoptic Problem

THE FACT   The first three gospels are closely related; John goes his own way. The narratives and discourses of Matthew, Mark, and Luke have common or corresponding passages which may be arranged in parallel columns. Thus, the reader gets a double or triple form of the same gospel event or saying and he may see at a glance, and in detail, the resemblances and differences. The text so arranged is called by the Greek term *synopsis* ('seeing together'). This is the reason the name 'synoptics' has been applied, since the end of the eighteenth century, to the first three gospels.

The relationship between the synoptics is a strange combination of agreement and disagreement (often described as a *concordia discors*). It pervades the gospels in such a way that there are variations in important matters and perfect accord in mere details. This fact, and the problem it raises, is not just academic. No attempted solution has been generally accepted, but the discussion of the problem, and the indication of the lines along which the solution must lie, are of real help in understanding the gospels. We shall first consider, briefly, the agreements between the gospels and their differences.

1. AGREEMENTS   A study of the synoptic gospels readily brings to
light the impressive similarity between the three narratives. Such
agreement cannot be the result of chance; the contacts are too
numerous and the agreements are too marked and continuous. On
the other hand, we must be careful not to overplay the extent of
agreement. We may find partial agreements within passages that
differ on a wider showing (e.g. Mk. 1:21-45 and Mt. 7:28-8:16;
Mk. 2:1-22 and Mt. 9:1-17; Mk. 2:23-3:6 and Mt. 12:1-14). We
may just as easily encounter disagreement in a generally similar
grouping (e.g. the order of Mk. 1:21-39; 1:40-45 and that of Mk.
4:13-24; 13:25 is inversed in the corresponding passages of Matthew). Luke follows the order of Mark closely; yet, we find the call
of the first disciples after the preaching at Capernaum (Lk. 5:1-11;
cf. Mk. 1:16-20 – the call comes before the preaching); the visit to
Nazareth is set in a different context (compare Lk. 4:16-30 with
Mk. 6:1-6). Differences are multiplied in the Passion-narrative. This
fact of numerous transpositions within a common framework
should be kept in mind.

2. DIFFERENCES   The agreement between parallel texts is manifest. On the other hand there are differences that are no less
marked and no less characteristic. Here again we have to advert to
the fact that the combination of disagreements and agreements can
be very complicated. We may find that, while the structure of a
narrative remains identical in different gospels, the details may
have changed. In the parables of the Talents (Mt. 25:14-30) and the
Pounds (Lk. 19:11-27), and again in the two versions of the Great
Feast (Mt. 22:1-10; Lk. 14:16-24) the basic plan is the same but
the words are quite different. The exact opposite may happen: in
the same episode words can remain identical but they have
changed place or even meaning. Crying out 'with a loud voice', the
unclean spirit came out of the possessed man (Mk. 1:26); in Lk.
4:33 the spirit cried 'with a loud voice' in addressing Jesus. The
crowd present at the exorcism was amazed at the authoritative
teaching of Jesus (Mk. 1:27) – or at the authority displayed in the
exorcism itself (Lk. 4:36). Jesus *raised up* Peter's mother-in-law
(Mk. 1:31); in Mt. 8:15 she *rose*. In Mk. 1:45 *logos* means 'news'
while in the same episode in Lk. 5:15 it means 'renown.' The same
Greek word *basanizō* signifies in Mt. 14:24 that the boat 'was
beaten by the waves' and in Mk. 6:48 that the disciples 'were *distressed* in rowing.' In the discussion on divorce, reference to Moses'

authorization of a certificate of divorce appears at an early stage in the discussion as an objection put to Jesus (Mt. 19:7). This sort of thing pervades the gospels.

THE PROBLEM   The existence of such a welter of agreements and differences constitutes the synoptic fact; the explanation of the strange relationship between the three gospels is the synoptic problem. It is clear, even from our hurried presentation of the data, that there can be no simple solution of the problem. It is here that all we have written above about the oral tradition and the respective roles of community and evangelists is drawn together. Key elements of the solution lie in the prehistory of the gospels; it will not do to study the evangelists alone. On the other hand, the oral tradition by itself will not account for the intricate relationship that exists between the three gospels: there are literary contacts between them. An immense amount has been written on the question since it came into prominence in the nineteenth century. The discussion of this problem has greatly contributed to a better understanding of the three gospels. Here we shall content ourselves with two hypotheses.

Toward a Solution

1. THE TWO-SOURCE THEORY   This theory is held, in one form or another, by a great number of scholars. In general it asserts the following: Mark is the earliest of our gospels; Mark is followed by Matthew and Luke, independently of each other. Then, in order to explain the further agreement of Mt./Lk. against Mk., a special document is posited, one that contained sayings and discourses only. This hypothetical document, which must have been written in Greek, is named Q, from the German *Quelle* ('source'). Many attempts have been made to reconstruct Q, all are subjective, and no two authors agree on the extent or arrangement of the document. The Two-Document hypothesis, in its simplest form, may be set out in a plan:

Mk.   Q.

Mt.   Lk.

2. A NEW THEORY   While the Two-Source theory is still widely followed as a convenient working hypothesis many rightly maintain

that the theory is inadequate to explain the complexity of the development of the gospel tradition. M.-E. Boismard's recent work[6] represents a radical and brilliant reassessment of the whole situation. The new theory does not, by any means, solve all difficulties, but it boldly faces up to these difficulties. It is presented here in barest outline.

1. BASIC DOCUMENTS

DOCUMENT A.   Of Palestinian origin. A's accounts are generally simple and concrete. There is a marked difference between this primitive simplicity and the later developed tradition. At the same time, A re-interprets the primitive accounts by the addition of certain details: the simplicity of A is largely due to the simplicity of its sources.

DOCUMENT B.   Essentially a re-interpretation of A made in a Gentile-christian milieu. In many cases, the A accounts differ so little from B that it is impossible to distinguish them in our actual gospels.

DOCUMENT C.   Independent traditions, very old, probably of Palestinian origin. We are led to postulate the existence of C because of those passages where Mark joins together *three* different texts: he must have known a third source independent of A and B. Since C has greatly influenced John and proto-Luke, one attributes to C the passages where John and Luke follow a tradition independent of Mt./Lk.

DOCUMENT Q.   According to the Two-Source theory, all material common to Mt./Lk. but absent from Mk. comes from a special source: Q. In this theory, Mt. and Lk. are independent of each other. Boismard admits a relationship between proto-Lk. and Intermediary-Mt. And he maintains that it is not necessary to attribute to Q all the texts common to Mt./Lk. and not in Mk. In fact, Q may well cover different related sources. His conception of Q is much less rigid than that of the Two Source theory.

2. INTERMEDIARY DOCUMENTS

INTERMEDIARY MARK   (Mk.-i.) made use of the three basic documents: A, B, and C. However, the Marcan tradition has its principal roots in B.

INTERMEDIARY MATTHEW   (Mt.-i.) has A as its principal source, and contains elements of Q. Mt.i. has no knowledge of B and

C and is not influenced by the Marcan tradition. Like A, Mt.-i. comes from a Judaeo-Christian milieu.

PROTO-LUKE has used direcy or indirectly all the above-mentioned documents. Except for the passion-resurrection narratives where it follows C, its principal source is Mt.i. – but C is used sporadically throughout.

3. THE GOSPELS

MARK, as we know it, has almost the same form as Mk.-i. The final gospel was completed with reference to Mt.-i. and proto-Lk. and shows some influence of Pauline theology and vocabulary; it contains some non-Marcan words and expressions from the hand of its last redactor. The relationship between Mk. and Mt./Lk. is complex. One must distinguish two literary stages: Mk.-i. (which influenced Mt. and Lk.), and final Mk. (influenced by Mt. and Lk.).

MATTHEW. The Two Source theory holds that Mt. depends on Mk. for all common passages; the situation is more complex. In fact, Mt. as we know it came into being when the (independent) text of Mt.-i. was largely replaced by that of Mk.-i. in those sections where the two are parallel. The final Matthean editor also added new material.

LUKE grew out of a revision of proto-Lk. in the light of Mk.-i. – a large part of whose structure and forms were adopted by the Lucan editor. This Marcan intrusion into proto-Lk. (whose main source is Mt.-i.) explains how Lk. agrees sometimes with Mt., sometimes with Mk. Since the vocabulary of the Lucan redactor and of proto-Lk. are indistinguishable, Luke himself is the creator of his gospel.

JOHN. In this context, the fourth gospel is of interest only insofar as it is related to the synoptic problem. When John uses the same episodes as the synoptists he appears to follow common sources. He uses B and C; his principal source is proto-Lk., especially in the passion-resurrection narrative. Jn. was influenced by Mt. in its final stage.

This very complex theory is based on a very simple principle: the care of the gospel editors to harmonize one with another the gospel traditions which they knew. This concern for harmonization persevered after the definitive publication of the canonical gospels.

It explains in part the variants which one finds in a great number of gospel manuscripts.

It may be helpful to present these dates in the form of a plan:

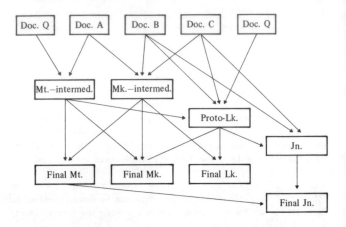

---

[1] See W. J. Harrington, *A Key to the Parables* (New York: Paulist Press 1964); *Stories Told By Jesus*. A Contemporary Approach to the Parables (Staten Island, N.Y.: Alba House 1974).

[2] Matthew and Luke go back to the birth of Jesus but the primitive preaching began with the Baptist and the baptism of Jesus. It was later that interest in the human origin of the Son of God gave rise to the infancy narratives.

[3] *Instruction on the Historical Truth of the Gospels*, issued by the Pontifical Biblical Commission, April 21, 1964.

[4] J. Macquarrie, *An Existentialist Theology* (London: SCM 1955).

[5] This study of redaction criticism is a contribution of my confrere Jerome Murphy-O'Connor, O.P., professor of Scripture at the Ecole Biblique, Jerusalem. For a fuller treatment see his article 'Redaction-Criticism,' *Scripture in Church* Vol. 5, No. 16, 1974.

[6] P. Benoit, and M.-E. Boismard, *Synopse des Quatre Évangiles en Français*. Tome II. (Paris: Cerf 1972). This volume is, in fact, the work of M.-E. Boismard.

TWO

The Gospel of St. Mark

AUTHORSHIP, DESTINATION AND DATE

THE STYLE OF ST. MARK

THE PLAN

THE PURPOSE OF MARK

THE MESSIANIC SECRET

1. AUTHORSHIP, DESTINATION AND DATE

1) The Testimony of Tradition

The tradition of the early Church is unanimous in attributing a gospel to St. Mark, who is regularly named as the interpreter and disciple of Peter. He is, likely, the same Mark who is frequently mentioned in the New Testament: Acts 12:12, 25; 13:5, 13; 15:37, 39; Col. 4:10; Phm. 24; 2 Tm. 4:11; 1 Pt. 5:13.

The gospel of St. Mark was written for non-Jewish Christians. This is evident from the explanation of Aramaic expressions (e.g. 'Boanerges, that is, sons of thunder' (3:17); ' *"Talitha cum"*, which means, "Little girl, (I say to you), arise" ' (5:41); cf. 7:11, 34; 14:36; 15:22, 34), as well as of Jewish customs (7:3 f.; 14:12; 15:42). According to early tradition, the gospel was written in Rome. In general, the many Latinisms found in Mark may be written off as current military and technical terms. Nevertheless, on two striking occasions a Greek expression is explained by its Latin equivalent: ... two *lepta* [Greek coins], that is, a *quadrans* [Roman coin]' (12:42); the 'interior of the palace, that is, the *praetorium*' (15:16). These suggest that the gospel was written in Rome.

There is wide agreement that the gospel was written before 70 A.D. (the date of the destruction of Jerusalem by the Romans) — a main reason being that chap. 13, which refers to this event, gives no hint that it had already come to pass. The date 65 A.D. is regularly suggested. Where there can be no certainty what does seem sure is that Mark is the earliest of our gospels; at latest, it cannot have been written long after 70 A.D.

2. THE STYLE OF MARK

Mark is written in a relatively simple and popular form of Greek that has striking affinities with the spoken language of everyday life. The evangelist uses only the simplest constructions; a glance at the gospel will show that sentences are most often strung together by the conjunction 'and,' while Aramaisms abound in his pages. The simplicity of the Greek can be deceptive: Mark is a far more skilful writer than has commonly been acknowledged. He is a consummate story-teller. The distinctive vivid touches which enliven his narratives are his own contribution — they do not reflect eye-witness influence.

SCHEMATIZATION   In this context we may consider a notable tendency in Mark, that of schematization, or the casting of narratives, miracle-stories especially, in the one mold. For example, the following are two distinct and quite different miracles described according to the same pattern and in almost identical terms.

The Tempest stilled 49:39-41	*An Exorcism* 1:25-27
And he awoke and *rebuked* the wind and *said* to the sea '*Be silent*, be still'	*And* Jesus *rebuked* him *saying* '*Be silent*, and go out of him.'
[Effect of the command: the sea stilled]	[Effect of the command: cure of the possessed person]
And they were filled with awe and *said* to one another, *Who* then is this?	And they were all amazed, and they questioned one another, *saying*, *What* is this?

In the same way we can compare the cure of the blind man at Bethsaida (8:22-26) and that of the deaf-mute (7:32-36); the preaching of Jesus in his own country (6:1-2) and in Capernaum (1:26-27); the preparation of the Supper (14:13-16) and the entry into Jerusalem (11:1-6).

DUALITY   A notable feature of Mark is the frequent, indeed pervasive occurrence of double expressions. These have been frequently explained either by the combination of two (or more) sources, or as redactional additions to one basic source. These duplicate expressions have been thoroughly analysed by F. Neirynck[1], who concludes that they represent an aspect of the evangelist's own style. He has examined with particular care three categories of the double phrases.

Temporal or Local Statements: Two-Step Expressions. It has been maintained that the text of Mark displays frequent redundancy, and the tendency has been to assign to different sources each half of such expressions. This leads to a rather mechanical distribution between tradition and redaction. But, if we accept the double expressions as part of the original text of the gospel, the situation is vastly changed. For example, in 1:32 ('That evening, at sundown'), the phrase 'at sundown' is not a synonym simply juxtaposed but gives further refinement and precision to the indication of time; the whole is a progressive two-step expression. Some local expressions reflect the same scheme of a vague indication followed by a more precise definition (e.g. 1:28, 38; 5:1; 11:1; 13:3). In this respect, the scheme of public teaching and private explanation delivered to the disciples in the *house* is generally accepted as typical of Marcan redaction (e.g. 4:1-9, 10; 7:14 f., 17:23; 9:14-27, 28 f., 10:1-9, 10 f.). Thus it would seem that apparent redundancy is not really such. Rather, in these temporal and local precisions we are faced with one of Mark's most characteristic features of style.

Double Questions and Antithetic Parallelism. The sequence of public teaching and private explanation provides a first example of the double step scheme in sayings material. The same scheme can also be verified in formulations that are closer to the duplicate *phrase*: the double question is perhaps the best illustration. It would appear that we have two separate questions in 13:4: 'When will this be, and what will be the sign when these things are all to be accomplished?' Yet, the broader formulation of the second part is better seen as an expression of the Marcan sense of climax. In 12:14 f. the theoretical question, 'Is it lawful to pay taxes to Caesar or not?' is completed by the practical one, 'Should we pay them, or should we not?' In these and similar cases we have further evidence for the double step scheme. While it is widely recognized that antithetical parallelism is a feature of Jesus' own style, Mark seems often to have reinforced the antithetical character of the sayings. He has done this by his distinctive device of *ou . . . alla* ('not . . . but'). e.g. '. . . receives not me, but him who sent me' (9:37); '. . . it is not you who speak, but the Holy Spirit'

13:11). The repetition involved in parallelism would have been congenial to Mark.

Oratio Obliqua and Oratio Recta. The study of temporal and local statements, of double questions and antithetic parallelism suggests that the progressive double phrase is indeed a characteristic Marcan usage. But duality is not restricted to these categories: it pervades the different parts and strata of the gospel. Mark shows a tendency to make a statement about Jesus' teaching activity and follow it up immediately with direct discourse (e.g. 4:2; 9:31; 11:17). The Gethsemane prayer is a striking case in point: 'he prayed that, if it were possible, the hour might pass from him. And he said: "Abba, Father, all things are possible to thee; remove this cup from me. . ." ' (14:35 f.). This is a progression from a first description of the content of the prayer to a more explicit expression of the prayer in *oratio recta*: v. 35 gives first, in indirect form the substance of the prayer and prepares the reader for the full impact of v. 36. This sequence is not unparalleled in the gospel and leads back to the double phrase in Mark and to the characteristic double-step scheme.

THE GOSPEL   St. Mark's gospel was long regarded as no more than an abridged version of Matthew. For this reason it was rather neglected, not coming into its own until recent times. Today it is recognized clearly that Mark is in no way an abridgment of Matthew; if anything, the opposite may be true in some few cases. Mark stands on its own merits, and indeed, as the earliest of our gospels, it is of special significance: it is nearer the source.

Still, Mark is quite obviously much shorter than the other synoptics. We note at once just how few of the sayings of Jesus are found in it. There are only three discourses, all of which are very brief: the discourse in parables (4:1-34), the community discourse (9:33-50), and the eschatological discourse (13:1-37). On the other hand, in narratives common to the three synoptics, Mark is usually richer in detail and more picturesque. We have a striking example of this in the account of the raising of the daughter of Jairus; it is certainly quite plain that here Mark is not abbreviating, as is obvious from a comparison of the texts of the three synoptists (Mt. 9:18-26; Lk. 8:40-56; Mk. 5:21-43).

This passage is no isolated case, for there are many other examples, especially in the first part of the gospel: for instance, the cure of the paralytic (Mk. 2:1-12; Mt. 9:1-8; Lk. 5:17-26); the stilling of the tempest (4:35-41; Mt. 8:23-27; 8:22-25); the first multiplication of loaves (Mk. 6:30-44; Mt. 14:13-21; Lk. 9:10-17). Mark is no abridgment. Although it is shorter than Matthew and Luke, this is due to the evangelist's own choice and method. Today, Mark has come into his own.

3. THE PLAN

The gospel of Mark is built up of two complementary parts. The first (1:14-8:30) is concerned with the mystery of Jesus' identity; it is dominated by the question, 'Who is Jesus? '. The second part (8:31-16:8) is concerned with the mysterious messianic destiny of Jesus.

INTRODUCTION   1:1—13

PART I.   *The Mystery of the Messiah:* Revelation of Jesus' Person 1:14-8:30.

Three sections, each *beginning* with a summary of the activity of Jesus and a narrative concerning the disciples and *concluding* with the adoption of an attitude in regard to Jesus.

A. Jesus and the Crowds   1:14 — 3:6 [1:14f, 16-20; 3:6]
B. Jesus and His Own   3:7 — 6:6a [3:7-12, 13-19; 6: 1-6a]
C. Jesus, the Disciples and the Gentiles
6:6b — 8:30 [6:6b, 6:7-31; 8: 27-30]

CONLUSION AND TRANSITION   8:27—33
Confession of Peter;
First Prophecy of the Passion;
Correction of Peter.

PART II.   *The Mystery of the Son of Man:* Revelation of Jesus' Sufferings   8:31 — 16:8.

A. The Way of the Son of Man   8:31 — 10:52

Signposted by three announcements of the fate of the Son of Man and three instructions on the lot of the disciples.

B. Jesus in Jerusalem   11:1   13:37
C. Passion and Resurrection   14:1 — 16:8
The Later Ending   16: 9 — 20.

4. THE PURPOSE OF MARK

Throughout the first half of the gospel the question of Jesus' identity has been repeatedly raised and has met with various answers. Some, the religious leaders, have rejected the evidence of his works and of his teaching; others have been impressed and have been prepared to acknowledge him as a prophet or as an Elijah-like figure (6:14 f.). The chosen disciples reacted with awe and wonder, but had failed to understand him. Only the evil spirits had acknowledged Jesus for what he was. But now we come to the point where the disciples do, at last, proclaim him as Messiah. The passage is the hinge of Mark's work, at once the climax of the first part, the Secret of the Messiah (the identity of Jesus) and the transition to the second part, the Mystery of the Son of Man (his destiny of death and resurrection). The second half of the gospel provides the answer to the question raised in the first half: 'Who is Jesus?' But this answer is not understood by the disciples who cannot grasp his suffering messiahship. We may look to that central passage (8:27-33) to find the purpose of Mark's gospel.

As a climax, the confession of 8:29 ('You are the Christ') is not to be seen as the explicit formulation of a conviction that had been gradually growing on the disciples. At least, it is not such in Mark's intention; in somewhat the same way, Matthew (16:16 f.) presents it as a divinely granted discovery by Peter. Mark has gone out of his way to stress the incredible blindness of the disciples. His miracle story of the healing of a blind man (8:22-26) is meant to declare that Jesus alone can bring light to the darkness of their understanding. And so it is that he takes the initiative (v. 27).

It is noteworthy that, in the first half of the gospel, the disciples, despite their privileged position, have shown themselves to be less perceptive than the 'crowds.' The Caesarea Philippi episode marks a turning-point. This is not to say that there is an improvement: Peter may acknowledge Jesus as Messiah (8:29), but he immediately shows that he cannot accept the idea of a suffering Messiah (8:32). The change is one from imperceptivity to misconception. Before, the disciples had failed to recognize Jesus as Messiah; now they misunderstand the nature of his messiahship. We must appreciate the importance of the Caesarea Philippi episode in Mark's theology.

It is evident that 8:29 stands out in high relief. Here Jesus is formally acknowledged as the Messiah of Jewish expectation and as the Christ of Christian worship — for this narrative is concerned with Christology. In the evangelist's eyes, the unique significance of Peter's confession rests upon the fact that here, for the *first* time, the disciples speak with Jesus as to what he is in their estimation. Jesus takes the initiative and asks the disciples about the opinion of 'men' — 'those outside' (4:11) — and learns that they would regard him not as a messianic figure but, at most, as a forerunner of the Messiah. It is very clear that not only was his teaching riddlesome to them but that they had missed, too, the import of his works. Peter, however, has at last begun to see: '*You* are the Messiah.' The sequel will show that this is but the first stage of his enlightenment; it is the risen Lord who will open their eyes fully. Again, the disciples are bidden to keep silence but now, for the first time, the prohibition is related to Jesus' own person. Mark, indeed, looks beyond Peter and the disciples to the Christian community of his concern and bids his Christians take care that they really understand who their Christ is. There has, indeed, been a studied psychological preparation of the reader. From the start, Mark has shown Jesus acting in an extraordinary manner which called forth the astonishment of the witnesses and led to a series of questions about him (1:27; 2:7; 6:2). Jesus himself heightens the effect (2:10, 18). Who, then, is this Son of Man? Who is this 'Physician' (3:16 f.)? Who is this 'Bridegroom' (2:19)? The themes of the amazement of the crowd and the incomprehension of the disciples stand as a constant question-mark over the first eight chapters of the gospel. And now, for the Christians who read Mark, the confession, 'You are the Christ' is *their* profession of faith. And it is precisely because it is the profession of christian faith that Jesus is depicted as accepting it without comment.

The central importance of Peter's confession in Mark's editorial structure is indicated by the brusque change of tone and of orientation after Peter has acknowledged the Messiahship of Jesus. In the actual structure of the gospel the prediction of the Passion (8:31-32a) is Jesus' response to the confession of Peter, and the evangelist sees an intimate link between this first prediction and Peter's confession. The following section of the gospel (8:31-11:10) is dominated by the prophecies of the passion (8:31; 9:12, 31; 10:33 f.); and the violent protestation of Peter in 8:32 shows clearly that this is a new and unexpected teaching. 'And he said this plainly' (8:32a) — it is indeed a turning-point in the self-revelation of Jesus: until now he has said nothing explicitly about his messiahship. If he still charges his disciples not to reveal his messianic identity (v. 30) – because their understanding of him is still so imperfect – he now speaks to them quite plainly of his destiny of suffering and death.

'And Peter took him, and began to rebuke him' (v. 32b). The idea of a suffering Messiah was entirely foreign to Peter; despite his confession he had not grasped the essential meaning of messiahship. In his surprise and his upset at the unexpected prospect he dares to 'rebuke' Jesus – something that no other disciple had ever done. In his turn Jesus rebuked Peter: 'Get behind me, Satan! ' (*hypage opisō mou, Satana*) – the words recall Mt. 4:10, 'Begone, Satan' (*hypage, Satana*). The temptation in the wilderness (Mt. 4:1-11; Lk. 4:1-13) aimed at getting Jesus himself to conform to the popularly accepted messianic role, to become a political messiah; it was an attempt to undermine his full acceptance of the will of God; here Peter plays Satan's role, Peter's acknowledgment of Jesus as Messiah had set him and the disciples apart from 'men' (v. 27); but now Peter is rebuked for thinking as men think. Peter, and all like him, who stand 'on the side of men,' stand opposed to God's saving purpose and align themselves with Satan.

Thus, we find that the passage is concerned not primarily with the historical situation of the ministry of Jesus but with the historical situation of the church for which Mark is writing. The reply to Jesus' first question refers to opinions available in the Palestinian situation of the ministry (v. 28); in the reply to the second question the title 'Christ' has christian overtones, and the prediction of the Passion is cast in language of the early Church (vv. 29,31). Peter's reaction and the sharp correction of it (vv. 32 f.) have much to do with an understanding of Christology. Historically, Jesus and Peter engage in dialogue. At a deeper level, 'Jesus' is the Lord addressing his Church and 'Peter' represents fallible believers who confess correctly, but then interpret their confession incorrectly. Similarly, the 'multitude' (v. 34) is the people of God for whom the general teaching (8:34-9:1) is meant. Thus, a story about Jesus and his disciples has a further purpose in terms of the risen Lord and his Church.

Here, then, more obviously than elsewhere, Mark is writing for his community. Here, above all, he is concerned with Christology. The confession of Peter is the facile profession of too many of Mark's contemporaries: 'You are the Christ.' Everything depends on what they mean by that profession and its influence on their lives. They cannot have a Risen Lord without a suffering Messiah;

they cannot be disciples without walking his road of suffering. Mark's admonition here is quite like that of Paul: 'When we cry "Abba! Father! " it is the Spirit himself bearing witness with our spirit that we are children of God, and if children, then heirs, heirs of God and fellow heirs with Christ, *provided we suffer with him* in order that we may also be glorified with him' (Rm. 8:15-17).

5. THE MESSIANIC SECRET

Throughout this gospel, Jesus is at pains to hide his messiahship. The devils know him and cry out: 'You are the Son of God' – and he commands them to be silent (1:25, 34; 3:11 f.). Silence is enjoined after notable miracles. For instance, after he had raised the daughter of Jairus, he turned to those who were present 'and he strictly charged them that no one should know this' (5:43; cf. 1:44; 7:36; 8:26). Again, when at Caesarea Philippi Peter had recognized his messiahship, and later when he was transfigured before Peter and James and John, he admonished them to tell nobody until he had risen from the dead (8:30; 9:9). From time to time he withdrew from the crowd on secret journeys (7:27; 9:30). He gave his disciples private instructions (e.g. 4:10 f., 33 f.).

Strictly speaking, the *secrecy* motif, at least in the direct form of the imposition of silence, is found only in the first part of the gospel. The related motif of the *incomprehension* of the disciples, on the other hand, spans both parts of the gospel and is integral to both sections. Thus the motifs, though related, are distinct. The disciples' lack of understanding prevails to the end and is even more prominent in the second part than in the first. The insistence on secrecy can lessen and disappear in the second part as it becomes clearer and clearer that the path of Jesus lies in one direction.

The *identity* of Jesus and the *nature* of his messiahship – these are the themes of the first and the second parts of the gospel respectively, and they are the stuff of the messianic secret. 'Those outside' (4:11), 'they' (4:33 f.), 'men' (8:27) are those who are hardhearted and who will not understand or accept the person of Jesus, his messiahship. They do not grasp the inner meaning of his parables – God has not revealed it to them because they are not receptive. Cf. Rm. 9-11. 'Israel failed to obtain what it sought. The elect obtained it, but the rest were hardened' (Rm. 11:7). In regard to his miracles they did not 'see signs' (cf. Jn. 6:26); they did not perceive the true significance of his works. The imposition of silence after the miracles makes that point: the bystanders have not understood, therefore they are to keep silent (cf. Mk. 1:44; 5:43; 7:36; 8:26). That the demons are forbidden to divulge his identity (1:34; 3:12) is perhaps meant to underline the fact that his exorcisms were a manifestation of his messiahship even though the demons alone were able to recognize this.

Twice (8:30 and 9:9) silence is enjoined on the disciples, but each time the situation is different. In the first case (8:30) they have perceived and acknowledged his messiahship. In the other case (9:9) they are given the limit of that silence: 'Until the Son of man should have risen from the dead.' However, the resurrection marks not only the limit of the secret: it lies at the centre of their failure to understand (9:10). Until they had recognized Jesus as Messiah they had nothing to reveal. But they are not yet ready to preach him: they must learn what his suffering, death and resurrection mean before they can give a true picture of him. The imposition of secrecy on the disciples is not permanent. Indeed, it will be their duty to proclaim not only the messianic identity of Jesus but also the nature of his messiahship – but this will be beyond the Cross and the Resurrection. Half-way through the gospel they discover the answer to the question, 'Who is Jesus? ' (8:29). And the gospel closes with the message (16:7) that will open their eyes to the full reality of his person. The messianic secret is concerned with Christology. It is another way of insisting that one cannot have Christianity without the Cross. 'Was it not *necessary* that the Christ should suffer these things and enter into his glory? ' (Lk. 24:26).

---

[1]F. Neirynck, *Duality in Mark*. Contributions to the Study of the Markan Redaction (Louvain: Leuven University Press, 1972).

THREE	*The Gospel of St. Matthew*

AUTHORSHIP, DESTINATION AND DATE

THE PLAN

THE STRUCTURE

MATTHEW'S MILIEU

THE COMMUNITY OR CHURCH IN MATTHEW

THE SERMON ON THE MOUNT

THE GREAT COMMISSION, Mt. 28:18-20

1 AUTHORSHIP, DESTINATION AND DATE

The unanimous tradition of the early Church is that Matthew, one of the Twelve, was the first of the four evangelists to write a gospel, and that he wrote it in Aramaic. However, the gospel of Matthew, as it has come down to us in the New Testament, was written in Greek; it is not a translation. The relationship between the traditional Aramaic writing and the later gospel is unclear. Matthew may have been the author of the Aramaic work; we are unable to name the author of the Greek gospel. As a matter of convenience we still continue to refer to it as the Gospel of Matthew.

This gospel was addressed to Greek-speaking Jewish Christians. An indication of this are a number of Jewish expressions: the parasceve (27:62), *raca, gehenna* (5:22), Beelzebul (10:25), and allusions to Jewish customs: ritual washing of hands before eating (15:2), the wearing of phylacteries — and the author rarely feels it necessary to give an explanation. Matthew is particularly interested in the fate of Israel; and he is concerned with the problem of the Law: which is now to be interpreted according to the principles of the higher law of love.

It is not possible to date the gospel with precision. Despite the common assumption, it is far from clear that Matthew used Mark; yet, it is reasonable to assume that it is the later of the two writings. The interest in Church structure would suggest a relatively late date. We might place it in the decade 80-90 A.D.

2. THE PLAN

The gospel of Matthew falls naturally into seven parts – with the
first part, the Infancy Narrative, forming a prologue. The structure
of chapters 3-25 is precise: five sections, each containing a narrative part and a discourse. Each of the discourses has a brief introduction (5:1-2; 10:1-5; 13:1-3; 18:1-2; 24:1-3) and each is closed
by a stereotyped formula: 'And it came to pass, when Jesus had
finished these sayings. . .' (7:28; 11:1; 13:53; 19:1; 26:1). These
five central parts of Matthew are not so many disconnected units;
there is a close link between them. The narratives indicate the progressive movements of events, while the discourses illustrate a
parallel progress in the messianic concept of the kingdom of
heaven.

I.	Prologue: Infancy Narrative	1-2
II.	The Kingdom Appears	
	The Preliminary Manifestation	3-4
	Sermon on the Mount	5-7
III.	Jesus' Saving Mission	
	Ten Miracles	8-9
	Missionary Discourse	10
IV.	The Hidden Kingdom	
	Opposition and Division	11-12
	Parables of the Kingdom	13
V.	The Kingdom Develops	
	Formation of the Disciples	14-17
	Community Discourse	18
VI.	Towards the Passion	
	Mounting Opposition of Judaism	19-22
	Judgment Pronounced	23-25
VII.	Passion and Resurrection	26-28[1]

3. THE STRUCTURE

We notice that the five discourses in the central part of Matthew
are addressed to: (1) His disciples (5:1-2); (2) The twelve (10:1,5);
(3) The crowd (13:2); (4) The disciples (18:1); (5) His disciples
(24:1). It has been convincingly argued that by 'the disciples' in
18:1, Matthew has in mind the Twelve. This means that the five
discourses fall into a pattern in which the first and fifth are addressed to 'his disciples,' whereas the second and fourth are

addressed to the authoritative group within the circle of disciples as a whole. This gives the chiastic pattern: a,b,c, b', a'. (The sections a and a', b and b' corresponding). Since the discourses are spaced regularly throughout the gospel, one can infer that the whole gospel was constructed on a concentric model. The significance of this is that it points to the evangelist's intention that the corresponding elements should be read in such a way that they throw light on each other.

The structure of the gospel, therefore, shows that the evangelist intended the title 'Son of Abraham' given to Jesus in the Prologue (1:1) to be related to the command given the apostles in the epilogue 'to make disciples of all nations' (28:19). Jesus is the realization of the promise made to Abraham: 'by you all the families of the earth shall bless themselves' (Gn. 12:3). We have here an evident stress on the universality of salvation. It has a place of high priority in the theological perspective of the evangelist, as is shown by its exposed position at the very beginning and at the very end of the gospel. What then of the position of Israel? To answer this we have to take into account two texts which are found only in Matthew. The first is the statement that Jesus 'was sent only to the lost sheep of the house of Israel' (15:24), and the second is the acceptance by the Jewish people of responsibility for the death of Christ (27:24-26). Taken together these two statements suggest that, for Matthew, Israel once had a privileged position which it has now lost. The stress on the universality of salvation indicates that its place has been filled by the Gentiles.

This is a sketch of the type of argument that the redaction-critic uses to support the conclusion that Matthew divided the history of salvation into *two* periods, namely, the time of Israel and the time of the Gentiles. He based his division on those to whom the divine call was addressed: Jews and Gentiles. If Matthew thus found the diversity in the history of salvation on the side of those who hear the word, is it not because he saw those who spoke the word as a unity? The answer would appear to be in the affirmative, because the first gospel exhibits an intention to assimilate both John the Baptist and the Apostles to Jesus.

Not only is the death of John presented in terms highly evocative of the death of Jesus (compare 14:5 and 21:45-46), but John and Jesus are depicted as saying the same thing to the same audience. Both proclaim, 'Repent, for the kingdom of heaven is at hand' (3:1 and 4:17). Once could be coincidence, but this hypothesis is excluded by the occurrence of the same phenomenon twice elsewhere in the gospel (John: 3:7 and 3:10 = Jesus: 23:33 and 7:19). The impact of this evidence is heightened by the fact that nothing parallel is found in the other gospels. John the Baptist is, for Matthew, a prototype of Jesus as an agent of salvation.

The same technique is used to assimilate the apostles to Jesus. They are ordered to say what Jesus said, 'Preach as you go, saying, "The kingdom of heaven is at hand." ' (10:7). But there is more, and this subtly differentiates the position of the apostles from that of John. They are also commanded, 'Heal the sick, raise the dead, cleanse lepers, cast out devils' (10:8). This is significant because Matthew in the two chapters immediately preceding this discourse has presented a series of miracles in which Jesus heals the sick (8:5-15), raises the dead (9:18-26), cleanses a leper (8:1-4), and casts out devils (8:23-34). The four-point agreement is too carefully worked out to be interpreted as coincidence. Moreover, it is confirmed by the arrangement of this section of the first gospel.

In the first discourse, the Sermon on the Mount, Matthew presents Jesus as Messiah in word (chaps. 5-7). The purpose of the narrative section which follows (chaps. 8-9) is to propose Jesus as Messiah in deed, because this narrative section is entirely made up of miracle stories. Then follows the Missionary Discourse addressed to the Twelve (chap. 10) which is succeeded by another narrative section beginning with the question raised by John the Baptist, 'Are you he who is to come, or shall we look for another? ' (11:3). The evangelist manifestly expects his readers to ask themselves the same question. Why, then, did he not place the question immediately after the presentation of Jesus as Messiah in word and deed (chaps. 5-9)? To put it another way, why did he insert a chapter concerning the Twelve between the question and the subject on which it bears? Given the careful structure of the first gospel one is forced to say that the arrangement is deliberate, and must have a meaning. The meaning can only be that Matthew believed that a decision regarding Jesus necessarily involved a decision concerning his Church represented by the Twelve. In other words, an authentic commitment to Jesus was possible only within the context of membership in his community.[2]

4. MATTHEW'S MILIEU

Matthew has a special interest in the role and fate of Israel in history. But he also feels that there is a single people of God in *both* Testaments which amounts to the true Israel. God exercises his Lordship in an uninterrupted saving pattern in the two covenants. One should speak, then, not of an old/new Israel but of a false/true people. Matthew exposes one aspect of this in describing Israel under judgment. This is notably evident in the parable of the Wicked Tenants (21:33-43) with its warning that the Kingdom will be given to another people of God, a new messianic community in place of the unbelieving Jews. Matthew's narrative of the passion accentuates the collective responsibility of the Jerusalem Jews in rejecting Jesus. The responsibility for Jesus' death rests wholly with the people of the Old Covenant; this reaches a climax when they accept responsibility in 27:25. There is a graphic paradox: the Jews demand Jesus' death, while the Gentiles affirm his innocence. The Jews are no longer *ho laos theou* (the people of God) but *Ioudaioi* — merely a race. They are contrasted with the Roman soldiers who confess that Jesus is the Son of God (27:54). The Messiah of Israel thus becomes the Messiah of the pagans. For Matthew, the gift of the Kingdom lies in recognizing Jesus as Messiah. The response given him decides true membership in the Community.

Connected with the question of Matthew's milieu are the two apparently contrasting viewpoints on the scope of Jesus' mission. Two texts proper to Matthew limit the mission to Israel (10:5 f.; 15:24), whereas 28:19 is clearly the great missionary command with all nations as its goal. This discrepancy has been variously explained. It could reflect the early christian tradition that the entry of the nations would result not of a mission *to* them, but of *their* coming to Zion as pilgrims. Or, Mt. 28:19 f. would be a development of 10:5, the commission to the disciples, in the light of the death and resurrection of Jesus. Jesus himself will now go to the nations in the person of his messengers and bring them the Kingdom. Thus, the universal mission becomes part of the Parousia which was initiated by his death and resurrection. Jesus confined his lifetime commission to the Israelite community, knowing that *God's* act of power would bring the Gentiles into the Kingdom. When he gives the command to 'make disciples of all nations' in 28:19, this implies that *God* no longer limits his saving grace to Israel but turns his mercy to the whole Gentile world.

5. THE COMMUNITY OR CHURCH IN MATTHEW

In this gospel it becomes exceedingly difficult to distinguish between the disciples and the Community (or Church) because in Matthew's eyes they blend into one. This is evident in the instructions given to the disciples in Mt. 18 which really form a *Gemeindeordnung*, a 'Community Rule.' Moreover, it is here that Matthew also brings together his significant ideas on the Church: true greatness in the Kingdom (vv. 1-4), scandal (5-10), the Lost Sheep (12-14), brotherly care and correction, authority in the Church (15-18), association in prayer (19 f.), and forgiving offences (21-35). For Matthew, the Church is a sociological reality centred on God with Jesus as its model. It is a family of children of the Father. Jesus is present in the *midst* of his Church — an idea framed by the Immanu-el promise of 1:23 and the promise to be 'with us always' in 28:20. We find he is *with* his followers, *present* in his missionaries (10:40), in all in need (25:35-45) in all received in his name (18:5), and in the assembly (18:20). When the disciples are persecuted, it is because they represent Jesus and imitate also his sufferings. Matthew too seems to see the community as a ship beaten by the waves, as he shows in the story of the stilling of the storm (8:23-27; cf. Mk. 4:35-41). In Matthew, this episode becomes a paradigm of discipleship for, even more than in Mark, his boat becomes a *navis ecclesiae* (the 'ship of the Church') and the cry *Kyrie sōson* ('Save, Lord') is at once a prayer and a confession of discipleship. 'Those of little faith,' the *oligoi pistoi*, are those in the boat of the Church. Matthew knows that, like the disciples in the gospel, his community has but 'little faith'; he himself had experienced the 'false prophets' of 24:11 f. The men who 'marvel' are those who learn of the good news in the preaching. But they do not know quite as Matthew does the lack of love and faith which menaces the interior of the Community in the apostolic Church.

The Church is not a secluded cenacle of the elect who are self-assured of salvation. It is a mixed body, comprised of men and women who are fully human, who will have to face a separation between good and evil at the last judgment. It is the completion of the disciple-group which Jesus formed around him during his ministry, to continue his mission with an ideal and a dedication identical with his own. This is why he gave authority in his own person to the closest of his disciples: he wanted them to preach and direct in his stead. The word *ekklēsia* occurs in the gospels only in Mt. 16:18 and 18:17, though it is frequent in the rest of the New Testament. (It has been pointed out that those who would argue that Jesus did not speak of a 'church' still must explain the wide use of the term by the early Christians). Matthew uses the term *ekklēsia* to designate the messianic community as distinct from the Old Testament community. This is the force of Jesus' saying to Peter, '. . . *my* Church,' in 16:18. For Matthew, only one standard settles membership in this messianic community: to have brought forth fruits of the Kingdom (21:43), to have done the will of God (5:16; 7:21), to have attained to the higher righteousness (5:20) and shaped one's life course to enter the Kingdom by the narrow gate (7:13). 'Let your light so shine before men that they may see your good works and glorify your heavenly Father' (5:16).

Matthew's Church is seen in the perspective of the coming judgment, and the task of discipleship is interpreted accordingly. The seven Kingdom-of-God parables (chap. 13) combine both ecclesial and eschatological motifs. Jesus rules over the Church, and from the Church over the world – thus realizing the Kingship of God in the present period of salvation. The Church is the link between accomplishment here and now and final consummation. The members of the Community are the personal members of the Church who have submitted to God's rule in Jesus. They keep it warm and alive as *persons*, rather than as an institution. In short, the Church is a preliminary stage and school preparing for and already representing the future *basileia* or Kingdom.

6. THE SERMON ON THE MOUNT

When the Sermon on the Mount (Mt. 5-7) is compared with the rest of the New Testament, it becomes clear that these words of Jesus – his moral teaching – were preserved primarily because they were part of the essential structure of the Gospel. Jesus did make demands, he did lay down the law of the Messiah. There is no conflict between Gospel and Law – the law of Christ. The Gospel is not only kerygma, not only kerygma and didache, it is also a moral code, and this was so from the beginning. We may put it another way and say that the kerygma involves the acceptance of Christ and of his demands, and that the didache includes precepts and rules of conduct for christian living. 'For some in the primitive Church, if not for all, the penetrating demands of Jesus, no less than the great kerygmatic affirmations about him, were part of "the bright light of the Gospel," that is, they were revelatory.'[3]

Jesus revealed himself not only in his works and words but also by the exigency of his demands.

The Sermon on the Mount is didache, a preaching to the christian community — to those already within the fold. But didache presupposes and contains kerygma: it sets out the basis of the faith, the saving events, and then goes on to teach; instruction in morals has a large part in it. The teaching will differ according to audience and circumstances (e.g. the instruction on prayer in Mt. 6:5-15 and Lk. 11:1-13). Matthew has four sayings which are concerned largely with how *not* to pray; in this context, the Lord's Prayer stands out as a model of a short prayer in contrast to long-winded effusions. In Luke, the Our Father is given in answer to the disciples' request to be taught to pray; the passage, then, goes on to urge perseverance in prayer and closes with the image of the father who will not turn a deaf ear to his son. Clearly, the Matthaean passage is addressed to men who have come from a milieu where prayer is not unknown, but where it has been open to misconceptions and abuses: it is a Judaeo-Christian didache. Luke is concerned with people who have to learn to pray and who need to be encouraged: it is a didache for converts from paganism.

The Sermon, then, is a classic example of didache. It is a collection of sayings of Jesus, compiled for the purpose of christian formation; it probably served for the instruction of catechumens or for the further direction of the newly baptized. It follows that something is presupposed; the proclamation of the Lord, crucified, risen, and to come — the declaration that Jesus has reconciled us with God and that he is our life. What is presupposed is the conquering attraction of the Good News, a sincere conversion; what has already taken place is the witness which Jesus has given, in words and works, to what he is; what is presupposed is faith in the Risen Lord.

This is the reason why Jesus is so demanding, why he goes so far beyond the Law (cf. Mt. 5:21-48). His teaching is addressed to men who have been rescued by the Good News from the power of Satan, men who already stand in the kingdom of God. He addresses men who have been pardoned, prodigal sons who have been received back into the house of their Father. Men who have received that gift and who have experienced the love and mercy of God are urged, by inner compulsion, to do the will of that heavenly Father. The demands of Christ are not further reminders of sin (cf. Rm. 7:7-13), but carry with them the divine help that enables men to obey and gives men the possibility of living as children of God.

The Sermon shows us the spirit and the demands of the Gospel of Jesus – demands far more exacting than those of the Law, and a spirit of freedom unknown to the most sincere observer of the Law. Above all, he who listens to the demands of Christ and earnestly seeks to live up to them is given the means to achieve that task, the liberal gift of grace. Here we put our finger on the difference between Law and Gospel; the Law makes demands, but does not give the means of carrying them out – it leaves man to himself; the Gospel sets man before the gift of God (salvation through Jesus Christ) and demands of him that he should make that ineffable gift the sole foundation of his life.

7. THE GREAT COMMISSION, MT. 28:18-20

This text, the final word in the gospel, has been seen to recapitulate the whole of Matthew, besides being one of the most comforting assurances which the Christian could hear that the risen Jesus lives on among us. Looking first at the literary value of the passage, one notes that it is connected with Dn. 7:14 and the image of the Son of Man there. It is not a direct quotation of Daniel, but rather presents a similar combination of authority, dominion and recognition by the nations. The form is like a *Gottesrede,* a 'divine discourse,' just as Yahweh's exhortations to observe the commandments in Deuteronomy. The sayings could have arisen as independent sayings or confessions of faith (cf. Eph. 5:14; Phil. 2:6-11). Although Jesus speaks as the *Kyrios* here, the kernel of his message is not his own person but the missionary command. He uses the language of Matthew and of the Lord living in Matthew's community. There are also the Matthaean concepts of Jesus' sovereignty, the universal destination of the gospel, the prominent role of the disciples. The sayings have not been spoken by Jesus on earth, but have been constructed by the apostolic Church. They are, however, (like the Johannine discourses) authentic expressions of his mind.

Jesus' saying that 'all power has been given to me' is directly influenced by Dn. 7:14; where we read that power was given to the Son of man. But in Daniel it is a matter of earthly power over humans, whereas in Matthew it is divine power in heaven and on earth. 'Power' (*exousia*) in the New Testament includes divine commission, authorization, and strength from above. It is inseparable from the proclamation that the Kingdom is near. 'Go, therefore, and make disciples of all nations' — *panta ta ethnē* implies, as we have seen, that God no longer limits his saying grace to Israel but turns his mercy to the Gentiles. Here (vv. 19-20a) we have Jesus' 'order of Mission,' whereas in the preceding verse (v. 18) we had the word of 'revelation.' *Mathētevein* normally has the meaning 'to be a disciple'; here, it takes on the meaning, 'to make disciples.' It suggests here finding membership in a community rather than any vague religious assent. Salvation will come to the peoples through their union in Jesus. While in Daniel the nations are ordained to serve the Son of man, here they will be invited to become disciples of Jesus. It is not a process of subjection, but of being drawn to Jesus through persuasion and grace. 'Teaching them all that I have commanded you': the baptized, the one taught or the 'disciple,' is he who observes Jesus' commands. 'All' his commands consists of the true life of God's people, as in Deuteronomy. God, through Jesus, is the true lawgiver.

Finally, we have Jesus' great promise of v. 20b: 'Lo, I am with you always, to the close of the age (the end of time)'. Here, in his very last words, Matthew opens out into the perspective of the Community, and the one who has spoken all the words of the gospel preceding this verse remains present to the community. They are not really left alone (cf. Jn. 14:18). Matthew does not speak of a 'departure' or of a 'farewell' of Jesus. Rather, he places the Community at the heart of the universal power of the Resurrection. The 'end of time' which he has in mind designates the time of the Community (cf. 13:39 f.; 24:3). It corresponds to the 'hereafter' of 26:64, where Jesus tells Caiaphas, 'hereafter you will see the Son of man seated at the right hand of Power. . .'. Jesus is promising his help as God himself, echoing all his assurances throughout the gospels: 'Fear not! '; 'I am with you! '; 'It is *I*! ' Whereas Luke closes with a farewell blessing and the ascension (Lk. 24:51), here in Matthew Jesus assures us that he will be abidingly present in the congregation. Moreover, what is present is not his static presence in one chosen group, but his dynamic and helping presence for a worldwide mission. It is the mission of salvation: the name of *Immanu-el*, 'God-with-us,' is perfectly realized in the name and work of *Jesus*, 'God saves.'

Thus, Mt. 28:18-20 both assigns to Jesus the functions of Yahweh in the Old Testament and sums up Matthew's view of the *Kyrios* in the New. He has universal lordship, he gives commands that determine the whole life of God's people and their relationship to him, and he promises to be the sustaining Lord at all times. Will he not keep his word? 'Where two or three are gathered in my name, there am I in the midst of them' (Mt. 18:20).

[1]H. Wansborough, 'St. Matthew,' in Fuller, R. C. (ed.), *A New Catholic Commentary on Holy Scripture* (London: Nelson 1969), 905.

[2]J. Murphy-O'Connor, 'Redaction-Criticism,' *Scripture in Church*, Vol. 5, No. 16, 1974.

[3]W. D. Davies, *The Setting of the Sermon on the Mount* (New York: Cambridge University Press 1964), 437.

| *The Gospel of St. Luke*

AUTHORSHIP, DESTINATION AND DATE

THE PLAN

THE MINISTER OF THE WORD

THE PURPOSE

THE MESSAGE OF LUKE

1. AUTHORSHIP, DESTINATION AND DATE

The testimony of tradition regarding the authorship of the third gospel is unhesitating: it is the work of St. Luke. Present-day scholarship, in general, is agreeable to accept the tradition. It follows that Luke is also the author of the Acts of the Apostles, for Luke and Acts are demonstrably two volumes of the one work. Luke is named three times in the Pauline letters: Phm. 23 f.; Col. 4:14; 2 Tm. 4:11.

Luke certainly wrote for Gentile Christians. Thus, he consistently avoids many matters which might appear too specifically Jewish. He omits whole passages: the traditions of the ancients (Mk. 7:1-23), the return of Elijah (Mk. 9:11-13), the antitheses in the Sermon (Mt. 5:21 f., 27 f., 33-37). Again, one cannot be precise about the date of this gospel. We may place it about the year 80 A.D. — whether before or after that date is impossible to say.

2. PLAN

Prologue 1:1-4

I. From the Temple to the Close of the Galilean Ministry
                                                    1:5 — 9:50

    The Infancy Narrative   1:5 — 2:52

    Preparation of the Ministry of Jesus
                            3:1 — 4:13

    The Galilean Ministry   4:14 — 9:50

II. The Journey from Galilee to Jerusalem   9:51 — 19:27

III. Last Days of the Suffering and Risen Christ
      in Jerusalem   19:28 – 24:53

      Ministry in Jerusalem   19:28 – 21:38

      The Passion   22 – 23

      After the Resurrection   24

Luke, like Mark and Matthew, has followed the primitive fourfold
gospel plan. However, he has made two important changes in this
order and so has given to his gospel quite a different bias. By
placing at the beginning the long Infancy narrative (chaps. 1-2) –
which balances the Passion and Resurrection narrative – he has
presented the story of Jesus in perfect equilibrium. By his insertion
of the long section (9:51-18:14), he has fitted cleverly into the
gospel narrative a very important collection of episodes and sayings
which are entirely absent from Mark and only partially represented
in Matthew. This Lucan section is dominated by the perspective of
the Passion, and the journey to Jerusalem is seen as a journey to
death (cf. 9:51; 13:22; 17:11). Thus, despite the general agreement
with Mark and Matthew, the third gospel has a distinctive character. But, while the main division is clear, it is not so easy to give
a satisfactory arrangement of the details.

3. THE MINISTER OF THE WORD

1. THE HISTORIAN Luke's careful wording of his prologue and his
dedication of the work to the 'excellent Theophilus' introduce a
work that does not purport merely to tell us about the Good
News; his object is to establish the soundness of the catechetical
teaching and, for that reason, his express intention is to weigh his
sources. In view of this he shows care in presenting historical data.
By the detailed synchronisms prefixed to his narrative of the birth
of Jesus (2:1-3) and of the ministry of John (3:1 f.), he sets these
events in the framework of general history. He can, on occasion,
correct the chronology of his sources. Thus, while in Mark we are
told that the Transfiguration took place six days after Peter's profession of faith at Caesarea Philippi (Mk. 9:2), Luke quietly modi-
fies the statement and says: 'about eight days after' (9:28); and he
regularly qualifies round numbers by adding 'about' (1:56; 3:23;
etc.). He speaks of Herod as 'tetrach' – his correct title – (9.7)
and not, as he was popularly described, as 'king' (Mk. 6:14).
Similarly, he speaks of the 'lake of Gennesaret' (5:1) rather than

of the 'sea of Galilee' (Mk. 1:6). He mentions contemporary facts:
the massacre of Galileans by Pilate (13:1-3) and the fall of the
tower of Siloam (13:4 f.). It is in the same spirit that he has had
recourse to new sources.

We may not, however, judge the work of Luke as we would
that of a modern historian; his gospel is not scientific history, nor
is it, any more than Matthew and Mark, a biography of Jesus. Even
though he has retouched his sources in this respect, he has scarcely
anything of the modern passion for precise chronology and detailed topography. He is interested in historical facts but he does
not have our regard for 'history.' If he does promise to write an
'orderly account' that order is primarily theological, for his concern is with the things delivered by those who were not merely
eyewitnesses of events but 'ministers of the word' (1:2).

2. THE EVANGELIST Luke himself is, first and foremost, a
'minister of the word,' an evangelist, and his work is, in the strict
sense, a 'gospel.' That is why he has remained faithful to the general plan of Mark, the consecrated plan of the apostolic kerygma.
But while Luke, no doubt because of his Greek background, is
somewhat more meticulous than the other synoptists about historical data, his intention remains, fundamentally, kerygmatic and
theological.

In short, we might say that Luke was a historian because he
was a theologian. His view of the *pragmata*, 'the things' (1:1), was
colored by his reflections on the relevance of the traditional *logoi*,
'teaching' (1:4) for his own time. If this teaching – the sayings of
Jesus about the importance of human relationships, about the
virtues of patience, perseverance, poverty of spirit, about the necessity of persistence in prayer – did have a far-reaching importance
for all time, then it meant that the period after the Resurrection
and Ascension had a value peculiar to itself as circumstantially influential for salvation, and not merely as a short interval before the
Parousia. This idea molded Luke's interpretation of the tradition
but immediately raised the question of the relationship between
Luke's contemporary situation and the life of Christ.

For Luke, salvation had come with Christ; after the Ascension,
men would be saved through him and because of what he had accomplished. The events of the life of Christ were decisive for the
world, constituting the beginning of the last days. For Luke, too,
Christ was the fulfillment of all the promises, in spite of the out-

ward circumstances of his life which blinded the eyes of the Jews to the reality before them. This implied that all that went before Christ was merely preparatory. Yet, preparation, fulfillment in Christ, and eventual universal salvation through him in these last days, though constituting quite distinct epochs, nonetheless, together form one divine plan for the salvation of the world, a plan progressively realized through history.

4. THE PURPOSE

Like Matthew, Luke was a second generation Christian, writing after the fall of Jerusalem (70 A.D.). His Jesus, too, is the risen Lord, the Savior. As a Gentile convert, he is not exercised, as was Matthew, by the relationship of Christianity to Judaism; for him, the break with Judaism is an accomplished fact. He does not look for an imminent return of the Lord (nor does Matthew, for that matter); his two-volume work (gospel and Acts) is written for Christians who live in the post-apostolic age. Indeed the Parousia is, in a true sense, a present reality, present in the risen Lord. Christ, the source of salvation, is in the christian community. The present moment is the time of fulfillment. This explains the frequency of the adverbs *nun* ('now') and *sēmeron* ('today') in the gospel (and Acts) – e.g. 2:11; 3:22; 6:21-25; 9:33, 12:52; 9:5, 9: 23:43. The 'today,' the 'now' of Christ's presence is the time of salvation. And now life is poured out in the Holy Spirit.

Luke is the theologian of salvation history. For him, that history falls into two periods: the period of Israel; the period of Christ and of his Church.[1] The first, the time of the Old Testament, is the time of preparation for the culminating event of Christ's coming: 'The law and the prophets were until John; since then the good news of the kingdom of God is preached' (16:16). The second period begins with Jesus and is supremely the whole time when he, as exalted Lord, is present in the Church. This is the perspective of Luke's great work. After his account of the infancies of John and of Jesus, he turns to the preaching of the kingdom of God in Palestine, first by the precursor and then by the Messiah; and at the close of the work he has Paul proclaiming the same kingdom at the centre of the Roman world (Acts 28:30 f.). The gospel tells of the mission of Jesus and of the saving event of his death and resurrection; it ends with his glorification in the ascension. Jesus had come as the Messiah of his people and had found himself rejected by them. But his mission had not failed; he had brought salvation to a new Israel – repentance and forgiveness of sins must be preached in his name to all nations, beginning from Jerusalem (24:47).

5. THE MESSAGE OF LUKE

UNIVERSALISM   Luke may be called the evangelist for all men, writing in a way that all men can understand. He knows that the risen Lord, so present to him and to his community, yearns to be present in every community of men. The note of universalism sustained throughout the gospel is first sounded in the infancy narrative. The angels heralding the birth of Jesus call for peace on earth 'among men with whom (God) is pleased' (2:14); this peace comes in the person of God's own Son, 'a light for revelation to the Gentiles' (2:32; cf. Is. 42:6; 49:6). Isaiah is also quoted in the words of the Baptist: 'All flesh shall see the salvation of God' (3:6), and it is in support of this view that Luke extends his genealogy of Jesus back to Adam, parent of all flesh (3:23).

To Jesus – and to the Christian who would follow him – no one is a 'foreigner'; no one is despised by him, and nothing is too mean for his all-embracing love. The last commission of Jesus is that 'repentance and forgiveness of sins should be preached to *all* nations, beginning from Jerusalem' (24:47) – a commission which Luke has shown in Acts as being already fulfilled, with the message offered to the Jews too, for it is *universal* – and which he himself is helping to fulfil even in writing his gospel. It 'seemed good' to Luke (1:3) to bring home his message of universalism most closely by including in his gospel, as none of the other evangelists do, the parable of the Good Samaritan (10:30-37). Surely Jesus felt that only through this poignant, vivid story, drawn from the everyday world of his people, could he convey to them the truth that all barriers, all distinctions of persons, fall before the absolute demands of *love*. By writing his gospel for all men – out of the love in his own heart – Luke had indeed learned well this vital word of his Lord, a word bringing newness of life and peace.

THE SAVIOR   If Luke's message is concerned with the gifts which the Lord's coming meant for the world, its specific impact is to be found even more directly in the presentation of the savior himself amidst his own. For, in Luke's eyes, Jesus was simply Savior of men. It is in this capacity that the evangelist, who had never met Jesus, had come most fully to perceive and to receive his Lord. He

saw that the whole ministry of Jesus was marked by understanding, forgiveness and compassion, all flowing form the
exquisite sensitivity of Jesus. The works proclaimed by Jesus at the
very beginning of his ministry (Lk. 4:18; cf. Is. 61:1 f.) are the
works of a Savior, the very deeds which he himself will perform:
preaching good news to the poor, proclaiming release to captives,
restoring sight to the blind, freeing the oppressed. Although the
title 'Savior' is used only once in his gospel (in the annunciation to
the shepherds, 2:11), yet, throughout, Luke portrays the poor, the
captive, the blind, the oppressed – of many kinds, of all sorts and
conditions of men and women – as being touched by the gentle,
saving power of Jesus.

Perhaps nowhere more than in the wonderful passage on the
'woman of the city who was a sinner' (7:36-50) do we see Jesus as
Luke saw him. The Lord does not hesitate between the self-right-
eous Pharisee and the repentant sinner and his words are clear and
to the point: 'I tell you, her great love proves that her many sins
have been forgiven' (7:47). Luke alone records the words of Jesus
to the 'good thief' (23:43) and his prayer for his executioners:
'Father, forgive them, for they do not know what they do'
(23:34). He alone tells of the look that moved Peter so deeply
(22:61). Everywhere, at all times, there is forgiveness. It has been
well said that the gospel of Luke is the gospel of great pardons.

It is typical of Luke that in his gospel he has paid special attention to women, for in the world of his day the position of women
was degraded, and the insistence of the third evangelist is all the
more striking when we compare his gospel with Matthew and
Mark. Among the women introduced by Luke are: Elizabeth the
mother of the Baptist (1:39-58), Anna, the prophetess (2:36-38),
the widow of Nain (7:11-17), the repentant sinner (7:36-50), the
women of Galilee who accompanied Jesus on the public ministry,
notably Mary Magdalene, Joanna and Susanna (8:2 f.) who were
with him at the end (23:55 f.), the sisters of Bethany, Martha and
Mary (10:38-42). There are, also, the woman who declared the
mother of Jesus blessed (11:27 f.) and the women of Jerusalem
who met Jesus on his way to Calvary (23:27-31). We find, besides,
two parables proper to Luke in which women figure: the Lost
Coin (15:8-10) and the Unjust Judge (18:1-8). Finally, it is impossible not to recognize that the person of Mary is shown in a vivid
light in the infancy narrative. God deigns to inform her of the

great thing he is to do in her, and the lingering echo of the angel's 'Rejoice! O favored one' is heard already in the *Magnificat*.

But the sinner, the outcast, the humble people, the distressed and the poor were asked simply for one thing: to place all their trust in a loving Father who provides for them so much more than for the birds of the air and the lilies of the field (12:22-32). And this could be asked of them because they had been given One who had been hailed as Savior at his birth and whose last message was of salvation, and of forgiveness in his name to all nations (24:46 f.). Luke who was deeply sensitive to sickness and whole- ness, to disquiet and joyful peace, and to the most elementary human needs – Luke was perfectly attuned to this Savior.

RICH AND   There is great gentleness, but there is nothing soft or
POOR   easy-going about this Jesus of Luke. Indeed, there is
something almost shocking about his call for total renunciation, his invitation to give up *all* one has. It is certainly shocking in the light of his Church's historical pact with capitalism. This demand is prepared for by sharp warnings on the danger of riches; Luke is far more emphatic than the other evangelists on this score: 6:24-26; 12:13-21; 14:33; 14:9, 11, 19-31; 18:22. The parable of the Rich Fool (12:16-21) gives the moral: 'So is he who lays up treasure for himself, and is not rich towards God.' A choice must be made, for no man can serve God and mammon (16:13). On the positive side, there is the fact that Jesus lived among the poor. At his birth it was shepherds who came to him (2:8), not the Magi of Matthew. His mother and Joseph gave the offering of the poor (2:24). In short, it is above all in the humble birth of the Son of God and the penury of his life that *voluntary* poverty is exalted: 'Foxes have holes, and the birds of the air have nests; but the Son of man has nowhere to lay his head' (9:58). And the example was effica- cious, for Simon and James and John – and so many others – left everything and followed him (5:11).

It is to be expected, then, that Luke insists on renunciation. Confidence is not to be placed on riches (12:13-21) but in God who will provide (12:22-32): 'Sell your possessions and give alms' (12:33). The followers of Jesus must renounce *all*: 'Whoever of you does not renounce all that he has cannot be my disciple' (14:33), and the ruler who came to him is bidden: 'Sell all that you have and distribute to the poor ... and come, follow me' (18:22). In both these texts, and in 5:11, 28, Luke stresses the completeness of the renunciation (cf. Mk. 10:21; Mt. 19:21). He, too, is the only one of the synoptists who includes the *wife* among the possessions of this world which call for renunciation or detachment on the part of the perfect disciple (14:26; 18:29).

There is another form of renunciation which the Lucan Christ demands; it is evident, for instance, in the parable of 12:42-48. The parable deals with the alternative conduct of a servant whom his master would place in charge of his affairs while he himself was absent on a long journey. Especially significant, in v. 42, is the change of 'servant' (*doulos*) to 'steward' (*oikonomos*) (cf. Mt. 24:45). When Luke wrote his gospel, hellenistic Christians viewed their leaders as God's stewards (cf. 1 Cor. 4:1 f; Tit. 1:7; 1 Pt. 4:10). They are God's deputies, acting not in their own name but in his. Hence, they are not masters of the community but men dedicated to its service. As stewards, God's stewards, they are more than ever *servants*. Cf. Lk. 6:39-45; 22:24-27. In Acts 20:17-35 Paul movingly outlines, in personal terms, the quality of community service. For Luke, service is the essence of office in the Church. And Jesus had asked for the setting aside of all ambition, for the renunciation of any desire to lord it over others.

PRAYER, JOY, PEACE — Luke is the gospel of prayer, and the supreme example of prayer is given by Jesus Christ himself. This fact is not neglected by Matthew and Mark. According to the three synoptists, Jesus prayed in Gethsemane; he prayed after the first multiplication of loaves (Mk. 6:46; Mt. 14:23); he prayed in Capernaum after he had cured many (Mk. 1:35). But Luke speaks of the prayer of Jesus in eight further circumstances. He prayed at the baptism (Lk. 3:21), he retired into the desert to pray (5:16), and before choosing his apostles he spent the whole night in prayer (6:12). He prayed before the confession of Peter (9:18) and later told Peter that he had prayed specially for him (22:32). He prayed at the Transfiguration, and it was the sight of him in prayer that moved his disciples to ask to be taught how to pray (11:1). He prayed on the cross for his executioners. Indeed, we might add that the surrender of his life to the Father was a prayer (23:46). Jesus often recommended prayer to his disciples: persevering prayer like that of the importunate friend (11:5-13) or of the widow before the unjust judge (18:1-8). They must pray to obtain the Holy Spirit (11:13) and, in short, they ought to pray at all times (21:36). Their prayer must be true prayer, like that of the taxcollector (18:13).

The personal example of Jesus is nowhere clearer than in Gethsemane. At his hour of trial (22:39-46), the Lord chose to drink the cup, he chose the cross; the disciples must pray that they, too, in their turn, will make the right choice. Here is the culmination of the prayer of Jesus: in anguish, vividly foreseeing and humanly shrinking from, the horrors of the passion, burdened above all by his love for his people and for all men, he prayed more earnestly. He himself in his hour of trial, this 'temptation,' put into practice his own recommendation to his disciples. If Paul could understand, so clearly, that the power of God can support our weakness (cf. 2 Cor. 12:10; Phil. 4:13), Jesus himself has experienced, with a clarity we cannot imagine, that weakness and that strength.

This passage on the agony of the Savior should not only remind us of the cost of our redemption but, above all, ought to be a powerful encouragement for us. Because, indeed, our High Priest is no stranger to suffering; he knows the demands it can make on our humanness and he can fully sympathise with our human lot (cf. Heb. 4:15; 5:7-9). And, in our own prayer, we should keep in mind the precious observation of Luke: 'being in an agony, he prayed more earnestly' (22:44), and of Matthew 'he went away and prayed for the third time, saying the same words' (26:44). The evangelists have given these words: '*Abba*, Father all things are possible to you; remove this cup from me; yet not what I will but what you will' (Mk. 14:36; cf. Lk. 22:42; Mt. 26:39). The prayer of Jesus was an *earnest* prayer, yes, but not a prayer of many words. It was a cry from the heart.

The coming of the Savior has created an atmosphere of joy and Luke is keenly aware of it. The annunciation of the birth of John includes a promise of joy (1:14), a promise that is fulfilled (1:58), and the unborn child leaps for joy in the womb at the presence of the mother of the Messiah (1:41, 44). At the greater annunciation the angel bids Mary rejoice (*chaire* = 'Rejoice! ') and her thankful joy finds expression in the *Magnificat* (1:46-55). The birth of Jesus is an event of great joy for the angels who proclaim it and for the people he had come to save (2:10, 13 f.). Later, the crowds rejoiced at the works they had witnessed (3:17). The seventy-two disciples returned, rejoicing, from their mission; Jesus pointed out to them the true motive of joy (10:20) and he himself 'rejoiced in the Holy Spirit' (10:21). Zacchaeus received Jesus joyfully (19:6). The disciples rejoiced on the occasion of the entry into Jerusalem (19:37) and after the ascension they returned to the city with great joy and praised God in the temple (24:52). The parables of chapter 15 depict the joy of God at the finding of a lost sheep, the return of a sinner.

Peace follows on joy, the peace which Jesus gives (7:50; 8:48), the peace that came into the world at his coming (2:14, 29). The song of the angels celebrating the birth of the *Rex pacificus* (2:14) is echoed by the disciples when the King of peace enters the holy city in triumph (19:38) – the city that did not receive his message of peace (19:42). It is this same gift of peace that the risen Christ gave (24:36), the peace which the disciples spread throughout the world (Acts 7:26; 9:31; 15:23). But peace and joy, both, are the fruit of prayer, of close personal union with Jesus Christ the Saviour.

---

[1] The well-known theory of Hans Conzelmann that the Lucan *Heilsgeschichte* falls into three periods: i) the period of Israel; ii) the period of Christ; iii) the period of the Church, has been convincingly disproved by Helmut Flender. Flender agrees with Conzelmann that Lk. 16:16 signals a division of epochs. The new replaces the old – the new includes both the period of Jesus' ministry and the period of the Church. H. Conzelman, *The Theology of St. Luke* (London: Faber & Faber 1961); H. Flender, *St. Luke, Theologian of Redemptive History* (London: S.P.C.K. 1967). See J. Kodell, 'The Theology of Luke in Recent Study,' *Biblical Theology Bulletin* 1 (1971), 115-144.

FIVE

The Acts of the Apostles

AUTHOR AND DATE

PURPOSE AND SCOPE

THE PLAN

THE SOURCES

HISTORICITY

THE DOCTRINE

1. AUTHOR AND DATE

In his preface, the author of Acts presents his writing as the continuation of a single work addressed to Theophilus (Acts 1:1; cf. Lk. 1:3). A consideration of the theme of both volumes and of the close similarity of style and vocabulary bears out the obvious meaning of the preface. The title of the work, 'Acts of the Apostles,' or 'Acts of Apostles,' adequately describes a book that forms a sequel to the 'Acts and Words of Jesus' (cf. Acts 1:1) — the Gospel. Early tradition is unanimous in attributing Acts to Luke, the author of the Third Gospel. As to date, this is determined by the date assigned to the gospel: about the year 80 A.D.

2. PURPOSE AND SCOPE

Since Acts is the second volume of one work, it cannot be understood except as a continuation of Luke's Gospel; it is more correctly seen as a sequel to the Gospel than as a history of the primitive Church. After his account of the infancy of John and of Jesus, Luke turns to the preaching of the kingdom of God in Palestine, first by the Precursor and then by the Messiah; and at the end of his work he has Paul proclaiming the same kingdom at the center of the Roman world. The Gospel tells of the mission of Jesus and of the saving event of his death and resurrection; it ends with his glorification in the ascension. Jesus had come as the Messiah of his people and had found himself rejected by them. But his mission had not failed: he had brought salvation to the new Israel — repentance and forgiveness of sins must be preached in his name to all nations, beginning from Jerusalem (Lk. 24:47).

Given the close relationship between Gospel and Acts, we are not surprised to find that the composition of both runs along parallel lines. The narrative of the ministry of Jesus is formed of two more or less equal parts: the first, covering the preaching in Galilee, centers in the Twelve and ends with the mission confided to the Twelve; it is very like the accounts of Matthew and Mark. The other part, the journey to Jerusalem, begins with the mission charge to the Seventy and has material not found in Matthew and Mark. Similarly, Acts has two parts: one in which Peter has the leading role, and which looks to Jerusalem; the second, centered in Paul, breaks out of this geographical framework and turns toward Rome. In following this plan, Luke had to strike a compromise between a systematic procedure and one which arose from the organization of the sources he followed. This causes — and explains — an unevenness in the composition.

In Acts, Luke is concerned with showing the triumphal progress of the Gospel throughout the whole known world. The plan of his work is dictated by the commission of the Risen Christ to his disciples: "You shall be my witnesses in Jerusalem and in all Judaea and Samaria and to the end of the earth" (Acts 1:8). He is especially interested in the passing of the preaching from the Jews to the Gentiles and in the progress of the Gentile mission. Behind the continuous progress of the Good News through the provinces of the Roman Empire, he sees the power of the Holy Spirit. Indeed, the theme of his book may be expressed in this manner: "Acts depicts the universal spread of the Christian religion as it was begun and maintained by the power of the Holy Spirit."

It is necessary, then, that the origin of the Gentile mission and its spread should be marked by the divine guidance. In view of this, it is not surprising to learn that the missionary activity was born of persecution: after the martyrdom of Stephen, the Hellenists fled to Samaria and elsewhere, but continued to preach the Gospel. It was a divine revelation that led Peter to baptize the Gentile household of Cornelius, an event of great significance for the future of the Church. Saul was dramatically confronted by the Risen Lord in person, and this former persecutor of Christians was transformed into the great Apostle of the Gentiles. Under his leadership, the mission penetrated Asia Minor and, at a later date, Europe; and he who had been set apart by the Spirit (Acts 13:2)

continued to be divinely guided (Acts 16:6-10). The sufferings of
Paul, his trial and imprisonment, were providential (Acts 20:22 f.);
and storm and shipwreck offered no hindrance to the design of
God (Acts 27:23 f.). In Rome, following his constant practice,
Paul preached first to the Jews; when they rejected the Gospel, he
turned to the Gentiles, confident that they would accept it (Acts
28:23-28). Thus, the book ends, its purpose achieved. The word
had gone forth from Jerusalem to the end of the earth for, in the
capital of the world, Paul was "preaching the kingdom of God and
teaching about the Lord Jesus Christ quite openly and unhindered"
(Acts 28:31).

Luke was aware that the Gentile mission had been set on foot
before Paul began to play his part, and he knew that Paul was not
the only architect of the Gentile Church. But, since his purpose
was to portray the progress of the Church, he could not have
chosen a more effective and dramatic way of doing so, and it is
typical of the genius of Luke that he should have gone about it in
this way. For it is true that Paul the missioner and Paul the theologian has set his stamp on Christianity for all time. The alleged
antithesis between the religion of Jesus and the religion of Paul is
based on a complete misunderstanding of the teaching of both; but
the fact that Paul could be put forward, with some plausability, as
the real founder of Christianity (or as the great perverter of the
Gospel of Jesus) is an indication of his stature. That stature Luke
has perceived. When he had written the acts of Jesus, culminating
in the great saving event, he turned to the emergence of a new
Israel; then, after his "Infancy-narrative" of the Church, he went
on to trace its progress in the "Acts of Paul." Just as Christianity
is grateful to him for his strikingly beautiful portrait of Jesus, it is
also grateful for his portrait of Paul.

Luke appears to have had a certain apologetical purpose, at
least when he turns his attention to the work of Paul. Important
Roman officials (Sergius Paulus, Gallio) attest that the Apostle's
preaching is not a danger to the State. Felix and Festus (as well as
Agrippa II) do not find Paul guilty of a capital charge, or of any
charge. The centurion Julius, to whom he had been committed as a
prisoner, treated Paul with great consideration. The latter's appeal
to Caesar's tribunal had saved him from assassination at the hands
of the Jews; and in Rome, until the statutory two years had elap-
sed, he was held under a remarkably lenient form of house arrest
(Acts 28:30 f.). The whole presentation has the effect of under-

lining the political harmlessness of the Christian religion: a matter of moment for the preaching of the Gospel in Rome and throughout the Empire. This was all the more necessary in view of Jewish attempts to present the new religion as a political danger. Nevertheless, the apologetical interest is never more than a secondary theme.

3. THE PLAN

Acts falls into two main parts. At the beginning of his second missionary journey (15:36), we find Paul, officially recognized as Apostle of the Gentiles, embarking on work that is truly his own. From that point on, the book may be regarded as the narrative of a journey which leads from Antioch to Rome (compare the analogous journey to Jerusalem in Lk. 9:51-19:46). The first part of Acts does not have the same marked coherency; rather, it is more like a mosaic of varied episodes, all serving to illustrate the progress of Christianity. A brief prologue (1:1 f.) indicates that Acts forms one work with the gospel and recalls the dedication of the whole to Theophilus. In Acts 1:3-11 the ending of the gospel (Lk. 24:13-53) is resumed, thus linking the volumes.

		INTRODUCTION (1:1-11)	
A.	I.	THE JERUSALEM CHURCH	(1:12—5:42)
	II.	THE FIRST MISSIONS	(6—12)
	III.	BARNABAS AND PAUL	(13:1—15:35)
B.	IV.	THE MISSION OF PAUL	(15:36—19.20)
	V.	THE PRISONER OF CHRIST	(19:21—28:29)
		EPILOGUE (28:30 f.)	

4. THE SOURCES

The problem of the sources of Acts is an involved one. In a brief source-study we shall find it convenient to take the two parts of Acts separately.

1:12 – The Semitic coloring of the first part of the book (in
15:35 particular chapters 1-12) is undoubted. Many attempts

have been made to explain considerable portions of chaps. 1–12 as the combination or juxtaposition of two parallel sources, but no delineation of these sources has stood up to penetrating criticism.

Some have seen in 2:41-5:40 a basic source, a single descriptive document, emanating from the community in Jerusalem. Other traditions have been linked with Caesarea (1:15-2:40; 8:1b-23, 26-40; 9:1-30; 9:31-10:48), and 1:1-14 has been regarded as a Galilean tradition. Nowadays, in the light of form-critical studies, scholars are loath to posit the existence of clearly-defined written documents; it is found preferable to speak of traditions, or of varied documentation on which Luke has built his narrative. It must always be kept in mind, too, that Luke has put his personal stamp on the material and that his whole work shows signs of considerable editorial activity. His composition has proceeded by stages: he wrote passages which he has later on fitted into his general plan by way of insertion or by means of link-passages. When, however, such a fragment is singled out, it must be seen as a passage edited by Luke; we cannot put our finger on the basic document as such.

The account of the first missionary journey seems a good example of a passage that has been artificially inserted into a redactional framework, for it can be shown that 12:25 and 15:1 f. are link-verses, anchoring the passage in its present context. It is not difficult to see that 11:27-30 plus 15:3-33 was originally a coherent narrative of the journey of Barnabas and Saul to Jerusalem, with an account of the discussion that followed their arrival, and their subsequent return to Antioch. This narrative is now interrupted by 12:1-23 which stands apart as a special Palestinian source, and by the Pauline tradition (13-14). Since this last describes a journey which began and ended in Antioch, the redactor, in combining the sources, had to leave Paul and Barnabas back in Antioch for the beginning of the missionary journey and had to give a reason for their going up to Jerusalem again; this he managed by the addition of 12:25 and 15:1 f. Strict chronology has yielded to reasons of literary composition.

It seems possible to discover three main sources in the first part of Acts: (1) Palestinian traditions (9:32-11:18; 12:1-23); (2) Pauline traditions (9:1-30; 13:3-14:28); (3) Antiochian traditions (11:19-30; 15:3-33). It should be kept in mind, however, that these passages, as they occur in Acts, had already been rewritten by Luke before he set about dovetailing them into his work. In order words, although the presence of different traditions may be noted, it is not wholly possible to distinguish between the basic sources and their editorial treatment. How far Luke's editing can go has been seen in the previous paragraph. But when cognizance of his method is taken, certain features of his work will seem less surprising. As a writer, Luke manifests a notable freedom in relation to his sources; as an historian, he is more concerned with the development of history than with the material details of events.

15:36 —   In the second half of Acts, the situation is far less com-
28:28   plicated; there is no real problem if Luke's authorship of the work is accepted. Granted that he is the author, it does seem hypercritical to deny that in the 'we-passages' (16:10-17; 20:5 — 21:18; 27:1 — 28:16) he writes as an eyewitness. It is reasonable to believe that here Luke had recourse to written notes — a kind of diary; some such source seems required by the vividness and graphic detail of these passages. For the rest of the material — all concerned with Paul — it is not unreasonable to suppose that Luke had questioned the Apostle and other companions of his. An obvious explanation is not to be despised just because it happens to be straightforward and simple. The further question, whether Luke's sources for his narrative of Paul's journeys were scattered notes, an itinerary, or a travel diary, is of secondary importance once we realize that, whatever form it may have taken, the source material was Luke's own.

THE   The discourses are an integral part of the book and
DISCOURSES   play an important role in bringing out the significance of the events described in the narratives. Each stage in the historical development of the Church is marked by an accompanying discourse which indicates the corresponding development of Christian thought.

At the very beginning, the Risen Christ specifies the role of his Apostles and maps out their activity; Peter's words in the supper room underline the importance of the Twelve. His discourse on Pentecost points to the meaning of the ecstatic phenomenon and the intervention of the Holy Spirit; it is also the first message addressed to the Jews by the group of Apostles. This message is further developed in Peter's subsequent addresses (Acts 3:12-26; 4:8-12; 5:29-32; 10:34-43). His reception of Cornelius marks a turning point, for now the admission of Gentiles must be justified (Acts 11:5-17; 15:7-11). Stephen's speech provides a valuable insight into the frame of mind of the Hellenists.[1] It also shows an incipient impatience with the demands of the Mosaic Law and with the Temple ceremonies that eventually will lead to a rupture with Judaism and bring Christians to a full consciousness of their own separate identity. Philip (Acts 8:30-33) explicitly identifies the Suffering Servant of Is. 53 with Christ.

Discourses effectively bring out the meaning of Paul's mission. After reading Acts 13:16-41, there is no doubt that the Apostle of the Gentiles anxiously longs for the conversion of the Jews of the Diaspora — he echoes the theme of Peter. His speeches at Lystra (Acts 14:15-17) and before the council of the Areopagus (Acts 17:22-51) show how he could accommodate himself to the style of Hellenistic religious propaganda which owed much to Stoicism. His farewell address to the elders of Ephesus at Miletus (Acts 20:18-35) is the Apostle's testament. His later discourses, at Jerusalem (Acts 22:1-21; 23:1-6), at Caesarea (Acts 24:10-21; 26:2-23), and at Rome (Acts 28:17-20, 25-28) are personal apologiae; yet, we may gather from them something of the situation of Christians in face of Judaism and of the Roman authorities.

5. HISTORICITY

Some may say that Luke's object was to trace the history of Christian beginnings. This is true, up to a point, for it is obvious that he had no intention of writing, in detail, the story of the primitive Church; we must not think that Acts is, or was meant to be, an ecclesiastical history. If he does trace the expansion of the Church, he is aware that its growth was due to the action of the Holy Spirit (2:47; 9:31); and the book shows us how the Holy Spirit has continued the work begun by Jesus, for it is he who guided the Apostles in their missionary task. Luke's whole work (gospel and Acts) is a theology of redemptive history.

But, since Christianity is an historical religion, it is necessary that Luke should deal with historical facts, although it does not follow that he should seek meticulous exactitude of detail. Much of Acts may be checked with information provided in the Pauline letters. From this it emerges that, although Luke has not used the epistles, he gives a picture of the missionary activity of the apostles which tallies with theirs. The trustworthiness of the historical data of Acts may also be measured by extrabiblical evidence; it has stood up to such verification. In most cases, what we know about contemporary history squares remarkably well with Acts. Luke is perfectly well acquainted with the religious, political, and social conditions of Paul's world.

An important factor, in this context, is Luke's taste for geographical details, at least when they fit in with the course of his narrative. He carefully locates places and towns he mentions; for example: ". . . the mount called Olivet, which is near Jerusalem, a sabbath day's journey away" (Acts 1:12); "Perga in Pamphylia" (Acts 13:13); "Lystra and Derbe, cities of Lycaonia" (Acts 14:6); "Myra in Lycia" (Acts 27:5); ", . . a place called Fair Havens, near which is the city of Lasea" (Acts 27:8). Similarly, Luke notes the addresses of people in his narrative: the place where they live, the house where they lodge. For example, in Damascus, Paul lodged in the house of Judas, situated in the street called Straight (Acts 9:11); in Joppa, Peter lodged with Simon, a tanner whose home was by the sea (Acts 10:6). At Philippi, Paul lodged with Lydia (Acts 16:14 f.), in Thessalonica with Jason (Acts 17:5-7), in Corinth with Aquila and Priscilla (Acts 18:3) and with Titius Justus whose house was next door to the synagogue (Acts 18:7); in Caesarea, he stayed with Philip the evangelist (Acts 21:8); and on a stage to Jerusalem in the house of Mnason of Cyprus (Acts 21:16). It is not credible that a writer with such an eye for detail would have been careless about historical facts.

Acts remains our most important source for the history of the primitive Church. At the same time, however, true to its real character, it shows us the beginning of Christian theology more effectively than any other document, and enables us (especially by means of the discourses of Peter) to grasp the primitive Christian message. Here history and theology go hand-in-hand, for Luke has desired to trace, in broad lines, a crucial phase of salvation history.

6. DOCTRINE
1) The Kerygma[2]

The semitic character of the first part of Acts is readily discernible. Sometimes this is due to Luke's conscious imitation of the style of the LXX which is so marked by Hebraisms. In other passages – in Peter's speeches for instance – it comes from an Aramaic substratum. This factor, taken in conjunction with Luke's quest of and respect for sources, makes it certain that the speeches attributed to Peter are based on material which proceeded from the Aramaic-speaking church at Jerusalem; in other words, they represent the primitive kerygma of that church.

The first four speeches of Peter (Acts 2:14-36; 38 f.; 3:12-26; 4:8-12; 5:17-40) cover substantially the same ground; they are complementary and give a comprehensive view of the content of the early kerygma:

1) The age of fulfillment has dawned. "This is what was spoken by the prophet" (Acts 2:16); "What God foretold by the mouth of all the prophets . . . he thus fulfilled" (Acts 3:18); "All the prophets who have spoken, from Samuel to those who came afterwards, also proclaimed these days" (Acts 3:24). Rabbinical exegesis of the Old Testament referred the predictions of the prophets to the "days of the Messiah"; hence, Peter declares that the messianic age has dawned.

2) Fulfillment has been achieved, in accordance with God's will and determinate plan, through the ministry, death, and resurrection of Jesus, the son of David; this is expressed quite emphatically, with proof from the Scriptures. The Davidic descent of Jesus is attested by David himself; "[David] being therefore a prophet, and knowing that God had sworn with an oath to him that he would set one of his descendants upon his throne, he foresaw [Christ]" (Acts 2:30 f.). The ministry is described: "Jesus of Nazareth, a man attested to you by God with mighty works and wonders and signs which God did through him in your midst" (Acts 2:22); "Moses said, 'The Lord God will raise up for you a prophet from your brethren as he raised me up' " (Acts 3:22). His death is proclaimed: "This Jesus, delivered up according to the definite plan and foreknowledge of God, you crucified and killed by the hands of lawless men" (Acts 2:23); "Him you delivered up and denied in the presence of Pilate, when he had decided to release him. But you denied the Holy and Righteous One, and asked for a murderer to be granted to you, and killed the Author of life" (Acts 3:13-15). His resurrection is boldly asserted: "God raised him up, having loosed the pangs of death, because it was not possible for him to be held by it" (Acts 2:24); "God raised him from the dead; to this we are witnesses" (Acts 3:15); "Jesus Christ of Nazareth, whom you crucified, whom God raised from the dead" (Acts 4:10).

3) By virtue of the resurrection, Jesus has been exalted at the right hand of God, as messianic head of the new Israel. "Being therefore exalted at the right hand of God . . . God has made him both Lord and Christ" (Acts 2:33, 36); "The Lord of our fathers

glorified his servant Jesus" (Acts 3:13); "God exalted him at his right hand as Leader and Savior" (Acts 5:31).

4) The Holy Spirit in the Church is the sign of Christ's present power and glory. "Being therefore exalted at the right hand of God, and having received from the Father the promise of the Holy Spirit, he has poured out this which you hear and see" (Acts 2:33); "We are witnesses to these things, and so is the Holy Spirit whom God has given to those who obey him" (Acts 5:32).

5) The Messianic Age will reach its consummation in the return of Christ. "That he may send the Christ appointed for you, Jesus, whom heaven must receive until the time for establishing all that God spoke by the mouth of his holy prophets from of old" (Acts 3:20 f.). Compare this with Acts 10:42; "He commanded us . . . to testify that he is the one ordained by God to be judge of the living and the dead."

6) The kerygma always closes with an appeal for repentance, the offer of forgiveness and of the Holy Spirit, and the promise of salvation. "Repent, and be baptized every one of you in the name of Jesus Christ for the forgiveness of your sins; and you shall receive the gift of the Holy Spirit. For the promise is to you and to your children and to all that are far off, every one whom the Lord our God calls to him" (Acts 2:38 f.); "Repent, therefore, and turn again, that your sins may be blotted out . . . and that he may send the Christ appointed for you, Jesus" (Acts 3:19 f.); "There is salvation in no one else, for there is no other name given among men by which we must be saved" (Acts 4:12).

Such is the Jerusalem kerygma. It is significant that its main points are indicated in a Gospel summary of the preaching of Jesus: "Jesus came into Galilee, preaching the gospel of God, and saying, "The time is fulfilled, and the kingdom of God is at hand; repent, and believe in the gospel' " (Mk. 1:14 f.). The kerygma follows the lines of this summary.

> The first clause, "The time is fulfilled," is expanded in the reference to prophecy and its fulfillment. The second clause, "The kingdom of God has drawn near," is expanded in the account of the ministry and death of Jesus, his resurrection and exaltation, all conceived as an eschatological process. The third clause, "Repent and believe in the Gospel," reappears in the appeal for repentance and the offer of forgiveness with which the apostolic *kerygma* closes. Whether we say that the apostolic preaching was modeled on that of Jesus, or that the evangelist formulated his summary of the preaching of Jesus on the model

of that of the primitive Church, at any rate the two are identical in purport. The kingdom of God is conceived as coming in the events of the life, death, and resurrection of Jesus, and to proclaim these facts, in their proper setting, is to preach the gospel of the kingdom of God.[3]

The discourse of Peter in Acts 10:34-47 differs from the others, not because it does not contain the principal elements of the kerygma, but because it concentrates on the historical facts concerning Jesus. We learn that, after the baptism of John, Jesus began to preach the Good News in Galilee and to proclaim it throughout Judaea. He went about doing good, healing the sick, casting out devils. He was crucified and was raised by God on the third day; he manifested himself to chosen witnesses and commanded them to preach to the people. The speech is addressed to a Gentile audience — Cornelius with his relatives and friends (Acts 10:24) — to people, unlike the Palestinian Jews, unacquainted with the main facts. "We may perhaps take it that the speech before Cornelius represents the form of *kerygma* used by the primitive Church in its earliest approaches to a wider public.[4]

Although Luke undoubtedly leaned on traditions that reached far back, it is Paul who provides our earliest extant written records. His writings, although not of the nature of kerygma, are a valuable basis of investigation, and in them we find a term of comparison with Acts. In 1 Cor. 15:3-7, Paul gives a brief summary of the kerygma, explicitly declaring that it is something he had received from his instructors in the faith. Passages in Galatians and Romans, as well as a speech in Acts (13:17-41), provide all the elements of the kerygma. Furthermore, it is clear that Paul regarded it as the outline of an apostolic Gospel which he believed to be common to himself and other Christian missionaries.

2) *The Holy Spirit*

Following on the Third Gospel, which, more than the other Synoptics, underlines the action of the Holy Spirit in the ministry of Jesus (cf. Lk. 4:1, 14, 18; 10:21), Acts gives the impression that the primitive Christian community lived entirely under the motion of the Spirit; Acts is like a "gospel of the Spirit." Before his ascension, the Risen Christ had assured his disciples that he would send upon them the promised gift of the messianic age, the Holy Spirit, who would empower them to carry out their task of witnesses to Jesus (Lk. 24:47-49; Acts 1:5, 8). The fulfillment of the promise was the "baptism in the Spirit" (Acts 1:5) of Pente-cost. This marked the beginning of the time of the Church, just as the baptism in the Jordan inaugurated the public ministry of the Savior; in both cases, Luke insists on the sensible manifestation of the Spirit (Lk. 3:22; Acts 2:3).

In his discourse, Peter explained that the ecstatic speaking in tongues was a sign that the Risen Christ had indeed poured out his Spirit upon them (Acts 2:33), thus fulfilling the prophecy of Joel (Acts 2:6-21). Since, however, Joel had spoken of "all flesh," the gift of the Holy Spirit is not for the circle of disciples alone but for all who will believe in Christ. Peter, then, can assure his hearers that they too will receive the Spirit if they will believe and be baptized (Acts 2:38 f.) — not only they but "all that are far off, every one whom the Lord our God calls to him" (Acts 2:39). Pos-session of the Spirit is part of the equipment of every Christian.

The activity of the Spirit is manifold. The charisms, especially speaking in tongues and prophecy, are an obvious expression of his activity. Not only at Pentecost, but also at other times, the Spirit gives the faculty of "speaking in tongues," that is, of praising God in the language of ecstasy, like Cornelius (Acts 10:46) and the dis-ciples of John at Ephesus (Acts 19:6). The Holy Spirit moves the prophets, like Agabus (Acts 11:28; 21:11 f.), who were to be found in many of the churches: in Antioch (Acts 13:1), in Jeru-salem (Acts 15:32), and at Caesarea (Acts 21:9).

If the charisms offer a striking manifestation of the Spirit's action, his role as guide and strengthener of the Christian preachers is of far greater importance. In the strength of the Spirit just re-ceived, Peter bore witness before the crowd of Jews and proselytes (Acts 2:5 f.) to Jesus as the Messiah sent by God (Acts 2:22-36). The witness of the Apostles is explicitly designated as the work of the Spirit (Acts 5:32). Stephen is filled with "wisdom and the Spirit," and his enemies cannot withstand him (Acts 6:10). The Spirit guides the Apostles and the leaders of the community and dictates their line of conduct (cf. Acts 8:29: "The Spirit said to Philip"; 10:19: "the Spirit said to Peter"). Peter was enlightened by the Spirit in the crucial matter of the acceptance of the pagan Cornelius into the Christian community (Acts 10:19; 11:12); and when the whole question of Gentile converts was in the balance, the Spirit guided the apostolic council (Acts 15.28). The Spirit called Barnabas and Saul to the first Gentile mission and directed the Church at Antioch to set them apart for that task (Acts

13:2-4). At the beginning of the second missionary journey, Paul was hindered by the Spirit from carrying out his original plan of preaching in the province of Asia (Acts 16:6 f.). In critical situations, the preachers, and the communities themselves, could look to the Spirit for support. Thus, Peter (Acts 4:8, 13, 21; 5-40) and Stephen (Acts 6:15; 7:55) spoke out boldly before the Sanhedrin, and the disciples were encouraged (Acts 13:52).

Acts has little to say about the manner of the outpouring and reception of the Spirit, and what it does say is sometimes difficult to understand. The visible descent of the Holy Spirit on the disciples at Pentecost and on the household of Cornelius was exceptional. Two passages are especially puzzling: 8:5-24 and 19:1-7. In ch. 8 the Samaritans baptized by Philip received the Spirit through the laying on of hands by Peter and John (8:15 f.). Luke's narrative is very compressed, and his interest bears on two points: the Samaritans received the Spirit only through the apostles' ministry, and the case of Simon, the former magician. It does emerge that Simon's conversion was not authentic, and that, even though the Samaritans had been baptized they had not received the Spirit. The group of twelve disciples in Ephesus (19:1-7) were not yet Christians – they lacked the vital factor: the Holy Spirit. They had yet to receive the complete initiation, therefore 'they were baptized in the name of the Lord Jesus' (19:5). Baptism presupposes and demands faith, and faith is shown to be genuine only by the gift of the Spirit. Luke asserts that it is God's giving of the Spirit which makes one a Christian.[5]

---

[1] The Greek-speaking Jews had always irritated the homelanders by their disdain for the physical elements of Israel's worship. Living in the Diaspora, they had found God away from the Temple and had worshiped him with a spiritual devotedness which spurned the smell of blood and burning flesh. In coming to know Jesus these Hellenists found the way of spiritual worship wide open to them in the 'Temple not made by hands.' When Stephen the Hellenist, therefore, spoke of Jesus, his hearers had ears only for that irritating sentence which echoed the old anti-Temple polemic: 'Solomon built him a house; yet not in houses made by hands does the Most High dwell" (Acts 7:47 f.)" (B. M. Ahern, *New Horizons*, Studies in Biblical Theology [Notre Dame, Ind.: Fides, 1963], p. 183).

[2] See C. H. Dodd, *The Apostolic Preaching and its Developments* (London: Hodder & Stoughton, 1963³), pp. 17-29.

[3] Dodd, *op. cit.*, p. 24.

[4] *Ibid.*, p. 28.

[5] J. D. G. Dunn, Baptism in the Holy Spirit (London: SCM 1970).

| SIX | *The Pauline Epistles* |

THE NEW TESTAMENT EPISTLES

1, 2 THESSALONIANS

THE MAJOR EPISTLES

THE CAPTIVITY EPISTLES

THE PASTORAL EPISTLES

HEBREWS

The title of this chapter implies nothing more than the existence of a traditional Pauline corpus; it does not follow that all the epistles treated here are truly Pauline. Thus, not only the Pastorals, Ephesians, and Colossians, whose authenticity is doubtful, but Hebrews too – certainly not written by the Apostle – find a place.

1. THE NEW TESTAMENT EPISTLES

1) Letter and Epistle

Many epistolary writings of antiquity have been preserved and are known to us. They fall into two classes: 1) *Letters* strictly so called; these were written on a particular occasion to a particular person or group of persons and are meant only for these readers. 2) *Epistles*; these are treatises cast in letter form and addressed to a wide circle or, simply, to any reader. The Pauline writings are true letters because there is always a special occasion and a definite group of receivers; but, with the exception of Phm., they are official, not private letters. Most of them are addressed to a single community, or to a small group of churches (Gal.; Eph.); three are addressed to the holder of an ecclesiastical office and through him to the church in his charge (1, 2 Tm.; Ti.). These letters deal with various aspects of the missionary activity: the instructing, confirming, and admonishing of the faithful; the settling of misunderstandings in the churches; and the refutation of false teachers. They are the writings of an apostle, instruments of his apostolic ministry; in them, he speaks with authority.

The other New Testament epistles are closer to the form of a theological treatise (Heb.), or are homiletical (1, 2 Pt.; 1 Jn.) or exhortatory (James). Yet, although we have pointed to, and are conscious of, the difference between epistle and letter, we shall continue to designate the relevant New Testament writings by the traditional term "epistle."

2) The Language and Style of Paul

The language of Paul betrays his background and training. A Jew of the Diaspora, born in Tarsus (a celebrated center of learning), he is marked by the influence of Greek culture. This is to be noted, for instance, in his use of the diatribe, that is, doctrinal or moral expositions in dialogue form, with questions and answers, apostrophes and exclamations (cf. Rm. 3:1-19, 27:31; 2 Cor. 6:4-10), in ideas borrowed from Stoicism (for example, the departure of the separated soul for the divine world [2 Cor. 5:6-8], the cosmic "pleroma" of Col. and Eph.), and in certain formulas (1 Cor. 8:6; Rm. 11:36; Eph. 4:6). At the same time, since he was a Pharisee, Aramaic-speaking from his infancy, a disciple of Gamaliel, the Jewish heritage is manifest and preponderant. Although he handles Greek with ease, as a second mother tongue, it sometimes seems that he thinks in Aramaic, and he is certainly indebted to the language of the LXX.

The Apostle's style is distinctive. "Never perhaps has the celebrated dictum *le style est l'homme même* been more truly verified than in the case of Paul whose style and eloquence are marked by the love of Christ and by a passion for the preaching of the gospel."[1] These influences not only account for the striking quality of so much of his work, but also explain its defects. Carried along by the pressure of his love and the urgency of his message, words can literally fail him (cf. 1 Cor. 9:15). More than once we get the impression that a passage was written or dictated at white heat (see Gal. and 2 Cor.). The complex character of Paul is mirrored in the many moods and shades of his writing.

1) 1 Thessalonians

THE THESSALONIAN CHURCH The city of Thessalonica was the capital of the Roman province of Macedonia; by special privilege of Augustus, it was a free city. As a seaport and a stage on the great Egnatian Way which led from Dyrrachium to Byzantium, the city was a flourishing commercial center, cosmopolitan in population. It had a democratic constitution and its chief magistrates bore the title of "politarchs" (Acts 17:8).

Paul visited Thessalonica for the first time in the course of his second missionary journey, probably in the year 50 A.D. He was accompanied by Silas. Both missionaries turned first to the Jews, preaching in the synagogue on three consecutive sabbaths. Their preaching won over many of the "God-fearers" (Gentile adherents of the synagogue) and some influential women. The exasperated Jews, cleverly adapting their tactics to the political situation, played on the feelings of the people and stirred up a mob against the preachers. The brethren prevailed on Paul and Silas to slip away by night to Beroea, a small town some miles to the west. It is manifest that the Thessalonian church was predominantly Gentile in composition.

It is not easy to determine the length of Paul's stay in Thessalonica. The account of Acts would suggest that it cannot have been long. The best we can say is that it may have been two or three months – scarcely more than that.

PURPOSE AND SUMMARY OF THE EPISTLE   Paul did not remain long in Beroea, but soon proceeded to Athens; Silas and Timothy, whom he had left behind, were expected to join him there before long. The Apostle was worried about the Thessalonian church which had so soon been left to itself; when the two arrived he sent Timothy back to Thessalonica (1 Thes. 3:1 f.). Timothy returned with a comforting report for the Apostle who now was in Corinth (51 A.D.). The latter straightway gave expression to his relief in a letter, but, pastor that he was, he seized the occasion to draw attention to certain shortcomings and to issue instructions.

The customary address (1 Thes. 1:1 f.) is followed by a long thanksgiving (1 Thes. 1:3-10) for the manifest fruits of a conversion wrought by the Spirit. Then, the integrity and disinterestedness of the Apostle's preaching and way of life are stressed (1 Thes. 2:1-2). On their part, the converts received his message as the word of God (1 Thes. 2:13-16). The passage 1 Thes. 2:17-3:13 outlines Paul's sentiments after he had left Thessalonica and the steps he had taken to keep in touch: his desire to see them again (1 Thes. 2:17-20), the sending of Timothy (1 Thes. 3:1-5), the Apostle's joy at his envoy's encouraging report (1 Thes. 3:6-10); his heartfelt prayer for their future progress (1 Thes. 3:11-13).

The second part of the writing, following the usual practice of Paul, takes up matters of personal import and exhorts the faithful to the practice of Christian morality. He urges the observance of chastity and brotherly love and advocates quiet attention to one's own affairs and work (1 Thes. 4:1-12). Evidently in reply to a problem of the community, he has comforting words on the fate of brethren who had passed away: they are with the Lord and will be witnesses of his Coming (1 Thes. 4:13-18). But, since the Lord will come unexpectedly, the living must be vigilant (1 Thes. 5:1-11). Finally, he has advice to offer on different aspects of community life (1 Thes. 5:12-22) and a concluding prayer (1 Thes. 5:23 f.). The letter ends in typical Pauline fashion (1 Thes. 5:25-28).

THE PLAN

THE ADDRESS (1:1 f.)		
INITIAL THANKSGIVING (1:3-10)		
THE APOSTLE AND THE THESSALONIANS (2—3)		
1) Paul's preaching and conduct		2:1-12
2) The reaction of the faithful		2:13-16
3) His subsequent solicitude		2:17—3:10
4) His prayer for them		3:11-13
INSTRUCTION AND EXHORTATION (4:1—5:24)		
1) Chastity and charity		4:1-12
2) Living and dead at the Parousia		4:13-18
3) Vigilance in view of the Day of the Lord		5:1-11
4) Various recommendations		5:12-22
5) Final prayer		5:23 f.
CONCLUSION (5:25-28)		

2) 2 Thessalonians

PURPOSE AND SUMMARY   It cannot be doubted that Paul's principal reason for writing a second letter to the Thessalonians was to set right certain erroneous views on the Parousia which had arisen in that church. Although it has been urged that these views may have sprung from a misinterpretation of 1 Thes. (especially 4:13-18), it is not easy to see how his words could have been so misconstrued. Reference to a "letter purporting to come from us" (2 Thes. 2:2) – frequently regarded as pointing to 1 Thes. – is, in its context, more readily understood of an hypothetical letter. There was also another reason for the Epistle, one apparently not unconnected with the other. Some of the Thessalonians no longer worked (2 Thes. 3:11 f.), probably because, believing in an imminent Parousia, they saw no point in work. The Apostle deals with both problems in forthright fashion.

2 Thes. opens with an address (2 Thes. 1:1 f.) followed by a thanksgiving for the faith and fidelity of the Thessalonians (2 Thes. 1:3 f.). Next comes a statement on God's final retribution (2 Thes. 1:5-10) and a prayer for the faithful (2 Thes. 1:11 f.). The letter then takes up the question of the Parousia and its preceding signs (2 Thes. 2:1-12): the Day of the Lord has not yet come because, beforehand, there will be a great apostasy and the "man of lawlessness" (Antichrist) must appear. But, the Lord Jesus will overcome all his enemies. The Apostle again thanks God for the Christian vocation of the Thessalonians and urges them to persevere in their calling (2 Thes. 2:13-15), and he prays for that end (2 Thes. 2:16 f.). He asks for the prayers of the faithful and expresses his confidence in their regard (2 Thes. 3:1-5). This sounds like a conclusion but, abruptly, Paul turns to another matter, probably just come to his notice (see 2 Thes. 3:11). The brethren must not live in idleness; they should work, following the example of the Apostle (2 Thes. 3:6-15). The writing ends with the customary salutation (2 Thes. 3:16) and a greeting and blessing added in Paul's hand (2 Thes. 3:17 f.) – his authentication of the letter.

PLAN

ADDRESS (1:1 f.)	
INITIAL THANKSGIVING (1:3 f.)	
1) The retribution of God	1:5-10
2) Prayer for the faithful	1:11 f
3) The Parousia and its Signs	2:1-12
4) Exhortation to perseverance	2:13–3:5
5) Warning against idleness	3:6-15
CONCLUSION (3:16-18)	

3. THE MAJOR EPISTLES

1) Galatians

THE GALATIAN   The Galatians (*Galatai* = *Keltai*) were a Celtic
CHURCH   people which in the fourth century B.C. had emi-
grated from Gaul to Asia Minor, eventually settling in the territory
round about Ancyra (Ankara). The last Galatian king, Amyntas (d.
25 B.C.), willed his kingdom to the Romans; at his death, it became
a Roman province with its capital at Ancyra. By Paul's time the
province had embraced a much wider area, incorporating Pisidia,
Phrygia, Lycaonia, Paphlagonia, Isauria, Pontus Galaticus, Pontus
Polemonianus, and Armenia. Although a few Roman writers did
refer to the whole province as "Galatia," it does seem that, in
practice, the current language of the first century A.D. reserved the
name for the *region*, that is, the original Galatian kingdom.

Therefore, we may reasonably regard the Galatians as not the
inhabitants of Pisidia and Lycaonia, but inhabitants of the Galatian
region visited by Paul on his second and third missionary journeys.
The Epistle was probably written during the Apostle's stay at
Ephesus (54-57 A.D.). Because of its close affinity with Romans, it
cannot have been written long before that Epistle. On the other
hand, we cannot be sure if it was written before or later than 1
Cor. The most likely date would seem to be 57 A.D. Its authenticity
has never been seriously contested.

PLAN

ADDRESS (1:1-5)
REPROOF (1:6-10)
PERSONAL APOLOGIA (1:11—2:21)
THE GOSPEL OF PAUL (3:1—4:11)
EXHORTATION (4:12—6:10)
EPILOGUE (6:11-18)

OCCASION AND   The purpose of Gal. is clearly defined: to refute
SUMMARY   the errors of Judaizers who had come to disturb

the faith of the Galatians by teaching the necessity of the observance of the Mosaic Law, and especially of circumcision; and, positively, to justify Paul's gospel. The Apostle argues that the Law is a provisional institution and that with the coming of Christ its role has ended; since Christ is now the only Mediator, the Mosaic observances are obsolete. These Judaizers had appealed to the authority of the Apostles and leaders of the Church, like Peter and James, who themselves observed the Law. They attacked the apostolic authority of Paul: since he had been converted after the resurrection, he was not a true Apostle. Besides, his doctrine differed from that of the true Apostles: before the Galatians he denied the necessity of the Law merely to win them more easily; elsewhere he accommodated himself to the customs of the Jews. As the result of the campaign, the Galatians were shaken in their allegiance to Paul and had begun to observe the rites of the Law.

When Paul learned that the Galatian community was in danger of falling under the sway of judaizers and was looking to the false security of observance, he reacted violently. He insists on his authority, not to browbeat the Galatians, not to awe them into submission, but in an almost desperate effort to get them up off their knees, to get them to accept the burden of responsibility and take the risk of making decisions. They were welcoming judaizers because these were offering them security. They could henceforth cling to the 613 precepts of the Torah, and were freed of the burden, and the risk, of personal decision. Henceforth, their life would be mapped out for them: they had only to do or to avoid what the Law prescribed. They were ready to shrug off their responsibility and let a moral precept carry the burden of decision.

The address (Gal. 1:1-5) is unusually solemn. It stresses two points: the divine origin of Paul's apostolate and the saving power of Christ's sacrifice. The indignation of the Apostle accounts for the fact that this is the only one of his Epistles that does not contain an initial thanksgiving; instead, he starts off abruptly with an expression of pained surprise at the fickleness of the Galatians and with a sharp reproof. His adversaries cannot accuse him this time of trying to win favor with men (Gal. 1:6-10). Then he proceeds to assert and to justify his apostolic authority (Gal. 1,11-2:21). When Paul states (Gal. 1:11 f.) that his "gospel" has come to him by direct revelation, he has in mind not all of his knowledge of the faith, but the particular doctrine of justification without the works of the Law. His gospel could not have come to him from the primitive community because he who, before his conversion, was a fanatical upholder of the Law (Gal. 1:13 f.), first came in contact with the leaders of the Christian community only three years after his conversion (Gal. 1:15-20), and after that brief visit to Jerusalem he preached, far from the city, in Syria and Cilicia (Gal. 1:21-24). On the other hand, his gospel had been formally approved by the Jerusalem church (Gal. 2:1-10); further-more, he had openly defended that gospel of freedom in a con-frontation at Antioch with Peter himself (Gal. 2:11-21). In Gal. 2:15-21, we find a clear exposition of his doctrine of justification by faith alone.

The following section (Gal. 3:1-4:11) develops the doctrine. The Galatians should know from their own experience that the Spirit came to them by faith in Jesus, and not by the works of the Law (Gal. 3:1-5); the history of Abraham supports this doctrine (3:6-14), for he had received the promise that cannot be annulled by the later Law (Gal. 3:15-18). Since it was nothing more than the pedagogue or tutor of the people of God who were still in a state of childhood, the role of the Law was transitory (Gal. 3:19-24); but now, by their faith in Christ, Christians are the true descendants of Abraham, heirs of the promise, sons of God (Gal. 3:25-4:7). How, then, can the Galatians dream of going back to the old way of life? (Gal. 4:8-11).

In Gal. 4:12-6:10, Paul turns to his children with words of affection, with remonstrance, and with practical advice. An illness of the Apostle was the occasion of the conversion of the Galatians — a striking example of God's way of doing things (Gal. 4:12-20). This passage gives a precious insight into Paul's character; the stern words of Gal. 1:6-10; 3:1-5 must be understood in the light of these verses. In order to inherit the promise, it is not enough to be a son of Abraham: one must be a son not like Ishmael but like Isaac, a son of the free woman and not of the slave (Gal. 4:21-31). But, by accepting circumcision, the Galatians would again become slaves and turn their backs on Christ (Gal. 5:1-12). On the other hand, Christian freedom is not license, and the fruits of the Spirit are opposed to the works of the flesh (Gal. 5:13-26). The Christian outlook is not vague; rather, it demands practical charity (Gal. 6:1-6) and the sowing of good seed in view of a harvest (Gal. 6:7-10). Paul, who had dictated the letter, now takes the pen him-self and concludes with a warning against the Judaizers and an avowal that, for him, Christ is the center of all things (Gal. 6:11-18).

2) 1 Corinthians

THE CORINTHIAN CHURCH   The celebrated city of Corinth had been destroyed by the Roman consul L. Mummius in 146 B.C.; a century later it was rebuilt by Julius Caesar as a Roman colony (*Colonia laus Julia Corinthus*). Soon it had become the capital of the Roman province of Achaia and the seat of the proconsul. Lying on the narrow isthmus between the ports of Cenchreae in the East and Lechaeum in the West, it was a vital stage in traffic between West and East. Because of its position and commercial status, it had an extremely varied population. Famous for its temple of Aphrodite on the summit of Acrocorinth – the steep hill above the city – it was, by the same token, a byword for sexual immorality, and that even in the world of Paul's day (cf. Rm. 1:26-32).

Paul visited Corinth for the first time on his second missionary journey; there he founded a church and remained for eighteen months, from the winter of 50 A.D. to the summer of 52 A.D. As usual, he began his preaching in the synagogue – on the sabbath. When Silas and Timothy arrived from Macedonia, he was able to devote himself entirely to preaching; but soon the Jews rejected him. Then he went to the house of a Gentile "God-fearer" called Justus. Many Corinthians were subsequently converted and baptized. The Corinthian church was mainly Gentile in composition (although there were some Jews [cf. Acts 18:8]) and was recruited mainly among the poorer classes (although not exclusively [cf. 1 Cor. 1:26-28; 11:22-32]). Shortly after Paul's departure from Corinth, a gifted Alexandrian Jewish convert named Apollos came from Ephesus and preached with notable success (Acts 18:24-28; 1 Cor. 3:5-9).

PLAN OF THE EPISTLE

ADDRESS (1:1-3)

THANKSGIVING (1:4-9)

PARTY STRIFE AND SCANDALS AT CORINTH (1:10—6:20)

1)	The rival parties	1:10—4:21
2)	A case of incest	5:1-13
3)	Christians before pagan courts	6:1-11
4)	On fornication	6:12-20

SOLUTION OF PROBLEMS SUBMITTED (7:1—11-1)

1)	Marriage and virginity	7:1-40
2)	Meats offered to idols	8:1—11:1

ON LITURGICAL ASSEMBLIES AND CHARISMS (11:2—14:40)

THE RESURRECTION OF THE DEAD (15:1-58)

CONCLUSION (16:1-18)

GREETING (16:19-24)

OCCASION AND SUMMARY   While Paul was at Ephesus during his third missionary journey (54-57 A.D.), he wrote what may be termed a "pre-canonical" letter — not extant — to Corinth, warning the converts "not to associate with immoral men" (1 Cor. 9:1; cf. 5:9-13). Some time later he was informed by "Chloe's people" of rival parties in the Corinthian church (1 Cor. 1:12-17). He learned, too, perhaps from the same source, of some who challenged his apostolic authority (1 Cor. 9:1-3). It had also come to his notice that the brethren submitted their differences to the judgment of pagan courts instead of regulating their own affairs (1 Cor. 6:1-8), and he was told of scandals in the church (1 Cor. 5:1; 6:12-20). Besides, the Corinthians, in a letter to the Apostle, had submitted a number of problems (1 Cor. 7:1); this letter was probably carried by a delegation comprised of Stephanas, Fortunatus, and Achaicus (1 Cor. 16:17). The questions involved regarded the relative merits of marriage and virginity (chap. 7), the use of meats offered to idols (chaps. 8-10), and the matter of charisms (1 Cor. 7:1-11:1). Paul had also heard of disorders in the cultic assemblies, notably in the celebration of the Eucharist (chap. 11), and of doubts concerning the resurrection of the dead (chap. 15). The Epistle faces up to the various problems.

In the address (1 Cor. 1:1-3), Paul insists on his own standing as apostle and on the vocation of the Corinthians; the thanksgiving (1 Cor. 1:4-9) regards the riches that the converts have received from God in Christ.

The first part of the letter (1 Cor. 1:10-6:20) is concerned with party spirit among the Corinthians. Rival parties in a Christian community are a contradiction, because Christ is not divided (1 Cor. 1:10-16). Who were those followers of Paul, of Apollos, of Cephas, and of Christ? If the fourth group was made up of those who claimed that, as followers of Christ, they were independent of any human intermediary, it seems clear that three of the parties challenged the authority of Paul while the other group, in reaction, would have gone too far in their attachment to him. The wisdom of God — the folly of the Cross — proclaimed by Paul stands in contrast to the human wisdom that had motivated the dissensions (1 Cor. 1:17-2:5). True Christian wisdom is revealed by the Spirit (1 Cor. 2:6-16). Party strife is further denounced and the proper role of preachers emerges (1 Cor. 3:1-17). The converts must turn from human wisdom which had led to strife and realize that they are all one in Christ (1 Cor. 3:18-23). Paul does not stand trial before the Corinthians — some of whom believe that they have become kings! — he looks only to the scrutiny of the Lord (1 Cor. 4:1-13). With a sudden change characteristic of him, he switches from irony to a paternal appeal (1 Cor. 4:14-21).

Paul then turns to the question of abuses in the community (1 Cor. 5:1-6:20). The Corinthian church had tolerated a case of incest, a man living with his stepmother; he orders the excommunication of the culprit, in the hope of bringing him to his senses (1 Cor. 5:1-5). A warning that a little leaven can ferment a whole lump of dough introduces the theme of the new pasch (1 Cor. 5:6-8) In a previous letter, he had warned them of associating with immoral men (1 Cor. 5:9-13). It is unseemly that Christians should appear before pagan courts; besides, it is shameful to have lawsuits at all. Unrighteousness excludes from the kingdom and should be unheard of in those who had been washed and sanctified in the name of Christ (1 Cor. 6:1-11). In urging freedom from the Mosaic Law, Paul had taught his converts that "all things are lawful"; this does not mean, as some of them had thought, that Christian liberty is license. It does not imply that fornication is licit, for this is a profanation of the body, that temple of the Holy Spirit (1 Cor. 6:12-20).

In the second part of the letter (1 Cor. 7:1-11:1), the Apostle answers the queries raised in the letter of the Corinthian community; in the first place, the merits of marriage and of celibacy. He favors the celibate state, but he acknowledges that marriage is good and he insists on the mutual conferring of conjugal rights (1 Cor. 7:1-9). Concerning divorce, Paul reiterates the Lord's teaching (1 Cor. 7:10 f.), but he gives his own view on mixed marriages (1 Cor. 7:10-16). Then, by association of ideas, he turns to exhort Christians to remain in the way of life which the Lord has assigned to each (1 Cor. 7:17-24) and follows this general admonition with further advice on virginity (1 Cor. 7:25-38) and for widows (1 Cor. 7:39 f.).

A particular problem exercising the community was the use of meat offered to idols. It appears that some at Corinth, arguing that an idol had no real existence, maintained that the meats in question were clean. Paul granted that, theoretically, they, 'the strong,' were right (cf. 10:14-22) but warns that, in practice, knowledge is not enough (8:1-11:1). The attitude of the 'strong' was based on a misunderstanding of christian freedom. Only what is 'helpful' or 'builds up' is consonant with christian freedom (6:12; 10:23). Freedom to act is circumscribed by love and concern.

The third part of the letter (11:2-14:40) is taken up with instructions concerning the liturgical assemblies of the community and the relative importance of spiritual gifts. In chaps. 12-14 Paul treats of the final question raised in the letter of the Corinthians, one concerning the 'charisms' or spiritual gifts granted to members of the community. Their number, and the rather disturbing character of some of them, tended to cause confusion. Hence Paul intervened and clarified the situation: All these gifts come from the same Spirit; they are granted in view of the good of the community; their relative importance is based on the importance of the services they render; charity stands far above the gift of speaking in tongues (*glossolalia*), a gift of which the Corinthians were inordinately proud; in fact, charity surpasses all the charisms. The long reply contains an important statement on the Body of Christ (1 Cor. 12:12-30) and the famous hymn to *agapē* – fraternal charity, a love which is selfgiving, which seeks the good of others. Its source is God, who has first loved us (1 Jn. 4:19) and who has given his Son in order to reconcile sinners with himself. The love of Christians is to be modeled on this love of God and of his Son.

Chapter 15, no longer a reply to a specific question in the Corinthian letter, is an instruction on the resurrection of the dead. Paul had heard of a tendency at Corinth, one influenced by the Greek outlook, to think of the afterlife in terms of the immortality of the soul apart from the body. He argues that the fundamental fact is the resurrection of Jesus (1 Cor. 15:1-11). Christ's resurrection is the guarantee of the resurrection of those "in Christ"; for, if Christ has not risen, his work had failed – he cannot help those who believe in him. And the Christian life, which involves so much self-denial, is foolishness if it ends with death (1 Cor. 15:12-19). At his Second Coming, those who belong to Christ will rise; then he, to whom all things have been made subject, will hand over the kingdom of the Father (1 Cor. 15:20-28). Arguments *ad hominem* support the reasoning (1 Cor. 19:29-34). Verse 29 refers to a practice at Corinth, perhaps vicarious baptism undertaken by Christians on behalf of dead friends and relatives. Paul does not commend the practice, but uses it as an argument.

Next, the manner of the resurrection and the nature of the risen body are considered (1 Cor. 15:35-58). On the analogy of the seed that dies and springs to new life, the resurrection will bring about a profound transformation of the body (1 Cor. 15:35-44). What is sown a physical body, sharing the natural and corruptible principle of life common to all creatures, like that of the first Adam, will be raised a spiritual body, like that of the last Adam, freed from the laws of earthly matter, incorruptible, immortal (1 Cor. 15:45-49). In 1 Cor. 15:50-53, Paul refers to the common belief that the Parousia would come soon and that many would be alive at the Lord's Coming (cf. 1 Thes. 4:13-17). The chapter closes with a hymn of thanksgiving for Christ's victory over death (1 Cor. 15:54-58).

The final chapter comes almost by way of an appendix. Paul gives instructions about the collection for the faithful of Jerusalem (1 Cor. 16:1-4); outlines his projected travel plans (1 Cor. 16:5-9); recommends Timothy to the Corinthians (1 Cor. 16:10 f.); and announces that Apollos will not return to the city (1 Cor. 16:12). After a call to faith, courage, and love (1 Cor. 16:13), he recommends the three envoys (1 Cor. 16:15-18) and sends greetings (1 Cor. 16:19 f.). The concluding words are written by the Apostle himself (1 Cor. 16:21-24).

No other epistle gives so clear an idea of life of a primitive community and of the problems that faced the converts. At the same time, it gives us a precious glimpse of Paul, for it is the letter of a man of action who goes right to the heart of things, of a leader who rigorously combats error and gives precise directions, of a father who loves his children despite their faults, and of an apostle whose only care is to win men to Christ.

3) 2 Corinthians

OCCASION AND DATE   Shortly after he had written 1 Cor., a sudden crisis demanded a brief and painful visit of Paul to Corinth (2 Cor. 1:23-2:1; 12:14; 13:1 f.). He returned to Ephesus, promising to go back for a longer stay (2 Cor. 1:15 f.); but soon a fresh incident, in which it seems that the authority of Paul was flouted in the person of his representative (2 Cor. 2:5-10; 7:12), called forth a "severe letter" (2 Cor. 2:3 f., 9), which had a salutary effect (2 Cor. 7:8-13). It was in Macedonia, not long after his arrival from Ephesus (1 Cor. 15:22; 2 Cor. 1:8-10; Acts 19:23-40), that Paul received this comforting assurance from Titus (2 Cor. 2:12 f.; 7:5-16); and there, toward the close of 57 A.D. he wrote 2 Cor. It was the fourth time – or at least the fourth time – that he had written to Corinth; the other letters being the "pre-canonical letter" (1 Cor. 5:9), 1 Cor., and the "severe letter."

There is no reference in 2 Cor. to the problems raised in 1 Cor.; hence, this letter seems to have been effective. When he wrote 2 Cor., Paul was planning to visit Corinth "for the third time" (2 Cor. 12:14; 13:1). He did in fact arrive in the city in 57 A.D. and spent the winter there (Acts 20:3). The intermediary visit (2 Cor. 13:2) was short, and painful – both for the Corinthians and Paul. This visit had not brought order to Corinth. The severe letter, written "with many tears," makes mention of a situation involving "one who did wrong" and "one who suffered a wrong" (2 Cor. 7:12). It is not the case of the incestuous man (1 Cor. 5:1-13), for the circumstances are notably different. As we have suggested, it seems to concern one who had challenged the authority of the Apostle's representative. Judaizing missionaries had arrived (cf. 2 Cor. 11-22) – the "arch-apostles" (2 Cor. 11:5) or "false apostles" (2 Cor. 11:13) who strove to undermine Paul's prestige and authority. The culprit of 2 Cor. 7:12 was, very likely, one of these "superlative apostles." Paul's severe letter had a salutary effect; and his relief found vent in 2 Cor., although it does seem that chapters 10–13 were occasioned by reports of further unrest in the community.

PLAN

ADDRESS (1:1 f.)	
THANKSGIVING (1:3-11)	
PAUL'S APOLOGIA (1:12 – 7:16)	
1) The Journey to Corinth 2) The apostolic ministry 3) Appeal and consolation	1:12 – 2:17 3:1 – 6:10 6:11 – 7:16
THE COLLECTION FOR THE JERUSALEM CHURCH (8 – 9)	
POLEMICAL APOLOGIA (10-1 – 13:10)	
1) Reply to accusations 2) Paul's apostolate 3) The third visit	10 11:1 – 12:18 12:19 – 13:10
CONCLUSION (13:11-13)	

SUMMARY   The address (2 Cor. 1:1 f.) is followed by Paul's thanksgiving to God for support in the trials of the ministry and for deliverance from grave danger (2 Cor. 1:3-11). His explanation of his former conduct toward the Corinthians forms the first part of the letter (2 Cor. 1:12-7:16). He explains why he had changed his travel plans. Refuting a charge of duplicity, he declares himself to be not a man who answers "yes" and "no" in the same breath. It was to spare their feelings that he had not come to Corinth; one painful visit was more than enough. Instead, from Macedonia he had written a severe letter, "with many tears." Now that the culprit had been duly punished by the community, it was time to pardon him. But Paul was still anxious for his Corinthians and he had left Troas for Macedonia in order to meet Titus who would bring him news of them. He joyfully thanks God for the good tidings received (2 Cor. 1:12-2:17).

Next he turns to the grandeur and the demands of the apostolic ministry (2 Cor. 3:1-6:10). Paul needed no recommendation to or from the converts, such as his adversaries doubtlessly required; the community at Corinth was his recommendation, an open letter for all to read. He is a minister of the New Covenant, one of the Spirit and not of the letter; the administration of the New Covenant is more glorious than Moses' administration of the old. Basing himself on a free exegesis of Ex. 34:33-35, he argues that the Jews fail to see that the Old Testament had reached fulfillment. Yet, they have only to turn to Christ for the veil to be removed. The role of an apostle is to preach Jesus Christ as Lord, to bring to men the knowledge of God revealed in Christ (2 Cor. 3:1-4:6).

Apostles, it is true, are earthen vessels, to show that divine, not human power is at work in them. Paul may be worn down by the tribulations of the ministry, but the life of Jesus flows from him to other men, and he is confident that he will share in the resurrection of Jesus. All the while, his spiritual life is being renewed and his sufferings are a prelude to his reunion with Christ (2 Cor. 4:7-5:10). The climax of the apologia is reached in 2 Cor. 5:11-6:10. He does not commend himself to the Corinthians, but he would wish them to be proud of him – this is why he has explained his conduct so fully. It is the love of Christ that stirs him and he, in his turn, proclaims Christ dead and risen again. For, in Christ, God has reconciled the world to himself. It was for our sake that God made him "to be sin" (2 Cor. 5:21); that is, God had sent his Son "in the likeness of sinful flesh" (Rm. 8:3), in order to become a sacrifice for sin. By dying in his flesh, the sensible sign of the sinful world, and by rising in a body made new, Christ himself and in him, virtually, all humanity passed from the carnal to the spiritual life. Paul commends himself by the sufferings he has undergone in the service of Christ; he entreats his faithful not to receive the grace of God in vain.

A tender appeal (2 Cor. 6:11-7:4) is unexpectedly interrupted by an exhortation not to associate with unbelievers and a warning to have no part with Belial (2 Cor. 6:14-7:1). The Apostle declares that his mind is now fully at rest. Titus has brought good news; he realizes that the severe letter had produced a salutary effect and he is confident that he can depend on his Corinthians (2 Cor. 7:5-16).

The letter passes to the question of a collection for the church of Jerusalem (chaps. 8-9).

Each of these chapters is concerned with the collection for the Jerusalem church and both cover the same ground; it appears that they represent two distinct letters. In 2 Cor. 9:1, Paul declares that it is "superfluous for me to write to you about the offering for the saints"; coming just after a whole chapter devoted to the collection, this rings strangely. Then, in 2 Cor. 8:1-5, he seeks to stir the Corinthians to emulation by recalling the eagerness and liberality of the churches of Macedonia, while in 2 Cor. 9:1-6 he tells the Corinthians how, in Macedonia, he had boasted of their zeal and generosity. Also, the motives for a ready response are presented twice and differently (2 Cor. 8:7-15; 9:6-14). On the evidence, it seems that we may reasonably regard chapter 9 as a letter, or part of a letter, originally written to churches of Achaia other than Corinth. Its insertion after chapter 8 must have occurred very early, because all extant manuscripts contain it as part of the Epistle.

This matter of a collection in favor of the "saints" of Jerusalem was of great importance in Paul's eyes (cf. Gal. 2:10; 1 Cor. 16:1-3; 2 Cor. 8-9; Rm. 15:25-27). Since, for him, the Christian is a member of the Body, and life in Christ is the life of the people of God, the unity of the Church is essential. He developed his theology of unity especially in the face of differences between Judaeo-Christian and Gentile converts and under the impetus of internal strife in the Corinthian community. In view of this, and of his great regard for Jerusalem as the holy city of the new people of God, the collection was much more than a work of charity.

> The carrying into effect of this project of the collection was perhaps the happiest stroke of genius in the whole of his life as an apostle. By it Jerusalem won a religious empire and the Gentile Christians saved not only their unity, but also their living connection with the center of monotheism and purity of life.[2]

Paul holds up for imitation the churches of Macedonia which, in spite of their difficulties and extreme poverty, had contributed voluntarily and liberally to the needs of the brethren of Jerusalem. Titus had been urged to complete the work already begun in Corinth. The Corinthian church, outstanding in every way, also must be foremost in this. Paul's ultimate argument is not friendly emulation, but the self-abasement of the Incarnation, the great charity of Jesus Christ, for the only driving motive that he knew, the only motive that really matters to a Christian, is the example of Christ and the imitation of him. The Corinthians are not expected to impoverish themselves, but they should give generously whatever they can spare. Paul is sending two delegates besides Titus (one is very likely Luke [2 Cor. 8:18 f.]); they should be warmly welcomed at Corinth (chap. 8).

Chapter 9 covers the same ground as chapter 8; we have suggested that it was originally addressed to churches other than Corinth. Paul has pointed to the churches of Achaia in order to stir the generosity of the Macedonians (in 2 Cor. 8:1-6, it was the other way about). Generosity is urged: almsgiving is a sowing of seed, and there exists between the seed and the harvest a strict law of proportion. But it is a question of one's attitude rather than of the amount one gives; the important thing is that the gift, whether big or little, should be given freely, gladly: "God loves a cheerful giver" (2 Cor. 9:7). God will see to it that the generous giver will not suffer on account of his generosity. He will receive spiritual blessings, but he will be blessed in temporal matters too – so that he may be able to give more liberally still! This work does not end with the relief of those in need; the benefactor will benefit from the prayers of those he has helped, and glory is given to God (chap. 9).

In the final part of the letter (chapters 10-13), Paul turns again to a personal apologia, but this time with a marked polemical tone. It seems that Titus, sent by Paul to organize the collection (2 Cor. 8:6, 17 f.), had found that the Apostle's adversaries had renewed their attacks on him. When Paul had received word of the latest development, he quickly wrote chapters 10-13. His adversaries had accused him of weakness: Paul can speak boldly when he is at a safe distance, but is timid and wavering when confronted. He assures them that he is quite prepared to take strong action whenever it is necessary. He will not class himself with those who so love to blow their own trumpet. He is not trespassing when he exercises his authority at Corinth, a church founded by himself. The Lord has called him to the apostolic ministry – this is approbation and praise enough; self-praise would sound foolishly beside it (chap. 10).

Although much of chapter 11 is bitingly sarcastic, Paul begins by excusing himself for his self-defense. He had been called a "fool"; then, they must be prepared to put up with his "folly." He had been driven to this self-defense by the fickleness of the Corinthians who were ready to accept a different gospel. He is not a whit inferior to the "super-apostles," those self-styled representatives of the mother-church to whom the Corinthians have turned; his unyielding insistence on financial independence marks him off from those others. Now he is obliged to boast in order to prove his apostleship genuine (2 Cor. 11:1-21a). While he cannot compete with the arrogance of his adversaries, he can match their claims of race (Hebrews), religion (Israelites), and inheritance (descendants of Abraham). And if they claim to be servants of Christ, his litany of sufferings *proves* him to be a true minister of Christ (2 Cor. 11:21b-33). Although boasting about visions is out of place, Paul is compelled to recall an extraordinary experience he had fourteen years previously; he had found himself caught up to the divine presence. However, a keen reminder of his human weakness kept him from being carried away by the experience. We do not know the nature of the "thorn in the flesh"; most likely it was a recurring illness; there are no grounds for regarding it as the urge of concupiscence (2 Cor. 12:1-10). Again he is forced to justify himself (2 Cor. 12:11-18). He fears that he will have to take strong action when he visits them anew, and he is quite ready to do so. But he hopes that the sinners will repent, because he has no desire to lord it over them. The Corinthians are strong when their conduct is fully Christian, and in this case Paul is weak since he does not have to invoke his apostolic authority against them (2 Cor. 12:19-13:10). The conclusion (2 Cor. 13:11-14) makes a final appeal for a Christian life in the joy of union. The closing wish, trinitarian in form, is possibly a liturgical formula.

4) Romans

THE ROMAN CHURCH   The origin of the Roman church is shrouded in darkness, but it is unquestioned that Christians had gained a footing in Rome in the early days of the Church. Most probably, the foundation of a church there was not due to a planned mission, but was the result of the migration of Christians to the capital of the empire. Some of the early converts were to be found among the Jews and proselytes who had heard the preaching of Peter at Pentecost (Acts 2). It is not likely that Peter himself was the founder of the Roman church, for he seems to have come to Rome for the first time in the decade 50-60 A.D.

Some have contended that the Roman community was predominantly Judaeo-Christian in composition. Paul addresses self-satisfied Jews (Rm. 2:17-3:8); he contrasts faith and the Law (Rm. 3:21-31); he speaks of "Abraham, our forefather according to the flesh" (Rm. 4:1); he answers objections against his doctrine of freedom from the Law (Rm. 6:1-7:6); he dwells at length on the fate of Israel (chaps. 9-11); finally, the "weak" of Rm. 14:1-15:13 are said to be Judaeo-Christians. To all this evidence must be added the weighty fact that the main doctrine of Rm. is this: Not circumcision and the Law, but faith without the works of the Law brings salvation.

Yet, strong as these indications seem, they are outweighted by arguments in favor of a Gentile-Christian majority. In his prologue and at the close, Paul expresses his desire of visiting Rome and insists on his vocation of Apostle to the Gentiles. He addresses the Romans as Gentile-Christians; he had received from Christ the mission of the apostolate among the nations, "including yourselves" (the Romans) (Rm. 1:5 f.). Hitherto he had been prevented from visiting Rome, where he would wish to bear fruit "as among the rest of the Gentiles" (Rm. 15:16). He addresses them quite deliberately as Gentiles: "Now I am speaking to you Gentiles — inasmuch as I am an apostle to the Gentiles" (Rm. 11:13). These texts are conclusive. The Roman church was composed, for the greater part, of Gentile-Christians; the evidence to the contrary indicates no more than a minority of Judaeo-Christians.

OCCASION AND DATE Paul had long desired to visit Rome. He had proclaimed the name of Christ in the East, and in Europe as far as Illyricum; now he wanted to preach in the West, especially in Spain. On the journey to Spain he planned to pass through Rome. As Apostle to the Gentiles he was more anxious than ever to establish contact with the Roman church for, in view of that apostolate, its position as church of the empire's capital was of paramount importance. He who did not wish to build on foundations laid by others, nevertheless saw clearly that the roads which led from Rome to all parts of the *orbis Romanus* could become so many roads of missionary expansion. Romans, then, was written to prepare the way for the visit of Paul: he wished that the Romans should know beforehand the main lines of "his" gospel.

For Paul is concerned to expound his gospel, his manner of presenting the Good News of Christ. From the moment of his conversion, he had perceived with clarity the unique role of Christ in the salvation of men. His work among the Gentiles had colored his attitude to Jewish law and practice; the enmity of Jews and the opposition of Judaeo-Christians further sharpened his appreciation of the central truth of salvation through faith in Christ. The writing of Gal. had given an opportunity of stating his thesis, but in a polemical atmosphere; now he can take it up again in a calmer fashion and more leisurely. It is not, however, a synthesis of his theology – there are too many omissions for that. But Paul does

PLAN

THE ADDRESS (1:1-7)	
THE THANKSGIVING (1:8-15)	
PART I. SALVATION BY FAITH (1:16 – 11:36)	
A. THE DOCTRINE OF JUSTIFICATION (3:21 – 31)	
THE THEME (1:16 f.)	

1) The universal sway of sin and retribution	1:18 – 3:20
2) The justice of God and faith	3:21 – 4:25
a. The doctrine of justification	3:21-32
b. The example of Abraham	4:1-25

B. SALVATION	
THE THEME (5:1-11)	

1) Liberation from sin, death, and the Law	5:12 – 7:25
a. Adam and Christ	5:12-21
b. Union with Christ in death and resurrection	6:1-14
c. Freedom from sin	6:15-23
d. Freedom from the Law	7:1-6
e. The role of the Law	7:7-25
2) Life in the Spirit	8:1-39
3) The situation of Israel	9 – 11
a. The privileges of Israel	9:1-5
b. Divine sovereignty	9:6-29
c. Israel's responsibility	9:30 – 10:21
d. God has not rejected his people	11:1-32
e. Hymn to the divine mercy	11:33-36

PART II.
THE JUSTICE OF GOD IN CHRISTIAN LIVING
(12:1 – 15:13)

1)	Sacrifice of self	12:1 f.
2)	Proper use of charisms	12:3-8
3)	Charity	12:9-21
4)	Christians and the state	13:1-7
5)	Love fulfills the Law	13:8-10
6)	The Christian is a child of light	13:11-14
7)	The "Strong" and the "Weak"	14:1 – 15:13

EPILOGUE (15:14 – 16:27)

1)	Personal explanations	15:14-33
2)	Recommendation of Phoebe	16:1 f.
3)	Greetings to friends in Rome	16:3-16
4)	A final word of warning	16:17-20
5)	Greetings of Paul's companions	16:21-23

DOXOLOGY (16:24-27)

take occasion to expound a theme which he had pondered at length: The salvation of God, presented by the preaching of the Gospel first to Jews and then to Gentiles; salvation, a divine force, necessary for all and offered to all (Rm. 1:1 f., 16 f.).

-Rm. was written at Corinth toward the close of the third missionary journey, during the winter 57/58 A.D. That Corinth was the place of origin is indicated by Paul's recommendation of Phoebe, deaconess of Cenchreae, the eastern port of Corinth (Rm. 16:1), and by the fact that he is the guest of Gaius who is, very likely, the same man named in 1 Cor. 1:14 (Rm. 16:23). We may add that, according to Acts 20:2 f., Paul left from Corinth on his last journey to Jerusalem (cf. Rm. 15:25).

SUMMARY   The address (Rm. 1:1-7) is unusually solemn: Paul presents his credentials to a church where he is unknown and over which he has no authority. He is a servant of Jesus Christ, called to be an apostle. He preached to the Gentiles that gospel foretold by the prophets and realized in Christ, a descendant of David, but now by his resurrection established Son of God in the glory of his power according to his spirit of holiness – our Lord. Christ is presented in his salvific role: the Risen Lord has become "a life-giving spirit" (1 Cor. 15:45). The thanksgiving (Rm. 1:8-15) acknowledges the good name of the Roman church and expresses the Apostle's eager desire to preach among them. In Rm. 1:16 f., we find the theme of the Epistle: The Gospel (the revelation of God's justice), the very power of God, working for the salvation of all who receive it by faith. It is preached first to the Jews whose historical role as Chosen People entitles them to hear it first; after that there is no distinction between Jew and Gentile.

In contrast to the revelation of God's justice, is the manifestation of his anger against Gentile and Jew (Rm. 1:18-3:20). In a passage inspired by Wis. 13:1-9, Paul declares that contemplation of the wonderful works of God should have led the Gentiles to an acknowledgment of the Creator; instead, men have perversely worshiped creatures. Idolatry is punished by depraved morals (cf. Wis. 14:22-31). The Apostle is passing judgment on the pagan world as such, not on individuals (Rm. 1:18-32). Then he turns to the Jews (Rm. 2:1 3:20). The Jew who sets himself up as a judge of other men will not be spared if he acts like them. Neither the Law, nor circumcision, nor the Scripture will dispense him from interior righteousness. All men, Jews and Gentiles, must face the judgment of God and will receive reward or punishment according to their deeds. The Gentiles who have not the advantage of a Law positively revealed can still follow the law written on the heart of every man. Paul does admit that the Jew has the honor of belonging to the Chosen People, but this alone is not sufficient to save him. Many Jews have, in fact, proved unfaithful, but then the failure of men cannot hinder the fulfillment of God's promises. The Law, an external norm of conduct, has not, in God's plan, the role of remitting sin; rather, it brings the sinner to an awareness of sin.

After the preliminary stage of his argument — apart from the Gospel all that is to be found in the world is sin and its retribution — Paul can turn to the thesis announced in Rm. 1:17: "The righteousness of God is revealed through faith for faith" (Rm. 3:21-4:25). The plan of God is presented in Rm. 3:21-26. Paul combines three metaphors: from the law-court (justification), from the institution of slavery (emancipation), and from sacrificial ritual (expiation by blood): "They are justified by his grace . . . through the redemption which is in Christ Jesus . . . and explation by his blood" (Rm. 3:24 f.). He describes an act of God for men, the metaphors serving to emphasize the change of status involved.

But what he is here concerned to make clear is that by no possible effort of his own could man alter his status before God, any more than a guilty prisoner could acquit himself, or a slave free himself, or an "unclean" person become "clean" without supernatural means; but that God, by a sheer act of grace, has made this change possible.[3]

For man is justified by faith alone and not by the works of the Law. Paul contrasts two regimes; one consists in believing, that is, in submitting oneself to the justifying activity of God; the other is a vain striving to find grace through works (Rm. 3:27-31).

Paul now brings Abraham forward in support of his doctrine of justification by faith (Rm. 4:1-25). In Jewish tradition, Abraham, by his constancy in trial, had become the model of justification by works. The Apostle argues that the faith of Abraham was his justification, and that even in Abraham the faith and justice of the Christian Era were prefigured; he is the first of believers. According to Genesis (15:6), Abraham was declared justified before he had been circumcised. It was only afterward that circumcision was imposed as a seal on the justification he had received through faith. Spiritual descent from Abraham is not based on circumcision, and the rite so valued by Jews and converts from Judaism is of no advantage to them. The promise made to Abraham did not reach him through the Law but through the "righteousness of faith," that is, through a justification which consists in believing or, quite simply, through a living faith. Paul argues that Abraham is the father of Gentiles too, and specifically of Christians. As their father he is the model of Christians, of all who are justified by faith in Christ. Abraham believed in God and trusted in the power of God who could vivify, miraculously, his body and the body of Sarah; hence, he reached, by anticipation and in type, the object of the Christian faith. For justification is a first participation in the life of the Risen Christ.

We come to the central section of the letter. We have learned that men are justified, freely, by God (chaps. 1-4); henceforth (chaps. 5-11), we shall see that the Christian, justified through faith, finds in the love of God and the gift of the Spirit the guarantee of salvation. Christ has won for us the entry into the friendship of God; the love of God for us bears the hallmark of divine love: it is while we were sinners that Christ died for us (Rm. 5:1-11). Paul is desirous to show that Christ has repaired, in superabundant fashion, the sin of the first man and its consequences. He describes with complacency the great contrast between the ravages of sin, however fearful, and the grace of God conferred on men through Jesus Christ. The Law was not able to remove sin; instead, it made men more conscious of sin (Rm. 5:12-21).

Paul takes up the objection that, if the work of salvation is entirely God's, and we can do nothing of ourselves, then why not remain on in sin so that there may be all the more room for grace (Rm. 6:1). First, he shows how baptism, the sacramental initiation into the Christian life, brings about a death and a renewal. Baptism by immersion symbolizes the effect of the sacrament; the baptized person is "buried" in the water and is dead to sin, but then coming out of the water, he "rises" to share the new life in Christ. The Christian, dead and risen with Christ, now lives in the Spirit. Although baptism destroys sin in men, still, until his body has "put on immortality" (1 Cor. 15:54), sin can again gain possession of this "mortal" body (Rm. 6:1-14). Next, he represents liberation from sin as freedom from slavery. No man can serve two masters; justification means the service of God and the free gift of eternal life in Christ (Rm. 6:15-23). The Christian, however, is free not only from sin but also from the Law; the argument is in terms of the laws of marriage. By their link with the death of Christ in baptism, Christians have died to the Law; a new life in the Spirit follows the old regime of the letter (Rm. 7:1-6).

Having introduced the Law, the Apostle, in Rm. 7:7-25, goes on to discuss its role. The Law is itself good and holy, but it has not justified men. It is a light which enlightens men's consciences, but does not give interior strength; it is powerless to prevent sin. In a certain sense, it is an occasion of sin, since it makes sin more obvious and more culpable. The argument is scriptural: it is inspired by the biblical description of the sin of Adam, the type of all sin (Rm. 5:12-21).

> Translated into terms of individual experience the story runs: *I lived at one time without law myself, but when the command came home to me, sin sprang to life and I died; the command that meant life proved death to me. The command gave an impulse of sin, sin beguiled me and used the command to kill me.* It fits like a glove; and there are enough verbal echoes of the Greek translation of Gn. 3 to make it likely that Paul actually had the passage in mind.[4]

Of course, Paul is not thinking merely of the person of Adam, but takes him as a type of humanity. What he has said can be applied, with the necessary nuances, to every man; yet, it is not drawn from personal experience or from abstract speculation, but from the story of Adam. Left to himself, then, man is in a hopeless state: "Who will rescue me from this body of death? " But, Paul knows that deliverance has been won and thanks God for it (Rm. 7:24-25a). Verse 25b is clearly an afterthought, and would be more in place before verse 24.

Having traced the unhappy state of a man in the bondage of sin and death, Paul now turns to the Christian already justified and filled with the Spirit. For, the new regime of the Spirit – the law of the Spirit of life in Christ Jesus – has replaced the regime of sin and death (chap. 8). The Mosaic Law, an external norm, was not a principle of salvation. Christ, by coming into the world "in the likeness of sinful flesh," and by offering himself as a sacrifice for sin, broke the power of sin and the stranglehold of the flesh. Henceforth, united to Christ, man is spiritualized. Because of sin the body is destined for physical death and is the instrument of spiritual death, but the spirit has life in Christ. The body, however, will rise again, and already the Spirit of God dwells in it (Rm. 8:1-13; cf. 1 Cor. 15:35-55). By the indwelling of the Spirit, Christians are made sons of God, sharing the divine life; this is the reason they can address their Father with the intimate title used by Jesus himself (Rm. 8:14-17; cf. Mk. 14:36).

The material world, created for man, shares in his destiny. Cursed by reason of man's sin (Gn. 3:17), it will share in man's redemption. Whereas Greek philosophy would liberate spirit from matter, regarded as something evil, Christianity sets matter itself free.

Like nature, Christians wait for the final redemption; salvation remains an object of hope. The image of God in man was tarnished by sin; Christ, the Image of God, enables men to acquire again, more fully, the divine likeness: he and Christians form the one family of the Father. God has destined his elect for glory and has ordered everything to that end (Rm. 8:18-30). Paul ends with a hymn of Christian hope: the certainty of salvation. The fact of the redemption and justification wrought by God gives the faithful the assurance of triumphing in the midst of the tribulations of the present life: nothing can part them from God's love in Christ Jesus their Lord (Rm. 8:31-39). "There is no arguing with such a certainty. Either you simply don't believe it or you recognize it as the word of God."

Paul has sketched the universal saving plan of God, but, in that plan, what has become of Israel, the people of the promises? As it is, the Jewish resistance to the Gospel seems to be a flat contradiction of all he has said. Hence, in diatribe style, he discusses the historical role of Israel (chaps. 9-11). First, he points to the privileges which the people of Israel, as chosen race, enjoys: adoption as sons of God; the glory of God's dwelling in their midst; the covenants with the patriarchs and with Moses; the cult of the true God; the Law that is the expression of his will; the messianic promises; and the fact that Christ was born of their race (Rm. 9:1-5).

After this short introduction, Paul deals with the problem in three stages:

1) God is absolutely sovereign and is completely free to chose the recipients of his favor and the instruments of his purpose. The freedom of God's plan is illustrated by the constant biblical theme that the heir of the promise is not necessarily the first born; thus, Isaac is chosen and not Ishmael. Man cannot take God to task for the free manifestations of his mercy or of his anger. Nor does his treatment of Pharaoh and of the Israelites conflict with his justice; while the mercy of God is manifest, in that the promises rejected by the Jews are now offered to the Gentiles – as the Scriptures had foretold (Rm. 9:6-29).

2) Next, Paul stresses human responsibility in the mystery of Jewish infidelity. Israel, in fact, has stumbled over Christ, a stumbling block for them, and has taken a wrong course. They have not submitted to God's plan; rather, seeking their own justification in works of the Law, they have missed the justification that Christ has brought. Salvation is won through profession of faith in the Lord Jesus (Rm. 9:9 f.); this gospel has been proclaimed, and if the Israelites as such have not called upon the Lord, it can be only because they are "a disobedient and contrary people" (Rm. 9:30-10:21).

3) Finally, it follows from God's free choice of his people and his own faithfulness that Israel cannot be rejected by him. All is not lost: although the Chosen People as a whole are now unfaithful, they will yet enter upon their true destiny. As it is, some Jews – the "Remnant" of which the prophets spoke – have attained the promise, and this Remnant is the guarantee of a future restoration. The Jews' actual rejection of Christ has opened the way to the conversion of the Gentiles, and if the latter, branches of a wild olive, have been grafted on to the parent stock of Israel, how much easier it will be to graft on the converted Jews. The Gentiles

can take salutary warning: they must realize that they, by the divine mercy, have won the inheritance that should have been Israel's; and they can learn from Israel's sad history that they too can be cut off if they prove unfaithful. But the Chosen People has not been rejected, and the Apostle announces the eventual conversion of Israel (Rm. 11:1-32). As he contemplates the final return of his people, Paul breaks into a hymn in praise of the great mercy of God (Rm. 11:33-36).

The great dogmatic themes of the Epistle now stand in the background as Paul takes up the moral demands of the Christian life (Rm. 12:1-15:13). It is his own person, not the animal sacrifices of Judaism or paganism, that the Christian offers to God (Rm. 12:1 f.). Charisms are to be used properly, for the common good of the whole Body (Rm. 12:3-8). Charity, love of the brethren and love of enemies, is the principle of Christian living (Rm. 12:9-21). Christians owe allegiance to the state, for civil authority is of divine origin; presuming, of course, that it is legitimate and has the common good in view (Rm. 13:1-7). Again charity is stressed: it is the fulfilling of the Law (Rm. 13:8-10). Awareness of the Parousia will remind the Christian that he is a child of light and should live in the light (Rm. 13:11-14).

In the long passage, Rm. 14:1-15:13, the Apostle considers a concrete moral problem (cf. 1 Cor. 8-10). The "strong" are those who can judge things in the light of Christian liberty; the "weak" are Christians with an insufficiently enlightened faith and who lack the conviction that would enable them to act with a sure conscience. Such a one, following a Jewish or pagan custom, will believe that he is bound to abstain from meat or to observe certain days as solemn festivals. Paul points out that there is room for both "strong" and "weak" in the Christian community (Rm. 14:1-12). The "strong" however, are bound, in charity, to take cognizance of the troubled conscience of the weak; he invokes (Rm. 14:15) the very highest motive for avoiding scandal (Rm. 14:13-23). All should take example from Christ (Rm. 15:1-13). The verse 15:13 gives the central themes of the first page of the Epistle and the conclusion of the writing; the rest is epilogue.

Paul again justifies his writing to Rome, a church he had not founded (Rm. 15:14-21). He plans soon to make a journey to Spain and will visit the Romans en route; he asks their prayers (Rm. 15:22-33). The recommendation of Phoebe – very likely the bearer of the letter (Rm. 16:1 f.) – is followed first by a long litany of personal greetings (Rm. 16:3-16) and then, unexpectedly, by a warning against those who create dissension and difficulties, probably Judaizers (Rm. 16:17-20). Then come the salutations of Paul's companions – Tertius is named as the secretary who wrote the letter (Rm. 16:21-23) – and the closing doxology (Rm. 16:24-27).

4. THE CAPTIVITY EPISTLES

The four letters, Philippians, Colossians, Philemon, and Ephesians, are called the "Captivity Epistles" because Paul informs us that he wrote them in prison (Phil. 1:7, 12-17; Col. 4:3, 10, 18; Phm. 1:9 f., 13, 23; Eph. 3:1; 4:1; 6:20). Although 2 Tm. was also written during an imprisonment (2 Tm. 1:8, 16: 2:9), it is grouped with the Pastoral Epistles. We learn from Acts that Paul was a prisoner for two years in Caesarea, 58-60 A.D. (Acts 23:33-26.32), and again in Rome (Acts 28:16, 30), apparently also for two years (61-63 A.D.). But Acts does not give a complete picture of Paul's missionary activities and, indeed, tells us little of his three-year in Ephesus. Hence, in recent times, many scholars have postulated a captivity of the Apostle in that city. This hypothesis, however, applies more directly to Phil. alone.

1) Philippians

THE PHILIPPIAN CHURCH Philippi was built by Philip of Macedonia, father of Alexander the Great, on the site of the ancient Krenides. In 42 A.D., it became a Roman military colony and received from Augustus the title of *Colonia Iulia Augusta Philippensis*. Its population was made up principally of Roman veterans and the town was administered in the Roman fashion (Acts 16:21). The Jewish element was evidently very small, since there was no synagogue (Acts 16.13). Paul visited Philippi for the first time in 50 A.D., during his second missionary journey; he was accompanied by Silas, Timothy, and Luke. It seems likely that the first community assembled in the house of Lydia, a native of Thyatira in Asia Minor, who was profitably engaged in the purple dye trade. The church of Philippi – inevitably in view of the small Jewish population – was predominantly Gentile in composition (cf. Acts 16:12-40; Phil. 2:15 f.; 3:3 f.; 4:8 f.). The Apostle visited the city again on his third missionary journey (57 A.D.) Luke had been in charge of the community in the meantime – and, for a third time, on his way back from Corinth (58 A.D.) when he took

Luke with him to Jerusalem (Acts 20:1-6). We gather that the church of Philippi was expecially dear to Paul. This is the reason he made an exception in the case of the Philippians and, for once waiving his rigidly-maintained independence, accepted material help from them (Phil. 4:16; 2 Cor. 11:19).

INTEGRITY   The authenticity of Phil. is not in question; the internal evidence is so clear as to put the matter beyond reasonable doubt. But, since the beginning of critical study of the Epistle, its unity has been seriously in doubt. A reading of the letter reveals breaks in tone and subject matter at the beginning of chapter 3 and again at Phil. 4:10. The hypothesis that most satisfactorily accounts for these facts is that Phil. is a collection of letters – all emanating from Paul and all addressed to the church at Philippi.

Recent studies distinguished three letters, although there is not always agreement in defining the limits of each letter. For our purpose we may designate them as follows:

A. 4:10-20; B. 1:1-3:1 + 4:2-9; C. 3:2-4:1.

While there is agreement that letter A is earlier than the others, both the relative dates and the extent of B and C are uncertain.

Apart from the break between verses 9 and 10 of chapter 4, the claim of A to be an independent letter (or part of one) rests on two considerations:

1) Its place at the very end of the letter. In this section, Paul thanks the Philippians for their generosity in his hour of need. He shows himself so deeply grateful that it is highly unlikely that this sentiment would not have manifested itself earlier in the Epistle (but all we find are two allusions, Phil. 1:5; 2:30).

2) To suppose that the section belonged to the letter carried by Epaphroditus on his return to Philippi is to assume that Paul had neglected to thank the Philippians promptly and has even failed to avail of the earlier messengers to the community who could so easily have conveyed his letter. In view of the close bond of friendship that bound Paul to the Philippians, this assumption is unlikely. Hence the passage (A) should be considered as the letter – or part of one – which the Apostle sent on receipt of the gift.

C is considered a separate letter because it presupposes a situation other than that implied in A and B. In A and B, although we gather that all is not perfect in the church at Philippi, we are given no hint that matters are as serious as C would suggest. Paul's attitude toward his adversaries in Phil. 1:28 (B) is almost magnanimous, but in Phil. 3:2, 18 f. (C), it is harsh, and the terms he uses are deliberately insulting. The impression that he is not dealing with the same opponents is confirmed by other indications.

In Phil. 1:28 he exhorts the Philippians not to be "frightened" by their adversaries, thus suggesting that they operate by means of threats. When confronted by Jewish opponents, Paul is never worried that his Christians will be terrified into compliance, but rather that they will be seduced from the true faith. Hence, it is legitimate to conclude that the allusion in Phil. 1:28 is to persecution by *pagans*. This accords with what we know of the historical situation at Philippi, for it would appear that the pagan community there was particularly devout. Reference to circumcision in Phil. 3:2 (C), makes it certain that the second group of adversaries was Jewish in origin and upheld this central demand of the Law. The violence of Paul's reaction is readily explained by the insidious nature of the propaganda of this group.

These considerations do seem to establish a basic difference between C and A + B. In conclusion, we may suggest that Phil. is a collection of three letters, to any of which the ending Phil. 4:21-23 may belong. When the fusion of these letters took place is a matter of conjecture. It may have been at the moment when the Philippians passed on their Pauline correspondence to another church. In fairness, however, we must observe that the distinction of three letters rests on internal criticism alone: the manuscripts of Phil. show no variation in their presentation of the Epistle.

PLACE OF ORIGIN AND DATE *Phil. was written from prison (Phil. 1:14, 17) and, until the end of the nineteenth century, it* was taken for granted that the first Roman captivity of Paul (61-63 A.D.) was in question. But since the beginning of this century, Caesarea and Ephesus have been proposed as alternatives to Rome. Caesarea, however, has found few supporters, because all the reasons adduced in its favor may be applied with greater cogency to Ephesus.

Dependable, direct evidence in favor of an imprisonment of Paul at Ephesus does not exist. However, the epistles to Corinth prove that Paul was imprisoned more frequently than Acts has recorded 2 Cor. 11:23) and that his ministry in Ephesus was much more troubled by persecution than Acts permits us to see. The brevity of the account of an Ephesian ministry that lasted nearly three years is accounted for by the fact that Luke was apparently not with Paul: he is not mentioned in Phil. and a 'we-passage' terminates at Philippi in the narrative of the second missionary journey (Acts 16: 10 f.), while the next 'we-passage' commences with a mention of Paul's visit to Philippi on the return stage of his third journey (Acts 20:6). Therefore, despite the silence of Acts, it is possible that Paul was imprisoned at Ephesus.

We may point to approximately the same date for all three letters that make up the epistle, and the indications are that this date is in the period of the major epistles. With some confidence, Phil may be dated in 56-57 A.D., and Ephesus put as its place of origin.

PLAN   While we may not ignore the form in which Phil. has come to us, it is important to have in mind, too, the probable genesis of the Epistle; hence, we give two plans of the writing.

1. ADDRESS (1:1 f.)	
THANKSGIVING AND PRAYER (1:3-11)	
1) Paul's situation	1:12-36
2) Exhortation	1:27-2:18
3) Apostolic ministers	2:19 – 3:1
4) The way of Christian salvation	3:2 – 4:1
5) Peace in the Church	4:2-9
6) Paul's acknowledgment of gifts received	4:10-20
FINAL GREETING (4:21-23)	
2. LETTER A (4:10-20)	
LETTER B (1:1 – 3:1 + 4:2-9)	
LETTER C (3:2 – 4:1)	
CONCLUSION (4:21-23)	

2) Philemon

Philemon was a Colossian who had been converted by Paul himself (Phm. v. 9). His slave Onesimus had run away – having stolen some of his master's goods (vv. 15, 18) – and had somehow reached Paul in prison (v. 10). The Apostle converted him. Paul wants to send him back to his master (he will return with Tychicus [Col. 4:9]), and he provides him with a letter for Philemon.

The introductory greeting (vv. 1-3), as in Col., associates Timothy with Paul. Apphia and Archippus are very likely Philemon's wife and son; we learn that their house was a place of Christian assembly. The thanksgiving (vv. 4-7) lauds the charity and faith of Philemon.

In the body of the letter (vv. 8-21), Paul, "an old man and prisoner for Jesus Christ," appeals to that charity of Philemon on behalf of Onesimus, the Apostle's spiritual son. In parenthesis, and with a touch of humor, he plays on the name "Onesimus," which means "profitable." Regretfully, he sends away such a dear and valuable disciple; nothing but a sense of justice would make him part with his child. We seem to detect a hint that Philemon should let Onesimus return (v. 15). Paul suggests that the whole episode was providential: Philemon had lost a slave only to gain a brother (vv. 15 f.) – surely a hint that the slave should be set free. Then, the Apostle, who writes this letter with his own hand, appeals to their mutual friendship; for that matter, Philemon, who had been converted by Paul, owes him more than this! He is confident, however, that Philemon will do even more than he asks, again hinting at the release and probably at the return of the slave. In conclusion (vv. 22-25), Paul expresses the hope that he himself will soon visit Philemon. Five fellow workers of Col. 4:10-14 are again listed; the same list is found in Col. 4:10-14.

Philemon formed part of the Pauline corpus from the beginning. Some elements in the early Church questioned its authenticity because of its brevity and because it was a private letter. In the last century, some critics maintained that Phm. was the work of a second-century forger who wanted to provide a Pauline ruling on slavery. Both contentions are irrelevant; nothing short of a lamentable lack of literary feeling would permit one to doubt for an instant the Pauline character of this charming letter. And because it is Pauline, we do not look in vain for an important doctrinal contribution: it puts before us the fundamental attitude of the primitive Church to slavery. In the social pattern of the age, the abolition of slavery was impossible; but the Christian slave should be regarded and treated as a brother and not as a chattel. For that matter, Paul would welcome the freeing of Onesimus (Phm. 14-16, 21). In time, the leaven of the Gospel would create such relations

between master and slave that the system of slavery would become
obsolete.

3) Colossians

THE COLOSSIAN   The town of Colossae lay in the Lycus valley
CHURCH   about one hundred miles east of Ephesus and
very close to the more important towns of Laodicea and Hiera-
polis; there was close contact between these three neighboring
towns (Col. 4:15 f.). It is practically certain that Paul had never
visited the towns (cf. Col. 2:1) and that he knew of their Christian
communities only by hearsay (Col. 1:4, 9). We learn that a disciple
of Paul, Epaphras, a native of Colossae (Col. 4:12), had evangelized
Colossae (Col. 1:7) and Laodicea (Col. 4:12). The community at
Colossae was mainly Gentile in origin (Col. 1:21; 27; 2-13). We
know, however, that Jews were numerous in these towns of
Phrygia and that here, as elsewhere, they tried to stifle the growth
of the churches. Their propaganda had brought about a crisis: a
dangerous error had won some acceptance and constituted a threat
to the community.

AUTHORSHIP   The traditional attribution of Col. to Paul is unhes-
AND DATE   itating. Since the nineteenth century, however, the
authenticity of the letter has been seriously challenged – though,
even today, perhaps a majority of scholars would defend Pauline
authorship. Arguments against Pauline authenticity are based on
considerations of language and style and on the christology of the
epistle. It has 34 words not found elsewhere in the New Testament
and 10 words found only in Ephesians, while some favorite Pauline
words are missing. More seriously, the style of Col. differs from
that of the earlier epistles; it is far less spontaneous. The christology involves the cosmic supremacy of Christ, and Christ as *Head*
of the Church; and the divine plan of salvation presented as the
'Mystery.' On the whole, this letter is notably different from the
certainly genuine Pauline letters. One may ask, then, whether Paul
has written Col., or whether another has written in his name and
has, to some extent, imitated Paul's style. Of course, there is the
link with Phm. Col. and Phm., both, do refer to Onesimus (Col.
4:9; Phm. 12) and list the same companions of Paul (Col. 4:10-14;
Phm. 23 f.). But, on the hypothesis of pseudonymity, this correspondence is due to the author of Col. – a later disciple of Paul.
By deliberately presenting himself as the Apostle (using the details

provided in Philemon) he won for his writing the stamp of apostolic authority.

If Col. is Pauline, it must have been written in the same place and at the same date as Phm., that is to say, Ephesus, 54-57 (or, Rome, (61-63). But if, as seems more likely, Col. was written by a disciple, then the place of origin and date remain wide open.

PLAN

ADDRESS (1:1 f.)	
THANKSGIVING AND PRAYER (1:3-12)	
CHRISTOLOGY (1:13-23)	
1) Transition	1:13 f.
2) Primacy of Christ	1:15-20
3) Reconciliation	1:21-23
POLEMIC (1:24 – 3:4)	
1) Paul and the Colossians	1:24 – 2:5
2) Error at Colossae	2:6 – 3:4
PRACTICAL ADMONITIONS (3:5 – 4:6)	
1) General admonitions	3:5-17
2) Particular admonitions	3:18 – 4:6
PERSONAL MESSAGES (4:7-17)	
FINAL GREETING (4:18)	

Pseudonymity. Pseudonymity (the attribution of a writing, by the author, to another than himself) was a well-known and accepted literary convention in NT times – in both hellenistic and Jewish circles. Among the Greeks, in the schools of Philosophy and medicine, it was normal for the disciple to publish his work under the name of his master – he thus acknowledged that he owed his knowledge and proficiency to his master. Pseudonymity was a constant feature in Jewish apocalyptic literature: an apocalypse was always attributed to a notable figure of the past, such as Daniel or Henoch. In the NT itself it has long been accepted that 2 Peter is pseudonymous. The question then is not *whether* there are pseudonymous writings in the NT, but rather, *how many* NT writings are pseudonymous.

We suggest that Col. is pseudonymous. This means that a disciple of Paul, one who held the great apostle in high reverence, faced up to the problems and difficulties of his later age, in the manner he believed Paul would have done in his day. In much the same way as the disciple in the Greek schools, he thereby acknowledged his debt to his revered master, and asserted his conviction that his own theological development was in the Pauline tradition.[5]

SUMMARY   Colossians, whether pseudonymous or not, is written in the name of Paul. The address (Col. 1:1 f.) presents Paul as an "apostle of Jesus Christ" and makes mention of Timothy. The Apostle thanks God for the faith, hope, and charity of the faithful and for the steady growth of the community founded by his disciple Epaphras. His prayer is that they may have the understanding that will promote their further progress and the patient endurance that will win for them a share in the inheritance of the saints (Col. 1:3-12). The "saints" may, perhaps, designate the angels (Jb. 5:1; Zech. 14:5; Dn. 4:10) with whom the elect will be associated (Mt. 22:30) in the eschatological light or brightness (Dn. 12:3; Mt. 13:43; Ap. 22:5). This interpretation is recommended by the Qumran writings with which Col. 1:12 f. presents striking literary analogies. God is the one who has delivered us from the dominion of darkness and who has brought us into the kingdom of light, the kingdom of his Son who has won redemption for us (Col. 1:13 f.). For, Christ holds the primacy in the order of creation and in the order of salvation (Col. 1:15-20). And the Colossians, once enemies of God, have been reconciled to him by his Son; now they must stand firm in the faith (Col. 1:21-23).

Paul, the prisoner, suffers for his converts: he has his share in the reconciling work of God in Christ. As Apostle of the Gentiles, he is a minister of that "mystery hidden for ages": the calling of the Gentiles to salvation and to heavenly glory through union with Christ. His solicitude reaches to the Phrygian communities he has never seen; he prays that they may be granted confidence and unity, and that they may be given understanding to penetrate the mystery of God, so that they may not be led astray (Col. 1:24-2:5).

Possessing Christ, they must live in him and not follow a human wisdom that would enslave them once more (Col. 2:6-8). He is the one true head of men and angels; in him alone God is revealed. Joined to him in his death and in his resurrection, the Christian, in Christ, is superior to the heavenly powers and he must never submit to them. The Law had made man conscious of sin and had stood in accusation against him; this incriminating document has "died"; it has been cancelled by the sacrificial death of Christ. According to Jewish tradition, angelic powers stood behind the Law (cf. Acts 17:53; Gal. 3:19; Heb. 2:2), which became for them an instrument of domination over men. Now they are seen in their true role, intermediary creatures subject to Christ, captives in his triumph (Col. 2:9-15). To follow the practices and to accept the beliefs of Jewish false teachers would mean to come again under the influence of the heavenly powers. This is because the ascetical and cultic practices in question give too much importance to the elements of the material world and thereby to the heavenly powers that control them. In Christ, the Christians have died to the elemental spirits and hence are free of human prescriptions and doctrines (Col. 2:16-23). Since they have been raised by Christ, then all the more reason they should turn away from the things of earth and seek the things that are above. As it is, their life in Christ, although real, is hidden, but at the Parousia it will be manifest and glorious (Col. 3:1-4).

This is followed by the moral part of the Epistle. The Colossians must flee the vices of paganism which incur the divine anger for, indeed, they have put on the new nature of those who have been re-created in Christ. Therefore, they must practice Christian virtues and be grounded in charity. Peace should reign and they should live in an atmosphere of thanksgiving, doing everything in the name of the Lord Jesus (Col. 3:5-17). Next come particular instructions (Col. 3:18-4:1) relating to family life, including the master-slave relationship (significant in view of Onesimus, the fugitive slave [Col. 4:19; cf. Phm.]). Assiduous prayer is urged and the Apostle recommends himself to the prayers of his faithful (Col. 4:2-4). He asks that they show wisdom and courtesy in their relations with non-Christians (Col. 4.5 f.).

Paul is sending Tychicus and Onesimus to Colossae. He sends the greetings of his companions. The Colossians are bidden to greet

the brethren at Laodicea and the two communities are to exchange
letters (Col. 4:7-17). 'Paul' adds the final greetings (Col. 4:18) in
his own hand.

THE COLOSSIAN   The author wrote this letter because of a dan-
ERROR   gerous error which threatened to disrupt the
Colossian community. Since the concrete situation was well known
to his correspondents, his references to it are vague and, to us,
obscure. It is widely held today that what was involved was a
syncretistic movement of Jewish-Gnostic character or, rather, the
infiltration of ideas from such a milieu. However, it can be argued
that this understanding of the situation does not, all, stand on very
firm ground. The alleged Gnostic or pregnostic nature of the ideas
combated by the author follows from an interpretation of certain
expressions of the Epistle in the light of second-century Gnostic
writings. It seems that the "Colossian error" should be sought in
another direction.[6]

What the disturbers propose to the Colossians, in the first place,
are observances touching the calendar (Col. 2:16b), dietary laws
(Col. 2:16a, 21-23), and circumcision (Col. 2:11-13); the Jewish
character of these observances is manifest. Paul lets it be clearly
understood that, behind all this, is the Jewish Law (Col. 2:14)
with its obsolete character and its air of "shadow of things to
come" (Col. 2:17). It is true that the other traits, like excessive
asceticism (Col. 2:23) and the pursuit of a human "philosophy,"
are less at home in orthodox Judaism, but may well mark the
esoteric aspect of a particular Jewish sect.

The "cult of angels" (Col. 2:18) raises a more delicate problem.
That the Colossian agitators showed excessive interest in the
heavenly powers is obvious from the author's care to place these
powers under the Lordship of Christ (Col. 1:16; 2:10, 15). It is a
long step, however – and in view of Jewish monotheism an
unlikely one – to postulate a true "cult" of the powers. What does
appear is that the author so chose to interpret the liturgical and
food observances of Judaism. It is significant that he substitutes
the term "angels" for those of "principalities" and "powers" (Col.
2:15), thus passing from the astral and cosmic forces of the Hellenistic world to a purely biblical angelology. The Jewish syncretists
he had in mind speculated on these heavenly agents and, on the
other hand, stressed the importance of Jewish observances. It was
Paul himself (or so it would appear), however, who linked the

speculation and the observances; he did so in accordance with the view already underlying Gal. 3:19; 4:8-10, that the Mosaic Law, given on Sinai by angels, leads to submission to the "elemental spirits," that is to the material elements of the world and the spirits who administer them. Hence, to set religion in material observances is, in fact, to render a cult to the angels who rule the cosmos – but, this inference is Paul's.

It does not follow, either, that the syncretists assuredly assigned to Christ a determined place among these "angels" within the divine "pleroma." Here again it was the author who pointed to the logical consequences of their views. And these views are erroneous because Christ has become, by his Cross and his triumph over death, the only Lord of the new world; all the angelic powers are necessarily subject to him. The author's one concern is to maintain the absolute primacy of Christ; his interest in the "powers" is secondary. He treats of them only because of the misleading speculation about them. One thing he is sure of: the powers in no way compromise the role and rank of Christ. For the rest, he is content to speak in vague terms. We cannot say with confidence how he would regard these heavenly spirits, whether as good or bad, angelic or demonic.

In conclusion, we may observe that the Epistle's description (such as it is) of the error at Colossae lacks the specific elements of Gnosticism: the ontological dualism of spirit (good) and matter (evil) and the emanations of eons from the divinity to material creation. We may add that, side by side with orthodox Judaism, there existed, notably toward the beginning of our era, a Judaism that was more or less heterodox. We know of one such sect in Palestine itself – Essenianism – which went further than the Law in ritual observance and professed a special interest in the angelic hierarchies. The Qumran discoveries have thrown fresh light on this situation. It is not at all beyond the bounds of probability that a syncretistic Judaism was to be found in Asia Minor, and especially in Phrygia which was a utopia for esoteric cult and speculation. Such a Jewish milieu was the breeding ground of the "Colossian error."

4) Ephesians

DESTINATION   Ephesus, capital of the province of Asia, was a natural center of missionary activity. Paul visited the city for the first time toward the close of 52 A.D. on the way to Jerusalem at the end of the second missionary journey (Acts 18:19-21). He was back during his third journey for a long stay of almost three years (Acts 19-20). From there he sent his disciples to other cities of Asia.

The title 'to the Ephesians' is not original, although it does reflect a traditional destination of the letter. Yet, it seems likely that the letter was, in fact, addressed not to one church, but to a group of churches. Even more likely, the impersonal nature of the writing, which makes it implausible that it could have been written to a community so well known to the Apostle, is due to the fact that it is pseudonymous.

Authorship. From the early Christian centuries onward, the Pauline authenticity of Eph. was taken for granted. Doubts were first raised at the end of the 18th century and denial of Pauline authorship became widespread in the following century. Today it is widely held that Eph. is the work of a disciple of Paul who sought to develop the ideas of his master in a markedly ecclesiological direction. It is agreed that the writing cannot be by Paul himself because of its developed theology, its unusual vocabulary, and its curious literary contacts with the other NT epistles and with Col. in particular.

The difficulties of a literary order are serious. The style of Eph. is labored and redundant; long periods (e.g. 1:3-14) are encountered which contrast strikingly with passages like Rm. 4:1-10. However, the most serious objection raised against Paul's authorship of Eph. always has been its literary relationship to Col. A comparative study of the two epistles reveals numerous similarities both in style and vocabulary, contacts of a very special nature. They make it appear that Eph. is a meticulous, imitative adaptation of Col. This procedure may even be quite awkward at times. In short, literary dependence of Eph. on Col. cannot be doubted. We may note, for instance, the following passages: (1) citations: Eph. 3:2 = Col. 1:25; Eph. 4:16 = Col. 2:19; Eph. 4:22-24 = Col. 3:9 f.; Eph. 6:21 f. = Col. 3:7 f.; (2) the conflating of two (or more) passages of Col. in one of Eph: Col. 1:14 + 1:20 = Eph. 1:7; Col. 1.25 + 1:20 + 1:12 = Eph. 1:10 f.; (3) a rather artificial reproduction in Eph. of expressions of Col: Eph. 3:1-13 = Col. 1:24-29.

This last example serves to highlight the problem. Four principal ideas occur in Col. 1:24-29: the sufferings of Paul; his vocation; the manifestation of the divine Mystery; and the content of

the Mystery. Eph. 3:1-13 has the same ideas, but tends to repeat
them. Thus, for example, Col. 1:25 is found once in Eph. 3:2 and
a second time in Eph. 3:7. It happens that a formula has been
broken up, so that the *ages and generations* of Col. 1:26 furnish
the *generations* of Eph. 3:5 and the *ages* of Eph. 3:9. Words have
changed meaning. Thus, *oikonomia*, which in Col. 1:25 has the
normal Pauline sense of 'office,' 'administration,' receives in the
parallel passage Eph. 3:2 the sense of 'plan,' 'disposition' (cf. Eph.
1:10; 3:9). The 'holy' (*hagioi*) apostles and prophets' of Eph. 3:5
is a combination of 'the saints' (*hagioi*) of Col. 1:26 with the
'apostles and prophets' (cf. Eph. 2:20).

It seems impossible to attribute to Paul himself these laborious
imitations; and, for the same reason, it seems impossible to attribute them to the author of Col. The reasonable assumption is
that Eph. is pseudonymous. It is the work of one who saw himself
as a disciple of Paul — not necessarily an immediate disciple of the
Apostle. This man built on Col. — which he may have taken to be

PLAN

ADDRESS (1:1 f.)		
DOGMATIC PART: THE MYSTERY OF SALVATION AND OF THE CHURCH (1:3 – 3:21)		
1) The divine plan of salvation		1:3 – 2:10
a. Contemplation of the plan		1:3-14
b. Realization of the plan		1:15 – 2:10
2) Union of Jews and Gentiles in one body		2:11-22
3) Revelation of the mystery		3:1-13
4) Prayer and doxology		3:14-21
MORAL PART (4:1 – 6:20)		
1) General principles		4:1-24
2) Particular applications		4:25 – 6:20
a. Individual morality		4:25 – 5:5
b. Social relations		5:6-20
c. Domestic morality		5:21 – 6:9
d. Spiritual warfare		6:10-20
CONCLUSION (6:21-24)		

a genuine letter of Paul. But, since he himself was conscious of writing pseudonymously, he may have been well aware of its true nature.

Recent studies have shown that Eph. has numerous contacts with the Qumran literature which cannot be explained on the basis of common dependence on the OT. There is, for instance, the theme of *truth*. It plays a very important role in the Qumran writings as the characteristic quality of the community and its members. It is applied in the same way in Eph. – a feature that makes this letter unique among the Pauline letters. In view of this and other contacts with Qumran, it is only reasonable to assume direct acquaintance with the writings of the Essenes on the part of the author of Eph. And, because of the strict prohibition of the *Rule of the Community* against the communication of the doctrines of the sect to outsiders (e.g. 1QS 9:16 f.), we are led to believe that the author of Eph., who evidently is familiar with these doctrines, must have been, at one time, a member of the sect. As for the date of Eph., it is later than Col., and may be put about the year 90.

SUMMARY   The address (Eph. 1:1 f.) is much like the address of Col. except that Timothy is not mentioned and no church is designated by name. Instead of the customary thanksgiving, a hymn (Eph. 1:3-14) – which reads like a baptismal hymn – introduces the divine plan of salvation, a plan which is unfolded in six stages: election, adoption, redemption, revelation, call of the Jews, and call of the Gentiles. The introductory verse of the hymn (Eph. 1:3) characterizes the stages as so many "spiritual blessings." God's choice of his elect is an act of his love ("in love" should be attached to verse 4 as in the RSV margin), a choice that obliges them to live holy and blameless lives (Eph. 1:4). Through Christ, the elect become sons of God; and this divine filiation, like the other blessings of God, has its source in the divine goodness and its end in the exaltation of his glory by his creatures. In this plan everything comes from him and returns to him (Eph. 1:5 f.).

Redemption is achieved by the blood of the Beloved Son shed on the Cross (Eph. 1:7 f.). The fourth blessing is the revelation to the Apostles, and by them to all men, of the "mystery" of the universal supremacy of Christ. And in the "fullness of time," the Messianic Age, the whole of creation, the world of men and the world of angels, is drawn under the authority of Christ (Eph. 1:9

f.). In him, Israel, a Chosen People, had been set apart in order to keep alive in a fallen world the expectation of a Messiah and the hope of salvation through him (Eph. 1:11 f.). The sixth stage is the call of the Gentiles to share the salvation formerly reserved for Israel, a salvation assured by the gift of the Holy Spirit long ago promised by the prophets (Eph. 1:13 f.).

Then, Paul turns to the realization of the divine plan (Eph. 1:15-2:10). First (after the introductory verses, 15 f.) he considers the great wisdom and efficacious power of God's plan (Eph. 1:17-19). That power is revealed in his raising of Christ, in his placing him over all the angelic spirits, and in his making him the Head of the Church. The Church is the Body of Christ because it contains all the saved, who are united to him; it is his Fullness because it indirectly embraces the whole new world, the setting of saved humanity, the world which shares in universal regeneration under the authority of Christ, Lord and Head (Eph. 1:20-23).

Formerly, not Gentiles only (Eph. 2:1 f.), but Jews too (Eph. 2:3) – subject to Satan, dead in sin – were objects of the divine anger. Now all of them, through God's love, have been brought back to life and reconciled in Christ. The baptized Christian is united to Christ dead and risen in a manner so real and intimate that he can be said to have shared in Christ's heavenly triumph. This sharing in the resurrection of Christ which Rm. 6:3-11 sees as something lying in the future is here presented as a reality already come to pass: it is realized eschatology, a characteristic trait of Eph. (2:1-6). In words that summarize the great thesis of Rm., Paul insists on the absolute gratuitousness of salvation (Eph. 2:7-10).

We pass to the theme of the reconciliation of Jews and Gentiles among themselves and with God (Eph. 2:11-22). The immeasurable grace of God has indeed reached to the Gentiles who, in Christ, are made inheritors of God's promises to his people, thus fulfilling Is. 57:19. Christ has broken down the "dividing wall of hostility" (an allusion to the barrier that marked off the court of the Gentiles from the Temple proper) by bringing to an end, on the Cross, the reign of the Mosaic Law that kept the Jews apart, and by substituting for it the universal regime of grace. Now, both peoples are joined together in the one Body of Christ that is the Church. This is the great Mystery known to Paul and of which he is the minister; this is why he is Apostle to the Gentiles.

Paul begins a prayer in Eph. 3:1, but then abruptly breaks into a long parenthesis (Eph. 3:2-13) which treats of his vocation and mission (Eph. 3:2-4, 7 f.), the revelation of the Mystery (Eph. 3:5, 9 f.), and the content of the Mystery (Eph. 3:6, 11 f.). We learn that the Mystery was made known to the Apostle by revelation and that he was especially commissioned by God to preach to the Gentiles. At best vaguely known to the prophets of the Old Testament, the Mystery is revealed to Christian apostles and prophets; hidden even from the heavenly spirits, it is now made known through the Church. The Mystery is this: the Gentiles are fellow heirs with Judaeo-Christians, members of the same Body. Then, the interrupted prayer is resumed and closes with a doxology (Eph. 3:14-21), a prayer for a better understanding in the Church of the Mystery; in effect, for a deeper knowledge of the love of Christ, the source of the Mystery.

The moral part of the Epistle (Eph. 4:1-6:20) is still bathed in the light of the sublime doctrine that went before. Paul first of all makes an appeal for unity (Eph. 4:1-16). Discord among Christians (Eph. 4:1-3) is opposed to the unity that should flow from the one Spirit, the one Body, the one Lord, the one faith and baptism, the one Father of all (Eph. 4:4-6). The necessary divisions of ministry (Eph. 4:7-11) are aimed at the building up of one Body into the fullness of Christ (Eph. 4:12 f.). Heretical doctrine (Eph. 4:14) is to be combated by means of close union with Christ, the Head who draws the whole Body together (Eph. 4:15 f.). Christian converts are called upon to put aside their former way of life and to live the new life in Christ (Eph. 4:17-24). Then follows a series of admonitions in the field of individual morality, all centered in charity (Eph. 4:25-5:5). Next come rules for social relations: contacts with non-Christians (Eph. 5:6-17) and the liturgical life (Eph. 5:18-20).

Rules for family living (5:21-6:9) comprise the magnificent passage on Christian marriage, the highpoint of NT teaching on marriage (5:22-35). Here the author presents the Christ-Church relationship as the archetype of christian marriage and it is precisely in view of the archetype (he explains) that the wife must be subject to her husband. The example of the Church's subjection to Christ, he who is *Savior* of the Church, should clearly set the recommendation in proper perspective. And husbands are exhorted to love their wives, not in any fashion, but after the manner of

Christ. Against this background the 'subjection' of the wife is offset, and even quite outweighed, by the love of her husband.

The author next passes to a new thought, one suggested by Gn. 2:24 — husbands should love their wives as they love their own bodies. Everyone loves his own flesh — so also Christ loves the Church, his Body. This is the meaning of Gn. 2:24 when one sees there a type of Christ and the Church. For the writer has in mind not the marriage relationship in general but the human prototype of marriage, that of Adam and Eve (for this is the *theological* view of the Genesis narrative); and Adam, who cleaves to his wife, is in his view a type of Christ who loves his Church. This is precisely the great mystery of which he speaks — great not because of its mysteriousness but because of its significance and sublimity. Adam and Eve, precisely in this relationship of husband and wife — for this is the sense of Gn. 2:24 — are types of Christ and his Church. And in the measure in which each earthly marriage of man and woman reflects the mystery of the marriage of Christ and his Church, it shares in that mystery.

Finally, we have a description of the spiritual arms worn and used in the fight against the devil and evil spirits, especially the mighty weapon of prayer (6:10-20). The epistle ends abruptly with the recommendation of Tychicus and a closing salutation (6:21-24).

DOCTRINE   The leading themes of Eph. are the cosmic dimension of Christ's salvation, the Church, and the divine Mystery. But these are also the themes of Col. and, in view of the close relationship of the writings, it is well to outline their treatment in the earlier Epistle. This will also help to highlight the notable theological advance made in Eph.

1. *The Cosmic Supremacy of Christ.* In Col., the person and work of Christ are considered from a point of view that is not only soteriological but cosmic as well. Now Christian salvation takes on the dimensions of the universe. Christ is not only head of the Church, whose members are his members and build up his Body; he is the head of all creation. To designate this situation Paul uses the term *pleroma*; and he finds the basis of Christ's universal supremacy in his divine pre-existence as Image of the Father and sees him as the source and end of creation.

The cosmic supremacy of Christ, head of the whole universe and even of the angels, has been so firmly established in Col. that

Eph. does not have to dwell on it at length. At most, the theme is recalled in some striking formulas. Thus, the term of the divine plan is to "recapitulate" the universe under one sole Head, Christ (Eph. 1:10). He is superior to all the heavenly powers (Eph. 1:21) because he has mounted above the heavens (Eph. 4:10). What is truly specific in Eph. is that the idea of Christ's cosmic supremacy has influenced the notion of the Church.

2. *The Church.* Col., with its cosmic view of the heavenly Christ, clearly distinguishes the Church from him who is its Head. Its character of "Body of Christ," which was already met with in the earlier Epistles, takes on a new relief and a stronger realism. The Church is the Body of Christ because it is made up of all Christians whose bodies are joined, by baptism, to the physical body of the Risen Christ and receive from him the new life of the Spirit.

Paul's horizon was broadened by his consideration of the Colossian error and by the need to refute it. Now that he has established the universal supremacy of Christ, he realizes that the Church, the Body of Christ, must be seen in a wider perspective. But what has struck him most forcefully is the idea of the collective salvation of humanity in Christ. And so his thought is concentrated on the Church which has grouped in one Jews and Gentiles; the Church which is a Body with Christ as its Head, or again which is the Spouse of Christ, and which ultimately so fills the renewed cosmos that it is to be identified with the "Pleroma" of Christ.

In Rm. 9-11, Paul had faced the problem of the reunion of Jews and Gentiles and had to be content with regarding it as a "secret" of the divine plan: the rejection of the Gospel by the Jews was necessary for the access of Gentiles to salvation, but ultimately Israel would return to the fold. Eph. takes up the problem anew. Already the two last strophes of the initial hymn (Eph. 1:11-14) suggest that Jews and Gentiles correspond to two stages of the divine plan, that of hope and that of faith in the Gospel. Then, in Eph. 2:11-22, the matter is explicitly and confidently treated. Separated formerly during the time of the old economy in which Israel was the bearer of the Promise (Eph. 2:11-13), the two people have been drawn together and have been reconciled with God by the blood of Christ which has suppressed the old economy (Eph. 2:14-18); henceforth, they are united as the component parts of a spiritual Temple where God dwells among men (Eph.

2:19-22). Gentiles and Jews have won the same salvation and form the same Body (Eph. 3:6).

The gathering together of the saved is made "in one Man" (Eph. 2:15), who is Christ, prototype of the new humanity; "in one Body" (Eph. 2:16), which is his body, crucified and dead to sin; and "in one Spirit" (Eph. 2:18), which is the Spirit of the Risen Christ. Here we have the theme of the Body of Christ at its most profound. And here, less than ever, can it be a metaphorical application of the profane image of the "social body." It is something very different: the expansion of the individual body of Christ, dead and risen, by the joining to it, through baptism, of the bodies of Christians; and hence it reaches out to the dimensions of the great Body of the Church. And, at the same time, a distinction is maintained between the Body which is built up on earth and the Head which directs its growth from heaven (Eph. 4:15 f.; cf. Col. 2:19). The whole structure of the Church is founded in unity and leads to unity (Eph. 4:1-6). Finally, Paul has brought out even more clearly the distinction of Head and Body (seen in the subjection of one to the other) and their union (achieved through love) when he presents the Church as the Spouse of Christ (Eph. 5:23-32).

The Church is not only the Body of Christ, it is his "pleroma" (Eph. 1:23). Beyond the Christians who are the "Body" properly so called, the Church embraces, in some manner, all the forces of the new creation that is filled by the power of the Risen Lord. For the Risen Christ is the initial cell of the new world; in him, God has created humanity anew (Eph. 4:24) and "united" the universe (Eph. 1:10). He thus contains in himself all the fullness of God and of the new cosmos (cf. Col. 2:9); and those who are united to Christ are, by that fact, plunged into this fullness (Eph. 3:19; 4:13; cf. Col. 2:10). The cosmic breadth of view of Col. is indeed maintained in Eph., but always in relation to the concept of the Church.

3. *The Mystery*. His contemplation of cosmic salvation, which embraces Jews and Gentiles alike and touches the whole of creation, filled Paul's soul with admiration. He sees here a "Mystery," that is, a secret long hidden in God but now revealed; and he insists on the need for supernatural wisdom in order to attain true knowledge of the divine plan (Col. 1:26-28; 2:2 f.). In Eph., too, the divine plan of salvation is presented as the "Mystery." Fundamentally, it is still the incorporation of the Gentiles into the

salvation of Israel: thus, in Eph. 3:3-6, 8 f. (a developed parallel of Col. 1:25-27), and in Eph. 6:19 (a parallel of Col. 4:3). Yet, we may say that the splendor of the Mystery of Christ and of the spiritual wisdom required for its understanding, are more firmly and explicitly affirmed in Eph. Here, Paul's wonder at the divine plan finds more moving expression (Eph. 1:3-14). Here, too, he speaks with pride of his own grasp of the Mystery and of his vocation in its service (Eph. 3:1-12). And he calls more urgently on his faithful to contemplate it and to pray to God for the light of his Spirit that they may understand it (Eph. 1:17 f.; 3:16-19).

5. THE PASTORAL EPISTLES

The two letters to Timothy and the letter to Titus from a distinctive group among the Pauline writings; since the eighteenth century they have been known as the Pastoral Epistles. Because all three of them are concerned with the qualities and responsibilities of those who administer to the Christian people, the designation is a happy one. But the three Epistles are closely related not only in their common interest and content but also in vocabulary and style. Hence, we may treat them as a group, rather than take them individually.

1) Common Characteristics of the Epistles

The Pastorals are addressed to two of Paul's most faithful disciples, Timothy (Acts 16:1-3; 19:22; 1 Thes. 3:2-6; 1 Cor. 4:17; 16:10 and the address of 1, 2 Thes., 2 Cor., Phil., Col., Phm.), and Titus (Gal. 2:1-5; 2 Cor. 2:13; 7:6-13; 8:6-17), and are almost exclusively concerned with the organization and direction of the churches which the Apostle committed to their care. The interest centers in consolidation, and no fresh doctrine is expounded as in the earlier Epistles. In style and vocabulary, too, there is a notable difference. Gone is the rich variety, the not unusual lack of coherence, of the other letters; instead, these letters flow smoothly, even sedately.

The Apostle charges his disciples to administer the churches founded by him, and for that purpose to set up overseers, elders, and deacons. Significantly, the first responsibility of the leaders is to teach: they must teach doctrine that is sound and, largely, of practical moral interest – prayer, good works, relations of family life. This doctrine, firmly set on the basis of the Old Testament, of Christ, and of the Apostles, is something that has been received and which must be safeguarded. The lines of transmission are clearly marked: from Christ to Paul who had confided the doctrine to his disciples; in their turn, they must pass it on to those whom they establish as teachers and guides of the churches.

True doctrine is recognized by its apostolic origin and by the sound piety which it engenders. There is no place here for sterile discussions concerning the Law, and for the venturesome speculation of doctors without mandate. It is noteworthy, too, that the charisms have slipped into the background. Nor is the concern with the Parousia so marked as in many of the earlier Epistles, and eschatological tension is almost absent. Indeed, Christianity is regarded as firmly installed in this present age, and as demanding from the world the conditions necessary for the expression and expansion of its own life. The Church has come of age.

The most pressing danger is from within. There are Christians who do not respect the solid traditional doctrine and who propagate false views; these Epistles have some harsh things to say about them. They are self-appointed — and self-opinionated — teachers, giving themselves the airs of deeply religious men, who win introduction into private homes and, apparently without much difficulty, win over to their views certain of the less enlightened faithful; women were particularly susceptible (2 Tm. 3:6 f.). These false teachers are boastful, controversialists tirelessly discussing vain problems (1 Tm. 1:4), mentally undisciplined, superficial, busy only with futile things (1 Tm. 6:4; Ti. 3:9; 2 Tm. 2:23), with fables and genealogies (1 Tm. 1:4; 4:7; Ti. 1:14; 3:9). Besides, they are self-interested, venal (Ti. 1:11), seeing in religion a "good thing" (1 Tm. 6:5). Hypercritical, disobedient, it can be said that they have made shipwreck of the faith (1 Tm. 1:19).

2) Authorship

Despite the strong traditional witness to the Pauline origin of the Pastorals, ever since the beginning of the 19th century their authenticity has been more and more assailed on critical grounds, and today very many scholars tend to accept their inauthenticity as an established fact. These scholars take their stand on the nature of the errors combated and on the hierarchical organization of the churches, both of which (they say) point to the second century, and also on the language and style which (they claim) are quite unlike those of Paul.

THE ERRORS   It is not easy (or even possible) to make an assured assertion on the basis of the incomplete and passing references to false teaching which the Pastorals provide. The danger threatens, not from a movement opposed to the Church, but from within the christian communities. We may, however, look to Judaism for the *source* of these errors. The preaching of the adversaries is the occasion of disputes on the subject of the Mosaic Law (Ti. 3:9, 1 Tm. 1:7); these false teachers distinguish between clean and unclean foods (1 Tm. 4:3; Ti. 1:15); their teaching is nothing more than 'Jewish fables' (Ti. 1:14). Titus is put on his guard especially against 'the circumcision party' which he must silence (Ti. 1:10 f.). It appears then, that the false teachers are Jews (or, rather judaizers, since they seem to be within the community). But 2 Tm. 3:8 seems to make a discreet allusion to magic practices, and the condemnation of marriage (1 Tm. 4:3) is certainly not in the line of orthodox Judaism; we may look to a syncretistic Judaism — as in the case of the Colossian error. This heterodox Judaism may be on its way to the Gnosticism of the second century, but the Pastorals give no hint of the characteristic traits of Gnosticism: dualism, the emanation of eons, opposition between the God of the OT and the God of the NT. However, the situation could fit the first decade of the second century.

CHURCH ORGANIZATION   The hierarchical organization of the churches, as it is presented in the Pastorals, demands a date considerably later than Paul's time. We find that the primitive Palestinian community, at its earliest stage, had, as leadership, the Twelve and the Seven (Acts 1:21-26; 6:1-6). Communities outside Palestine were under the direction of the apostle who had founded them; when absent, the same apostle would guide them by letter or by fully-accredited representatives. A local organization also began to take shape. It was modeled on the Jewish synagogue and especially on the synagogue's system of elders. Hence, already in Acts 11:30 we find 'elders' in the Jerusalem church itself, and in chap. 15 'apostles and elders' are named together. There is no evidence that, in the communities, one elder held pre-eminence over the others. (James' position was due to his unique standing as 'brother of the Lord'). At this stage the 'hierarchy' comprised the Apostles and their delegates, the elders and the deacons as assistants to the apostles. Besides in the Gentile Christian missionary city of Antioch, we find the community presided over by "prophets and teachers."

True, the term *episkopos* (whence our 'bishop') occurs, but as the equivalent of *presbyteros* ('elder'). Thus, for instance, Paul summoned to Miletus the 'elders' of the church of Ephesus (Acts 20:17) and assured them that the Holy Spirit had constituted them 'guardians' (*episkopoi*) to feed the church of the Lord' (20:28). Similarly, in saluting the leaders of the church of Philippi, Paul names 'the overseers (*episkopoi*) and deacons' (Phil. 1:1); unless the elders are included among the 'overseers,' their omission is inexplicable. Thus, in the middle of the first century, *presbyteros* and *episkopos* are, for all intents and purposes, synonymous.

The Pastorals reflect the same usage. In 1 Tm. 3:2, the author begins to outline the qualities and duties of an *episkopos* and then passes to those of the deacon – the qualities are much the same – with no mention of elders. And in Ti. 1:7 (the only other passage where *episkopos* occurs), the argument runs like this: v. 5: Titus will establish 'elders' in the towns of Crete; v. 6: each of them must be blameless; v. 7: 'for an *episkopos*,' etc. These texts show that *episkopos* and *presbyteros* do not yet stand for two clearly-distinguished degrees of the hierarchy. We are far from the 'mon-archical episcopate' of Ignatius of Antioch – but this does not mean that the Pastorals have therefore to be much earlier in time, for that development in Syria did not at once affect other churches. What is clear in the Pastorals is the dominant place of the 'hierarchy' and its role as a bulwark against error. This em-phasis is not found in the genuine Pauline letters and reflects a later stage of church organization.

STYLE AND VOCABULARY   The most serious objection to the Pauline author-ship of the Pastorals comes under this heading. The imposing total of 306 words (36%) which are not found in the other Pauline letters must raise a big question mark. Furthermore, while the Pauline letters are cast in the familiar, spoken Koine Greek, the Pastorals are written in the more stilted literary Koine. We are faced with thought patterns and notions that are properly hellenistic and that are not represented in the earlier NT writings. The result seems to be Pauline thought in hellenistic dress – and thought that is not typical of Paul.

These, and other, arguments are cumulative. If we have been prepared to accept that Col. and Eph. are not genuine Pauline letters, we cannot hesitate in regarding the Pastorals as pseudony-mous writings. Their author would not appear to have been an immediate disciple of the Apostle; he was a man of the second or, it may be, third christian generation. What he has to say about Timothy and Titus, shows them in a light very different from their standing as the stalwart and experienced associates of Paul, and the implied later activity of Paul is not easy to fit into the life-time of the Apostle. He has used the names of the well known disciples to deal with the problems of the community, or communities, of his

3) 1 Timothy

PLAN

ADDRESS (1:1 f.)	
THE GOOD WARFARE (1:3-20)	
1) False teaching	1:3-7
2) The role of the law	1:8-11
3) The vocation of Paul	1:12-17
4) The responsibility of Timothy	1:18-20
GUIDANCE OF THE CHURCH (2:1 – 3:16)	
1) Public worship	2:1-15
2) The ministers	3:1-13
3) The mystery of Christ	3:14-16
THE FALSE TEACHERS (4:1-10)	
TIMOTHY AND THE FAITHFUL (4:11 – 6:2a)	
1) In general	4:11-16
2) Men and Women	5:1 f.
3) Widows	5:3-16
4) Elders	5:17-20
5) (Advice to Timothy)	5:21-25
6) Slaves	6:1-2a
CONCLUSION (6:2b-19)	
1) False teaching and money	6:2b-10
2) Challenge to Timothy	6:11-16
3) True riches	6:17-19
4) Final charge	6:20 f.

concern. Paul is, for him, the ideal apostle. And the pastoral direct-
ives, needful for his situation, found greater weight when they
were presented as issuing from Paul. That situation may well point
to the early second century. The Pastorals are late among the NT
writings; we may date them about the year 100. All three letters
were written by the same author but their chronological order is
not clear. Such indications as there are would suggest the order: 1
Tm., Ti., 2 Tm.

SUMMARY   The greeting (1 Tm. 1:1 f.) presents Paul as an
"apostle of Jesus Christ by command of God our Savior"; the title
of "Savior" applied to God is frequent in the Old Testament and
occurs six times in the Pastorals (1 Tm. 1:1; 2:3; 4:10; Ti. 1:3,
2:10; 3:4), but not elsewhere in the Pauline Epistles He addresses
Timothy, his "true child in the faith."

Timothy is urged to remain in Ephesus in order to combat false
teaching. The "myths" and "endless genealogies" that formed part
of the false doctrine are Jewish legends, based on the Old Testament
narratives, and elaborate pedigrees, as we find them in the apoc-
ryphal literature; the self-styled doctors founded in their own sterile discussions. Timothy must inculcate charity, purity of conscience, and sincere faith (1 Tm. 1:3-7). The Jewish Law (abused
by the false teachers) is good, although limited in its scope. Under
its penal aspect, it is concerned with those who break the law,
those who act contrary to the sound doctrine that is in conformity
with the "glorious gospel" (1 Tm. 1:8-11). The idea of "soundness" of doctrine is found only in the Pastorals (1 Tm. 1:11; 6:3;
Ti. 1:9,13; 2:1, 8; 2 Tm. 1:13; 4:3).

Reference to the Gospel entrusted to him (1 Tm. 1:11) moves
Paul to thanksgiving for the great mercy and magnanimity Christ
had shown in calling a persecutor of the Church to his service. The
Apostle is a living proof of the truth of the claim that Christ had
come into the world to save sinners; he closes with a solemn
doxology (1 Tm. 1:12-17). Timothy is again commissioned to wage
war against the false teachers, this in accordance with the "prophetic utterances," that is, the testimony of Christian prophets which
accompanied Timothy's ordination. Already some have made shipwreck of their faith; Paul has excommunicated two of them (cf. 1
Cor. 5:5); one of the two, Hymenaeus, is named again in 2 Tm.
2:17.

Paul then puts forward recommendations for the ordering of
the public worship of the community. Prayer is to be offered for

kings and for all who are in high administrative positions, in order
that Christians may be able to lead peaceful and godly lives and
that all men may arrive at a knowledge of the truth; for God
desires all men to be saved (1 Tm. 1:1-4). The object of Christian
faith is this; one God, and one Mediator, Christ, who has died for
all. Paul, preacher and Apostle of the Gentiles, is the herald of the
testimony to the saving will of God made by Christ (1 Tm. 2:5-7).
In the communities, men alone should recite public prayers;
women will remain silent in church. It is their place to live mod-
estly, to perform good deeds, and to be submissive to their husbands (cf. 1 Cor. 14:34 f.; 1 Pt. 3:3 f.). Woman's vocation, in
conformity with Gn. 3:16, is to be a mother; this declaration is
directed against a false doctrine (1 Tm. 4:3) that depreciated marriage (1 Tm. 2:8-15).

The office of *episkopos* ("bishop") is a noble task, demanding
sterling qualities (cf. Ti. 1:7-9). Much the same qualities are
demanded of deacons (1 Tm. 3:1-13). Paul hopes to come to
Ephesus soon, but the instructions contained in this letter will
serve in case he is delayed. Meanwhile, Timothy is in charge of the
"household of God" — a "pillar and bulwark of the truth."[7] The
theme of "truth" keeps recurring in the Pastorals: 1 Tm. 2:4;
3:15; Ti. 1:1, 14; 2 Tm. 2:15, 18, 25; 3:7 f.; 4:4. The "mystery
of our religion" (cf. 1 Tm. 3:9) is great indeed: it is nothing other
than Christ. This idea is developed in a quotation from an early
Christian hymn which sings of the triumph of Christ's glorious
resurrection and ascension (1 Tm. 3:14-16).

The latter days will be marked by apostasy from the faith (cf.
2 Thes. 2:3-11), brought about by deceitful spirits who turn men
against the good things given to them by God. Condemnation of
marriage (if not necessarily abstinence from certain foods) appears
to point to Gnostic dualism; yet, the errors may be those of an
esoteric Jewish sect (cf. Col. 2:16-21). The true doctrine is that
everything created by God is good, and its use is consecrated by
prayer (1 Tm. 4:15). Timothy, faithful disciple, will instruct the
brethren along these lines; he will have nothing to do with godless
and foolish fables (1 Tm. 4:6-10). Although young in years, he
must set a good example to all. He will attend to the public
reading of the word of God and comment on the sacred text in
the public assemblies. He was consecrated for the ministry by the
imposition of hands: let him exercise the divine charism he has

received. If he is faithful to his ministry of the word, he will save himself and those who hear him (1 Tm. 4:11-16).

Timothy must be circumspect in his dealing with the faithful – there is no place for self-assertion (1 Tm. 5:1 f.). Then, his attitude toward different classes within the community is specified (1 Tm. 5:3-6:2a). Three categories of widows (1 Tm. 5:3-16) are distinguished: those who are cared for by their own families (v. 4); those who are "real widows," that is, really dependent (vv. 2-8, 16); those who have official standing and render special service in the churches (vv. 9-15). The elders are to be treated with honor, especially those who have acquitted themselves well as preachers and teachers. But Timothy is not to be hasty in appointing men to office in the Church (1 Tm. 5:17-22). Among sundry remarks (1 Tm. 5:23-25), he is advised to moderate his own asceticism. Finally, there are instructions for slaves and masters. Christian slaves owe respect to their pagan masters, so that Christian teaching will not be brought into dishonor. And they must not take advantage of Christian masters, but should respect them even more (1 Tm. 6:1-2a).

Timothy is urged to be mindful of the instructions he has been given and receives another warning against false teachers (1 Tm.

4) Titus

PLAN

ADDRESS (1:1-4)	
DUTIES OF TITUS (1:5 – 2:1)	
1) Appointment of elders	1:5-9
2) Opposition to false teachers	1:10 – 2:1
EXHORTATIONS (2:2 – 3:11)	
1) Christian conduct in the Church	2:2-10
The ground of this conduct	2:11-15
2) Christian conduct in the world	3:1 f.
The ground of this conduct	3:3-7
3) Final advice to Titus	3:8-11
CONCLUSION (3:12-15)	

6:3-5). Their erroneous view that godliness is a means of gain leads to a statement on the contrast between false and true riches (1 Tm. 6:6-10). A moving exhortation to Timothy to fight the good fight of the faith (1 Tm. 6:11-14) closes with a solemn doxology (1 Tm. 6:15 f.), reminiscent of 1 Tm. 3:16. In 1 Tm. 6:17-19 – a passage which should come, logically, after 1 Tm. 6:6-10 – there is a return to the theme of riches and the dangers of wealth. The final charge to the disciple reminds him yet again of his obligation to defend the true faith against the attack of false teachers (1 Tm. 16:20 f.).

SUMMARY   The address (Ti. 1:1-4) is long and unusually solemn in tone. The mission of Paul, Apostle of Jesus Christ, is, by means of his preaching, to lead the elect, by faith, to the eternal life promised by God in the Old Testament.

Titus is reminded that he was left in Crete to organize the Church, specifically by appointing elders in the local churches. The qualities and duties of an elder – an overseer ("bishop"), God's steward – are listed; his principal concern is the teaching and defense of sound doctrine (Ti. 1:5-9). False teachers – patently Jews or Judaizers – have been disturbing the communities; they must be refuted (Ti. 1:10-16). The saying (v. 12) of the sixth-century Cretan poet Epimenides fits these people exactly; Cretans had a reputation for lying (as Corinthians had for sexual immorality).

Then comes a series of exhortations to Titus. In the first place it should always be his concern to teach sound doctrine. He must instruct Christians in their duties. Five groups are distinguished, with specific counsels for each; older men, older women, young women, young men, slaves (Ti. 2:1-10). The ground of Christian conduct is the revelation of God's saving grace in Christ. Although they live in this world, the eyes of Christians are (or ought to be) turned to the Parousia of "our great God and Savior Jesus Christ" – a straightforward affirmation of the divinity of Christ – who by his death has won for himself the new people of God (Ti. 2:11-15).

Christians are reminded of their duty of submission to lawful civil authority and are exhorted to show gentleness and courtesy to all men (Ti. 3:1 f.). The ground of such conduct is presented in a statement that develops the teaching of Eph. 2:3-10 and summarizes the doctrine of Rm.: the goodness and loving kindness of

God our Savior who has saved us not by works but, through Jesus Christ, by the gift of baptism, renewal in the Holy Spirit. And once justified by the grace of Christ, we are heirs to eternal life (Ti. 3:3-7).

In conclusion, Titus is urged to insist on the matters that have been drawn to his attention. He must inculcate the practice of good works and, on the other hand, avoid futile controversies and shun entanglement with the factious (Ti. 3:8-11). When Artemas and Tychicus arrive in Crete, Titus is to join Paul at Nicopolis (in Epirus); also, he is to make arrangements for the journey of Zenas and Apollos (Ti. 3:12-14). The closing greeting (Ti. 3:15) is brief and conventional.

2) Timothy

PLAN

ADDRESS (1:1 f.)	
THANKSGIVING (1:3-5)	
THE CALL TO SUPPER (1:6 — 2:13)	
1) Fearless profession of faith	1:6-14
2) Disloyal and loyal friends	1:15-18
3) The will to suffer	2:1-13
FALSE TEACHERS (2:14 — 4:5)	
1) Advice to ministers	2:14-19
2) Personal advice	2:20-26
3) Perils of the Last Days	3:1-17
4) Solemn adjuration	4:1-5
CONCLUSION (4:6-22)	
1) Paul's testament	4:6-8
2) Paul and his friends	4:9-18
3) Personal greetings	4:19-23

SUMMARY   The address (2 Tm. 1:1 f.) is the same as in 2 Cor. and Col. Paul thinks lovingly of his beloved "son" and thanks God for Timothy's faith, a faith like that of his grandmother and mother (2 Tm. 1:3-5).

Timothy is called upon to rekindle the gift of God within, the grace of consecration which he received when he was officially invested as an apostle, a grace of courage and of power. He is urged to accept his share of suffering for the Gospel and to bear these sufferings cheerfully as Paul did (2 Tm. 1:6-8). For, God has called us not because of our deeds but freely, in virtue of his grace, now manifested through the appearance of our Savior Jesus Christ who has destroyed death and brought life and immortality to light (2 Tm.1:9 f.). Paul suffers for the Gospel, but he is not ashamed of his sufferings (so neither should Timothy). He had been appointed preacher and apostle and teacher of the Gospel and he is confident that he will stand firm in his charge to the end; Timothy, too, with the help of the Holy Spirit, will be faithful to the Gospel (2 Tm. 1:10-14). Paul's Asian friends have deserted him. By contrast, the fidelity of Onesiphorus is all the more welcome, and the Apostle expresses his gratitude with warmth (2 Tm. 1:15-18). At his inauguration as an apostle ("before many witnesses" [cf. 1 Tm. 4:14; 6:12]), Timothy had been entrusted by Paul with the sound tradition of the faith; in his turn he is to entrust it to dependable men who will instruct others. But, he must be prepared to shoulder his share of suffering, like the soldier or athlete or farmer who earns his reward only by facing up to the demands of the task in hand (2 Tm. 2:1-7). Faithful service will win fellowship with Jesus Christ. Again Paul points to the example of his own sufferings. The passage closes with a quotation (2 Tm. 2:11-13) from a baptismal hymn: at baptism the Christian dies and rises with Christ, but the sacrament imposes the obligation of endurance and fidelity (2 Tm. 2:8-13).

The central part of the letter (2 Tm. 2:14-4:5) is dominated by a concern for the dangers that false teachers and corrupting doctrine can give rise to in the communities. Timothy must remind his faithful of the demands of their Christian calling and get them to cease from futile discussions; he himself must set the example. Two false teachers, Hymenaeus and Philetus, are mentioned by name; the former had already been excommunicated by Paul (1 Tm. 1:20). Their teaching was that the resurrection is already past. We know that the Greeks had difficulty in accepting the idea of bodily resurrection (Acts 17:32; 1 Cor. 15:12), and these teachers interpreted it in a spiritual fashion, as referring to postbaptismal life in the Spirit (cf. Rm. 6:1-11; Col. 2:12; 3:1; Eph. 2:5). But the Church — which upholds the reality of the resurrection — stands on solid foundations that bear the inscription of God (2 Tm. 2:14-19). The metaphor of the Church as a building leads, naturally enough, to the further image of the utensils of a house, some for noble, some for ignoble, use; here, the ignoble utensils are false teachers, who must be avoided. Once again, Timothy is warned to abstain from sterile controversy. It is pointed out that, if he must oppose the false teachers, he must do so patiently and gently, for God may yet bring them to their senses (2 Tm. 2:20-26). "The true apostle does not condemn. He knows that the Lord can always straighten up the bruised reed and light the smouldering wick (Is. 42:3; Mt. 12:20)."

If there is to be a final wave of evil before the Parousia (2 Tm. 3:1-5a), it is implied (v. 5b) that the false teachers are already enemies of true religion. They may be able to lead astray silly women, but they will be no more successful in the long run than Pharaoh's magicians (cf. Ex. 7:11 f., 22; 8:7) — the names Jannes and Jambres come from late Jewish tradition (2 Tm. 3:6-9). Timothy, however, has been the faithful disciple of Paul from the beginning and knows what the Apostle has suffered. He had been well instructed in the Old Testament by his mother and grandmother (cf. 2 Tm. 1:5). In 2 Tm. 16 f., we have an attestation of the inspired character of Scripture while the whole passage is an important statement on the importance and profit of the reading of Scripture (2 Tm. 3:10-17). There follows a very solemn adjuration to Timothy: he must continue to preach the Gospel "in season and out of season." The fact that people will refuse to listen to the word, and turn to novelties is, paradoxically, a further reason for more earnest preaching still. In these difficult times and circumstances, the utmost loyalty is demanded of the disciple (2 Tm. 4:1-5).

Paul realizes that this, his second Roman captivity, will end with his execution; hence, he can speak of his blood about to be poured out as a libation to God (cf. Phil. 2:17). And he can declare in all sincerity that he has been faithful to his charge and that he is confident of the victor's wreath (2 Tm. 4:6-8). Demas — a companion of the first captivity (cf. Col. 4:14; Phm. 24) — has now deserted Paul, while Crescens, Titus, and Tychicus are absent on missionary work. Only Luke is with the Apostle, and now he dearly wishes to have Timothy and Mark come to him — these

three are like that choice inner circle of Jesus' disciples, Peter and
James and John. He wants Timothy to bring a cloak, books, and
parchments left at Troas, and the disciple is warned against a certain Alexander. Paul feels all the more lonely and abandoned
because, at a recent appearance before the tribunal, there was not
one voice raised in his defense; but the Lord saved him (2 Tm.
4:9-18). The letter closes with an exchange of personal greetings (2
Tm. 4:19-22).

6. HEBREWS

The Epistle to the Hebrews differs from the other New
Testament Epistles in that it ends like a letter (Heb. 13:18-25),
although it does not begin like one and lacks the customary opening address with the names of the writer and recipients. Although
1 Jn., which also begins without an epistolary formula, quickly
manifests (1 Jn. 1:4) its proper character of letter, Heb. presents
the first formally epistolary expression only in 13:22: "I have
written to you." But, references throughout the work suggest that
it is a letter. The apostrophes: "brethren" (Heb. 3:12; 10:19),
"holy brethren" (Heb. 3:1), "beloved" (Heb. 6:9) would be out of
place if Heb. were a treatise, and therefore impersonal in tone. The
recipients are well known to the writer with regard to their spiritual condition (Heb. 5:11-14; 6:9-12), the dangers to which they
are exposed (Heb. 2:1 ff.; 3:12 f.; 4:1, 11; 10:25 ff.), and the
merit of the good works which they have done (Heb. 6:11; 10:32
ff.). In short, it does seem that Heb. is indeed presented as a letter;
the writer is at a distance from his addressees and he intervenes in
a concrete situation.

All the same, Heb. has a distinct solemnity about it. Its author
describes it as a "discourse of exhortation" (Heb. 13:22) and uses
expressions proper to oratorical style (Heb. 2:5; 5:11; 6:9; 7:9;
9:5; 11:32). Hence, it has been regarded as a homily cast as a
letter, or a writing which is part homily and part letter. However,
the presence of undoubted homiletical elements does not prove
that this was originally a homily, afterwards set down in letter
form. This impression is due to the notable oratorical gifts of the
writer, which show themselves even in the framing of his letter.
Again, it has been suggested that Heb. is an epistle rather than a
letter, but, perhaps, it would be better not to overstress the differences between these two literary categories, as though there
could not be a varied form. And this seems to be just the case of

Heb.: it is a letter because of its setting, which never loses sight of a clearly-determined group of readers; and it is an epistle because of the loftiness of the subject treated and because of its style.

Occasion. Hebrews is written to a christian community. At first sight, because of the wide use made of the Old Testament, this would appear to be a predominantly Jewish-Christian church. In fact, this does not necessarily follow — Rm. and Gal., too, pre-suppose a good knowledge of the Old Testament. The author writes for a community which has grown discouraged and lax — a situation that would support a relatively late date for the epistle. They had been tempted (2:18); their spiritual life had suffered: they had grown sluggish and hard of hearing (5:11; 6:12). Some had lost heart (12:12).

All this explains the tone of the epistle and its repeated exhortations. The readers are first of all called upon to cling to the Word of God as revealed by Christ, lest they should stray from the truth (2:1). They must continue on their way perseveringly, like athletes (12:1). They must not be deceived (13:9), nor overcome by weariness (12:3); they must resist sin (12:4). On the positive side they must look to the joyful certainty of salvation (10:35); they must remain steadfast in hope (10:39). In a word, they must at all times preserve *pistis* ('faith') in its triple sense of docile acceptance of the revealed word, of confidence in Providence, and of persevering fidelity to the divine will (3:7; 4:13, chap. 11)

AUTHORSHIP,   Today it is practically unanimously accepted
ORIGIN AND DATE   that Hebrews is not Pauline: language, style and theology are distinctive and notably different from those of Paul. It is not possible to name the author. The place of origin of the writing is uncertain. The final salutation of 13:24 suggests Italy. But *hoi apo tes Italias* may mean: 'those who have come from Italy' (more simply 'the Italians' — whether still in Italy or not). Hence, some have argued from this text that the letter was written *to* Italy. The epistle is cited by Clement of Rome (c. 95 A.D.); hence it cannot be later than that date. It is most likely a document of the second christian generation and may be reasonably dated in the 80's.

The structure of Heb. has been much discussed in this century; it is, obviously, an important factor in our understanding of the writing. The remarkable study of A. Vanhoye[8] is the most detailed study of the literary structure of Heb. yet to appear.

1. *The Literary Structure.* The technique of catchwords as a linking device has not quite the importance that Vaganay attached to it; instead, the indication of a subject to be treated is more constant and has greater significance. This is done regularly before each of the five parts of the Epistle and points, according to the part in question, to its one, two, or three sections. Thus, for the central part, which has three sections preceded by a preamble, the indication of the subject is made in a single phrase before the preamble; it is then repeated, piece by piece, before the start of the three respective developments. For parts II and IV, each composed of two sections, the indication of these two sections is presented in an order that is the inverse of the two subsequent developments, thus enabling the author to introduce the first section by using as catchwords the very terms of the title. With regard to the second sections of the two parts, he judged it unnecessary, both times, to announce the subject again before going on to treat of it: he could hope that the reader would still remember it.

This structure gives a concentric symmetry that is clearly apparent. Corresponding to the number of sections in each, the parts are symmetrically arranged around a central part: part III. Parts I and V have one section each, while parts II and IV have two each, and the central part has three. This part III, in its turn, is built around a center – its second section – which is preceded by a preliminary exhortation and a first section, and followed by a third section and a final exhortation.

The whole Epistle is a combination of doctrinal exposition and parenesis (admonition, exhortation):

1) The single section of part I (Heb. 1:5-2:18) is doctrinal (apart from Heb. 2:1-4).

2) Part II has one section of parenesis (Heb. 3:1-4:14) and one doctrinal section (Heb. 4:15-5:10).

3) In part III, the two exhortations or pareneses (Heb. 5:11-6:20 and 10:19-39) frame the three sections (Heb. 7; 8-9; 10:1-18), all doctrinal, which together form one great exposition.

4) Part IV has one parenetical section (Heb. 11:1-40) and one doctrinal section (Heb. 12:1-13).

5) Part V has clearly the character of an exhortation (Heb. 12:14-13:19), although there are some doctrinal traits (e.g. Heb. 12:8-24; 13:11 f.).

It may be seen that the symmetry is not perfect; thus, for instance, part V, like part I, should be doctrinal. On the other hand, the actual arrangement gives a better over-all balance: six sections of doctrine and five of parenesis. Besides, it is fitting that this "word of exhortation" should close with practical exhortation.

PLAN

	1:1-4	Introduction	
I	1:5 – 2:18	The name more excellent than the angels	Doctrine
II	A. 3:1 – 4:14	Jesus, faithful	Parenesis
	B. 4:15 – 5:10	Jesus, compassionate High Priest	Doctrine
III	5:11 – 6:20	Preliminary exhortation Jesus, High Priest	Parenesis
	A. 7:1-28	according to the order of Melchizedek	Doctrine
	B. 8:1 – 9:28	arrived at fulfillment	Doctrine
	C. 10:1-18	cause of external salvation	Doctrine
	10:19-39	Final exhortation	Parenesis
IV	A. 11:1-40	Faith of the elders	Doctrine
	B. 12:1-13	Necessary endurance	Parenesis
V	12:14 – 13:19	The peaceful fruit of justice	Parenesis
	13:20 f.	Conclusion	
	(13:22-25	Final Greeting)	

2. *The Thought Pattern* 1) The central point: The structure of Heb. is designed to set the central elements in relief. Hence, part III (which is central [Heb. 5:11-10:39]) must be regarded as the most important of the five parts of the Epistle. In this third part, the section B (Heb. 8:1-9:28) is central; in this section, the subdivision Heb. 9:1-10 + 9:11-14 is central; and, finally, the first

word of Heb. 9:11 is the very center of the whole Epistle. This
word (in the Greek text) is the name *Christ*. Hence, Heb. is seen to
be "Christocentric" in the most literal sense. This external trait
corresponds to a profound reality: the doctrine expounded in the
Epistle is essentially a *Christology*.

2) The three themes: A study of the central section provides
the key to the Epistle.

(8:1 f.) Introduction	
8:1-9:10:	Insufficiency and Replacement of the Old Cult.
c 8:1-6:	the old cult, earthly and figurative
b 8:7-13:	the first covenant, imperfect and provisional
a 9:1-10:	the old, powerless cultic institutions
9:11-28:	The Sacrifice of Christ, Efficacious and Definitive
A 9:11-14:	the new efficacious institutions
B 9:15-23:	the new covenant
C 9:24-28:	access to heaven
(9:27 f.) Conclusion — transition	

We may recognize in the three couples of subdivisions *a* + A; *b*
+ B; *c* + C) three different themes. The theme of the central
subdivision (*a* + A [Heb. 9:1-14]), and therefore the most important of the three, is that of *sacrifice*: the Jewish rites, culminating
in the liturgy of the Day of Expiation (Heb. 9:1-10), give way to
the sacrifice of Christ (Heb. 9:11-14). From the central place given
to this theme, it follows that the Christology of the Epistle is not
meant to be a timeless speculation; rather, it is the revelation of an
event. It is by his sacrifice that Christ has been manifested (Heb.
9:26); and not only manifested, but "made perfect," as the title of
the section (Heb. 7:28) has it. The other subdivisions do no more
than develop certain implications of this decisive affirmation. In
the first and last of these (*c* [Heb. 8:1-6] and C [Heb. 9:24-28]),
the author defines the level of the reality which is attained. While
the old liturgy was confined to an earthly world which was only
figurative (*c*), the sacrifice of Christ reached heaven itself. Thus, it

is unique and definitive; it marks the end of time (Heb. 9:26) and will be followed only by the Parousia (Heb. 9:24-28). We recognize the *eschatological* perspective; it is the second theme.

The intermediary subdivision (*b* [Heb. 8:7-13] and B [Heb. 9:15-23]) expound a third theme, which is also in direct relationship with that of sacrifice, the theme of the Covenant. The old rites, powerless, belong to a Covenant destined to disappear; the fruit of the sacrifice of Christ, on the contrary, is the establishment of a new and better Covenant. We may call this the *ecclesial* theme.

Thus, in this central section we obtain the following concentric arrangement of themes:

c	Eschatology
b	Ecclesiology
a *A*	Sacrifice
B	Ecclesiology
C	Eschatology

This trilogy of themes is found throughout Heb. and is indeed the key to its composition:
- a) Part I, whose subject is "the name more excellent than that of the angels," speaks especially of the heavenly glory of Christ; it is predominantly *eschatological*.
- b) Part II, which presents Jesus as the "faithful and merciful high priest," is predominantly *ecclesiological* (fidelity and mercy are essential aspects of the Covenant).
- c) Part III is predominantly *sacrificial*.
- d) Part IV like the second part, is predominantly *ecclesiological*.
- e) Part V: its very title "the peaceful fruit of righteousness" (Heb. 12:11), has an undeniable *eschatological* coloring (cf. Heb. 12:14, 22-27; 13:4; 14).

We find, then, that the succession of the dominant themes in the five parts of the Epistle corresponds to the following schema:

I	Eschatology
II	Ecclesiology
III	Sacrifice
IV	Ecclesiology
V	Eschatology

Also note that, while one theme *predominates* in each part, the whole trilogy is present in each part.

3) The present age and the age to come. The subdivisions of the central part bring out another fundamental trait of the author's thought, a characteristic which also marks the whole of Heb.: the distinction of two phases of salvation history. This distinction is applied to each of the themes and enables one to penetrate them more deeply. Whether it is a question of sacrifice, Covenant, or eschatology, it is the comparison of these two phases that can shed full light on the theme.

In the opening lines of Heb., two periods are set in parallelism: *of old*, the period of multiform revelation; and *in these last days*, revelation "in the Son." The central section also notes that the sacrifice of Christ is situated "at the end of the age" (Heb. 9:26), and underlines the fact that it has opened the second phase. But consideration of the unique role played by the sacrifice of Christ, affirms the fundamental weakness of the Old Law; while, at the same time, the Old Law retains its value of prefiguration. Hence, a comparison of the two phases leads to the identification of three kinds of relations: *resemblance, difference,* and *superiority.*

In the central part, it is, in a particular way, the value of the sacrifice that is defined in this fashion:

a) The sacrifice *resembles* the old sacrifices: something is "offered" (Heb. 8:3); a death was necessary (Heb. 9:15 f.); blood was shed (Heb. 9:7, 14, 18, 22); there is question of "entering the sanctuary" (Heb. 9:7, 12).

b) Essential *differences* appear: between "offering gifts and sacrifices" (Heb. 9:9) and "offering himself" (Heb. 9:14); between the blood of victims and the blood of the priest (Heb. 9:12, 19, 25); between an entry "once a year" (Heb. 9:7, 25) and entry "once for all" (Heb. 9:12, 26); between access to the type-sanctuary and to the true sanctuary (Heb. 9:24).

c) There is evident *superiority* : Christ offers "better sacrifices" (Heb. 9:23); he has passed through "the greater and more perfect tent" (Heb. 9:11); the efficacy of his sacrifice is not in the realm of ritual purity, but purifies consciences (Heb. 9:13 f.); he wins an "eternal redemption" (Heb. 9:12).

The same relations exist between the Covenants: *resemblance* (Heb. 8:4, 6, 8-10; 9:1, 19-21); *difference and superiority* (Heb. 8:6-9). And, in the third theme, the old order is modeled on the heavenly: *resemblance* (Heb. 8:5). But, there is a greater *difference* between the tent "made with hands" and the tent "not made with hands" (Heb. 9:11, 24), between the earthly and the heavenly (Heb. 8:4, 9:23 f.), between the provisional and the eternal (Heb. 9:10, 12, 15). The *superiority* of the New Testament over the Old is shown in a decisive manner: only the New Testament gives access to the ultimate realities. The three kinds of relationship may be discerned throughout the Epistle.

4) Christ and Christians. Although Christians are situated in the same phase of salvation history, they are not there on the same title as Christ. This is brought out in Heb. In the matter of eschatology, for instance, part I treats only of Christ: it speaks of "the first-born" (singular) (Heb. 1:6); of the sceptre of *his* kingdom (Heb. 1:8); and *his* kingship (Heb. 1:6; 2:5). In the corresponding part V, there is question of the first-born (plural) (Heb. 12:23), the kingdom which *Christians* receive (Heb. 12:28); the city to come which will receive *them* (Heb. 13:14).

On the sacrificial theme, part I describes the movement which the Son has accomplished to place himself on the same rank as his brethren (Heb. 2:10-18); part V indicates the path which we take to find ourselves beside him (Heb. 13:11-13). The parallelism of parts II and IV takes the same line: part II has as subject the fidelity of Christ and his priestly compassion; part IV gives to Christians the example of faith and appeals to their endurance.

In a general way, we may say that the entire first half of Heb. is more concerned with Christ and the second half more with Christians. Thus, the relative positions of Christ and of Christians are not confused, even though they are comprised on the same plane of salvation history.

5) Exposition and parenesis. The author has used two literary forms, doctrinal exposition and parenesis, which alternate. It is more than a simple stylistic procedure, however, and has, in fact, a profound significance. It shows that Christian salvation is not a matter of knowledge alone, but demands a conversion (cf. Heb. 12:1-3). This is the reason the Christian apostle cannot limit himself to expounding the mystery of Christ; he must at the same time incite his hearers to receive this mystery into their lives by an ever-deeper commitment.

Although exposition and parenesis has each its proper consistency, their multiple and essential links will not permit us to present each as a separate organism; but we may consider them as two "systems" (in the sense in which we speak of the nervous system and the blood system) forming part of one same organism. The ensemble of the different exposés forms the "doctrinal system" of Heb., and the ensemble of exhortations forms its "parenetic system." If the summit of the one (Heb. 8:1-9:28) is like the head of the whole work, the vital core of the other (Heb. 10:19-39) is its heart.

---

[1] J. Cambier, "Paul", DBS, VII, col. 341.

[2] L. Cerfaux, *The Church in the Theology of St. Paul, op. cit.*, p. 261.

[3] C. H. Dodd, *The Epistle of Paul to the Romans*, London, 1959[2], p. 80.

[4] *Ibid.*, p. 124.

[5] For pseudonymity in the New Testament letters see A. Wikenhauser, J. Schmid, *Einleitung in das Neue Testament*, Freiburg; Herder, 1973[6], 462-613.

[6] Benoit has reacted against the commonly-accepted view, with justification I believe. I give an outline of his position. See Benoit, *op. cit.*, (BJ), pp. 50 f.; "Paul: Colossiens (Epître aux)," DBS, VII, cols. 159-63.

[7] Certain Fathers had referred the image "bulwark of the truth," that is, of the Christian revelation, not to the Church but to Timothy, an interpretation that is in harmony with the role of Timothy in the Pastorals. This interpretation seems to be supported by evidence from Qumran. See Murphy-O'Connor, *art. cit., Revue Biblique*, 67-76.

[8] See A. Vanhoye, *La Structure Littéraire de l'Épître aux Hébreux* (Paris/Bruges: Desclée de Brouwer, 1963).

| *The Catholic Epistles*

JAMES

1 PETER

JUDE

2 PETER

In addition to the collection of Pauline letters, the New Testament contains another group of seven epistles: James; 1, 2 Peter; 1, 2, 3 John; Jude. But these writings differ so widely among themselves that the mere fact of not being Pauline seems to be the only reason for grouping them together. The existence of this group was attested to by Eusebius early in the fourth century.

The seven writings are known as the Catholic Epistles. Although there is some doubt about the meaning of *katholikos* in this context (it was first used by the anti-Montanist writer Apollonius [c. 197 A.D.] with reference to 1 Jn.), it seems likely that it is meant to imply the "general" as opposed to the "particular" nature of these writings: the Catholic Epistles were addressed to Christians in general, in contrast to the Pauline Epistles which – for the most part – were addressed to individual churches. The adjective is appropriate in the case of Jas., Jude, 2 Pt., and 1 Jn., while 2, 3 Jn., although each is addressed to a particular church, were, naturally enough, grouped with the first Epistle and perhaps, in view of their brevity, may have been regarded as appendices. Although 1 Pt. is addressed to the churches of a definite region, it is at least general in comparison with the Pauline writings.

In view of their close relationship with the Fourth Gospel, we are justified in considering 1, 2, 3 Jn. in the following chapter, with the other Johannine writings.

1. JAMES

It is widely acknowledged that the James named in the address as author of this writing is James 'the brother of the Lord,' leader of the Jewish Christian community of Jerusalem. Internal evidence would seem to support this view. The author of Jas. writes with authority (3:1). Knowledge of the synoptic tradition is not surprising in one who was a close relative of Jesus and became his disciple. A profound influence of the Old Testament is inevitable in the James whom we know from Acts. And yet there is the Greek style of the writing. It is not easy to accept that a man of James' background, with his necessarily superficial contacts with Hellenism, could write such good Greek; in this respect the author of Jas. is not surpassed by any other New Testament writer. Once again, we appear to be faced with pseudonymity.

If Jas. is authentic, we may suppose that James composed his letter towards the end of his life, between 57 and 62 A.D. On the other hand, there is the remarkable affinity of Jas. with the first epistle of Clement (c. 96-98). Rather than mutal dependence in either direction, this fact may point to the existence of a common source. By the same token, it would suggest that Jas., too, dates from the last decade of the first century.

OCCASION   Jas. is addressed to a milieu in which social differences are marked. There are the rich, who expect, and receive, deferential treatment even in the liturgical assemblies (Jas. 2:1-3), men who are prodigal of generous words that cost them nothing (Jas. 2:16). Entirely absorbed in their business affairs (Jas. 4:13-17), they do not hesitate to cheat their workers and to squeeze the poor (Jas. 5:1-6). These same poor receive scant attention even from those who are supposed to be their shepherds and ought to be their servants (Jas. 2:2-6). Such conduct cannot but give rise to dissension: jealously (Jas. 3:14; 4:2); anger (Jas. 1:19); murmuring (Jas. 5:9); and cursing (Jas. 4:11). The exasperated poor may be driven to rebel against their lot (Jas. 4:2), or they may, enviously, be seized by the desire for worldly possessions.

All James' sympathy goes to the afflicted and to the weak; he has written mainly for them. Like the Old Testament prophets, he takes issue with social injustice; at the same time, however, he considers poverty to have a religious value which makes of the unfortunate the privileged friends of God – the 'anāwîm. And if he could, and did, turn to the sages and the psalmists to find expression of this outlook, his words have a fresh vigor from the practice and teaching of Jesus.

SUMMARY   James writes to the "twelve tribes in the dispersion," that is, either Jewish Christians "dispersed" throughout the Greco-Roman world, or all Christians, the new people of God, exiles from their true fatherland. In the Christian view, trials should be a source of joy, for they are the testing-ground of faith (in the sense of confidence in God and perseverance in action) and give rise to steadfastness (Jas. 1:2-8).

While the poor man (one of the *'anāwîm*) may exult in his discernment of true spiritual realities, the wealthy Christian must ponder on the precarious nature of riches (Jas. 1:9-11). From trials in general the author passes to a special trial: temptation (Jas. 1:13-15). While God permits temptation, he himself does not tempt; hence, one who succumbs cannot cast the blame on him. It is a man's own desires that set him astray, conceive sin, and lead to death (cf. Rom. 6:21-23). God sends, not temptation, but good and perfect gifts (Jas. 1:16 f.). His greatest gift to men is rebirth through the Gospel; verse 18 (cf. 1 Pt. 1:22 f.) seems to refer to a baptismal liturgy (Jas. 1:16-18). Nevertheless, one must be prepared to listen, to check hasty speech, to put away wickedness, and to attend with docility to the word of the Law written on the heart (Jas. 1:19-21). In Judaism, the Law was not regarded as a burden; in a much truer sense, the Gospel, fulfillment of the Old Testament, is a law of liberty which is gladly obeyed (Jas. 1:22-25). It is all too easy to imagine oneself a "religious" person; failure to control one's tongue (cf. Jas. 3:1-12) gives the lie to such an illusion. Genuine religion manifests itself in the service of those in need and in aloofness from the defilement of the world (Jas. 1:26 f.).

The passage, Jas. 2:1-13, is concerned with class distinction: it deplores favoring the rich and slighting the poor. This is the only passage (apart from the address) in which Jesus is named, and his title is solemn. "Our Lord Jesus Christ, the Lord of glory" (Jas. 2:1). The different treatment meted out to rich and poor is particularly reprehensible in the liturgical assemblies (cf. 1 Cor. 11). Besides, the *'anāwîm* are the truly rich. Christians must be ruled by the "royal law" of fraternal love; partiality and discrimination are sins against Christian love. But since the law is a unit, the breaking of one commandment (a *fortiori*, the "royal" commandment) is a violation of the law as such – an indication of the gravity of sin. Therefore, Christians must be mindful of the law under which they will be judged. One who does not show mercy cannot expect to be shown mercy at his judgment (cf. Mt. 6:14 f.); the merciful will meet with mercy.

When Paul uses the word "faith," he implies a trust in God, a personal commitment; for James, however, "faith" is a set of beliefs, a "creed." The profession of Christianity is of no avail unless one lives up to it; significantly, the works in question are works of charity. Whereas Paul (Rm. 4:2 f.; cf. Gn. 15:6) argues that Abraham was justified by faith and not by works, Jas. (2:21) – referring to the sacrifice of Isaac (Gn. 22:4), the culminating point of the trial of Abraham – argues that the patriarch was justified by his good works. Similarly, it was the action of Rahab (cf. Jas. 2) that won her justification (Jas. 2:14-26).

Control of the tongue, already referred to in passing (Jas. 1:19, 26), is now treated at length (Jas. 3:1-12). The brethren should not be overanxious to be teachers (cf. 1 Cor. 12:8, 28), unless they are prepared to be judged in the light of the greater obligation thereby incurred. Only a mature Christian can really control his tongue, for such control points to mastery of one's whole conduct. True wisdom, like faith, finds expression in works (cf. Sir. 19:20). Jealousy and ambition can lead to betrayal of the truth; this is not the "wisdom" of God, but of the devil, and entails disorders of all kinds. The wisdom from above (cf. Prv. 2:6; 8:22-31; Sir 1:1-4; 24:3 f.; Wis. 7:22-8:21) is pure, peaceable, merciful; a rich crop of righteousness is sown by the peaceful who possess wisdom (Jas. 3:13-18).

By contrast, Jas. turns from peace to warfare (Jas. 4:1-12). Strife is caused by unruly passions and uncontrolled desires; even prayer can be wrongly motivated (Jas. 4:1-3). Friendship with the world is "adultery," unfaithfulness to God, who is a jealous God and who opposes the proud (Jas. 4:4-6). Hence, the Christian must resist the devil, draw near to God submissively with sincere contrition, and be humble (Jas. 4:7-10; cf. 1 Pt. 5:5-9). He must not speak evil against or judge his neighbor (Jas. 4:11 f.).

The passage, Jas. 4:13-5:6, is a warning to the wealthy. First boastful self-confidence is censured (Jas. 4:13-17; cf. 1:10 f.; 2:9). The denunciation, Jas. 5:1-6, unlike the preceding verses, is eschatological in tone and the language is reminiscent of the Old Testament prophets (cf. Am. 5:11; Mi. 2:8 f.; Is. 5:8-10; Jer. 22:13 f.): judgment is stored up for the godless rich who have laid up treasure, kept back the wages of their workers (cf. Dt. 24:15), and lived in luxury. The brethren are to be patient, looking to the endurance of the prophets and the steadfastness of Job. Verse 9, summing up the ideas of 4:11 f., seems to be an isolated saying not quite in its context.

The letter closes with various admonitions (Jas. 5:12-20). A warning against swearing is in the spirit of Sir. 23:9-11 and, very close to Mt. 5:34-37, doubtless echoes the synoptic tradition. In the spirit of the Psalter – psalms of supplication and of thanksgiving – prayer is recommended both in suffering and in joy (Jas. 5:13). The scriptural basis for the sacrament of the anointing of the sick is found in Jas. 5:14 f.; the elders of the (local) church, summoned to a sick person, will anoint him with oil (cf. Mk. 6:13), while invoking the name of the Lord Jesus (cf. Mk. 2:7), and will pray over him. This rite, inspired by faith, will comfort the sick man and forgive sin. Then, by association of ideas, the author passes to (public) confession of sin and to prayer. Elijah is presented as an example of the efficacy of the prayer of a righteous man (Jas. 5:16-18). The Christian who guides an erring brother back on the right road will save a soul from death and cover a multitude of sins (Jas. 5:19 f.; cf. Prv. 10:12). And thus the writing ends abruptly.

2. 1 PETER

OCCASION   In the concluding greeting (1 Pt. 5:12-14), written in his own hand, the author indicates the purpose of his work: to strengthen the recipients in their faith. Like Heb., it is a "word of exhortation" (cf. Heb. 13.22), and, in a similar manner, builds its parenesis on doctrine. Peter addresses to Christians, recruited in large measure from the ranks of the poor (1 Pt. 2:18 f.), a letter of consolation and of encouragement. The readers are called upon to endure with steadfastness, and even cheerfully, the sufferings and trials that have come upon them and which will continue. They have to contend with slander (1 Pt. 2:12; 3:16), and they suffer simply because they are Christians (1 Pt. 4:16). The best answer to such charges and hostility is the leading of blameless lives (1 Pt. 2:12, 15; 3:2, 13-17). They will be comforted and strengthened by the example of Christ, of his meekness in the face of suffering unjustly inflicted (1 Pt. 2:21, 23 f.).

AUTHORSHIP   The epistle certainly purports to be the work of Peter (1:1; cf. 5:1 f., 13). Irenaeus tells us that the patristic tradition had always regarded the head of the Apostles as the author of this letter. Yet, its Greek style is comparable to that of Jas.; the author thinks in Greek and quotes from the LXX. However, we are told explicitly (5:12) that 1 Pt. was written down by a secretary — who may be responsible for the unexpected Greek style.

Nevertheless, there are indications that the writing is later than the traditional date of Peter's death (64 A.D.). The designation 'Babylon' for Rome (5:13) was known in Jewish and Christian tradition (cf. Ap. 14:8; 16:9; 17:5; 18:2, 10, 21), but there is no evidence that it was in use before 70 A.D. 1 Pt. envisages a persecution that affects or will affect Asia Minor cf. 1:1); this can hardly be the Roman persecution of Nero; it is, more likely, the later persecution of Domitian (81-96). On the whole, it seems that the epistle is pseudonymous and dates from the time of Domitian.

SUMMARY   The address (1 Pt. 1:1 f.) explicitly names the Apostle Peter as the author of the letter. He writes to "the exiles of the dispersion" (cf. Jas. 1:1), that is, to the new Diaspora, Christians exiled from their true homeland. The five provinces named cover the whole of Asia Minor except Cilicia. A trinitarian formula states the situation of Christians: called by the Father, sanctified by the Holy Spirit, for obedience to Christ and for salvation through him; the action of the Trinity is developed in 1 Pt. 1:10-12.

God in his great mercy has begotten Christians anew (cf. Jn. 3:3; Ti. 3:5) through the resurrection of his Son, that is, by means of baptism (1 Pt. 3:21; cf. Rm. 6:3-11), to a living hope (cf. 1 Pt. 1:13; 21; 3:5, 15) of salvation in Christ and of an imperishable inheritance (1 Pt. 1:3-5). That heavenly inheritance, although it is an object of hope, is yet seized by faith; even in the midst of trials, such faith and hope are the source of Christian joy. The basis of the faith of Christians and the object of their hope is one: Jesus Christ. Although they have not seen him, they love him; their faith in him is the source of "unutterable and exalted joy," for it is the guarantee of salvation (1 Pt. 1:6-9). The role of the prophets of the Old Law, inspired by the Spirit of Christ, was to announce the Christian mystery (cf. Acts 3:18; 7:52; Mt. 13:17; Lk. 10:24; 24:26 f.; Heb. 11:13, 39 f.) which is characterized by "suffering" and "glory" (cf. Lk. 24:26; Acts 17:3; 1 Cor. 15:3 f.). That gift of salvation, looked forward to by the prophets and not yet revealed even to the angels, has been made known to Christians, by the Holy Spirit, through the Gospel preaching (1 Pt. 1:10-12).

But, Christian faith makes demands for holiness, charity, and closer attachment to Christ (1 Pt. 1:13-2:10); the typology of the Exodus is in view throughout this passage. In the first place, Christians must set their hearts fully on the living hope and order their conduct accordingly. The God who has called them is holy (cf. Lv. 19:2); they cannot go back to their former way of life. They must recall that their heavenly Father is also a Judge and that they have been ransomed from the old ways by the blood of Christ (cf. Ex. 12:5). In short, their life must be lived, in faith and hope, in the God who raised Jesus Christ from the dead (1 Pt. 1:13-21). The way of holiness is a way of fraternal love, a characteristic of the new life into which they have been born, a life sustained by the abiding word of the Good News (cf. Is. 40:6-8). The newly baptized (a baptismal liturgy seems to be in view) must put aside malice and insincerity, and should desire the spiritual food that will enable them to grow as Christians. Reference to milk seemingly has in mind the ancient custom of giving milk and honey to the newly baptized; the quotation of Ps. 34 (33):9 probably refers to the Eucharist, received at baptism (1 Pt. 1:22-2:3).

Christians must come to Christ that they may be built, living stones, into the spiritual temple founded on him (cf. Eph. 2:20-22; Mt. 21:42 f.), that, as a holy priesthood, they may offer to God a true cult (cf. Jn. 4:23), and that they may become the new Israel (cf. Eph. 1:14). The gist of the whole passage (1 Pt. 2:4-10) is found in verses 4, 5, and 9: to come to Christ means incorporation into his community of the new Israel whose function is to offer cult to God through Christ and to manifest the saving mercy of God.

The principles have been established, and what follows (1 Pt. 2:11-4:6) is largely their application in daily living. Christians, as exiles in this world (cf. Phil. 3:20; Heb. 11:8-10, 13; 13:14), must first subdue in themselves the attraction of the alien world. Their good conduct toward pagans will be, at the Parousia, a reproach to their slanderers (1 Pt. 2:11 f.). Since it is God's will that Christians should live in harmony with all men, then, by that will, they are obliged to respect the laws and functionaries of Rome, their land of exile; but, if they honor the emperor they must fear God - their ultimate allegiance is to him.

Christian slaves should be submissive and respectful even toward overbearing masters; the patient acceptance of punishment unjustly inflicted is especially salutary in God's eyes. It is, however, the example of Christ that will enable the Christian slave to transform a degrading state into something noble and to attain an inner freedom (1 Pt. 2:18-25). The passage, 1 Pt. 2:21-25, is a Christian interpretation of the Servant of Yahweh theme (cf. Is. 53:5-12; Acts 3:13, 16; 4:25, 30).

Next, marriage is considered, with exhortation for wives (1 Pt. 3:1-6) and husbands (1 Pt. 3:7). Wives are to be subject to their husbands (cf. Col. 3:18; Eph. 5:22); this is all the more important in the case of an unbelieving husband (one who does not obey the word of the Gospel [cf. 1 Pt. 1:25]) who may be won by the conduct of his wife. Christian wives must not set store by external adornment (cf. 1 Tm. 2:9 f.), but in the interior beauty of a quiet and gentle spirit; they must look to the holy women of Israel: Sarah obeyed her husband and called him "lord" (Gn. 18:12). By following her example, they become the true children of Sarah. Christian husbands are urged to treat their wives with great consideration and gentleness and to show them honor as coheirs of the gift of eternal life; husbands and wives are on terms of complete spiritual equality. All Christians are again urged to live in unity of spirit, in fraternal charity (3:8-12; 4:7 f.); the exhortation is supported by the quotation of Ps. 34:13-17.

The passage, 1 Pt. 3:13-4:6, has to do with the conduct of Christians in face of persecution; but the development of the argument covers the most difficult part of the Epistle: the descent of Christ into hell (1 Pt. 3:18-4:6). No hurt can come to Christians who are zealous for good; even suffering in such circumstances is a blessing. Let them cling to the Lord Christ and not be troubled by those who persecute them (cf. Jn. 8:12 f.). They must be prepared, when challenged, to defend their Christian hope — but gently and respectfully; they must not descend to the level of their adversaries who revile them (cf. 1 Pt. 2:12), but should act in accordance with the will of God, in this way maintaining a clear conscience (cf. 1 Pt. 2:20). The practice of goodness will triumph over suffering (1 Pt. 3:13-17).

Christ himself suffered unjustly (cf. 1 Pt. 2:21-24), but his death saved us. It seems that 1 Pt. 3:18-4:6 preserves different elements of a baptismal Credo: death of Christ (1 Pt. 3:18); descent into hell (1 Pt. 3:19); resurrection (1 Pt. 3:21); session at the right hand of God (1 Pt. 3:22); judgment of the living and dead (1 Pt. 4:5). Christ died, but has made us alive in the Spirit (1 Pt. 3:18), the principle of his resurrection (cf. 1 Pt. 1:2; 3:21; Rm.

1:14). In the state of spirit quickened after physical death or, better, in the course of the process of death and resurrection described in verse 18 (for this seems to be the meaning of *en hō* ["in which"]), Christ "went and preached to the spirits in prison" (1 Pt. 3:19). This may mean (especially if taken in conjunction with 1 Pt. 4:6) that, in the interval between his death and resurrection, Christ preached to the spirits of the dead in Sheol. On the other hand, verse 20 seems to have in mind "those who did not obey"; it is these who are the spirits "in prison" — the just are not in question. On the whole, it seems better to interpret 1 Pt. 3:19-20a in the light of Gn. 6:1-6: the spirits in prison are the "sons of God" whose union with the "daughters of men" was the final wickedness that occasioned the Flood. They are the fallen angels who received notification of the domination of Christ over them (cf. Eph. 1:21 f.; 3:9 f.; Col. 2:15; Phil. 2:8; 1 Cor. 2:6 ff.; 1 Tm. 3:16), just as the heavenly powers were subject to the ascended Christ (1 Pt. 3:22). In 1 Pt. 3:20b-21, the ark of Noah is presented as a type of baptism: just as the family of Noah, thanks to the ark, passed unscathed through the waters of the Flood which buried sinful humanity, so also the baptized person passes safely through the waters of baptism, which bury his sins, to find a new life with Christ.

The theme of 1 Pt. 3:18 is taken up again in 1 Pt. 4:1 f. — the example of the suffering Christ. Christians have died to sin with Christ and now must live the new life in Christ (cf. Rm. 6:1-14). Let their pagan past be indeed a thing of the past. Gentiles, too, for that matter, will have to render an account to him who judges the living and the dead (1 Pt. 4:3-5). The preaching of the Gospel to the dead (1 Pt. 4:6) most likely refers to the descent of Christ. Yet, it does not necessarily follow that "the dead" of 1 Pt. 4:6 are "the spirits" of 1 Pt. 3:19. Hades was not the same for all: the place of rest and the place of torment were separate worlds (cf. Lk. 16:23, 26).

The imminence of the Parousia (1 Pt. 4:7-11) — a theme that recurs in 1 Pt. 4:17 and 1 Pt. 5:10 — is brought forward as a motive for virtue and watchfulness (cf. Phil. 4:5; Jas. 5:8; 1 Jn. 2:19), and especially for the love that covers a multitude of sins (cf. Jas. 5:20) and which can find expression in hospitality. Charity, too, must order the use of the charisms that manifest themselves in the course of divine worship (cf. 1 Cor. 12:4-11; Rm.

12:6-8). Persecution and suffering are taken up again in 1 Pt. 4:12-19, a passage which might be regarded as a synthesis of the Epistle. The "fiery ordeal" (cf. 1 Pt. 1:7) of persecution should not come as a surprise, for it is a feature of Christian life in this world. It not only tests the genuineness of the faith of Christians, but also is a sharing in Christ's sufferings; it is even a cause for joy as a pledge of a part in his glory (cf. 1 Pt. 1:21; 5:1, 10). The Spirit of God rests on those who bear reproach for Christ (1 Pt. 4:12-14). While they should do nothing that merits punishment, to suffer simply because one is a Christian (the name occurs elsewhere only in Acts 11:26; 26:28) is not something to be ashamed of. Judgment begins with the household of God (cf. Jer. 25:29; Ezek. 9:6) – persecution is a purifying trial – but it will be much more severe for unbelievers (cf. Prv. 11:31 [LXX]). Those who patiently endure suffering are in the care of a faithful Creator – only in this place in the New Testament is God so designated (1 Pt. 4:15-19).

The author, an elder of the Church, has a word of advice for his fellow elders (1 Pt. 5:1-4). Leadership in the Church must not be regarded as a road to profit or to power; true leadership is not achieved by brandishing authority, but by example, following the lead of the Chief Shepherd.

Next, the author turns to the faithful (1 Pt. 5:5-11) in a passage that is very close to Jas. 4:6-10. For the younger members of the community (cf. Ti. 2:6; 1 Jn. 2:12, 14) there is an admonition to obey the elders; all are to be humble (cf. Prv. 3:34). They must accept, as coming from God, the trials that humiliate them, but which will cause their greater glory (cf. 1 Pt. 1:6 f.); and they must trust absolutely in him (cf. Ps. 55 (54):22; Mt. 6:25-34). They must be sober and watchful (1 Pt. 1:13; 4:7), because the devil is at work; their resistance will be helped by the knowledge that they do not suffer alone, but share the common lot of Christians. Besides, God himself will speedily establish them in eternal glory. Another doxology (cf. 1 Pt. 4:11) concludes the Epistle proper. The final greeting (1 Pt. 5:12-14) was probably added in the author's own hand; Silvanus is presented as the secretary who has written the letter. The faithful of Asia receive the greeting of the Roman church (the "elect of Babylon"); Mark is mentioned specifically. The "kiss of love" may be a liturgical rite (cf. Rm. 16:16; 1 Cor. 16:20), and the very last word is an echo of the address (1 Pt. 1:2), the wish of peace.

3. JUDE

PURPOSE   Although it certainly takes issue with false teaching, this short writing does not offer us sufficient data to determine what form of heresy is in view. However, the indications are that it is incipient Gnosticism. The writer unmasks some — seemingly a small number — who pervert the traditional doctrine of the Church (v. 3) and put the faith of the community in peril. These men create divisions among the faithful (v. 19). They act as Cain the unbeliever or Korah the rebel (v. 11); they are like unreasoning animals (v. 10). They are like trees which, at the end of autumn, are still without fruit; rather, they are uprooted and dead trees (v. 12). Or they may be compared to wild waves of the sea (v. 13), to wind-driven clouds which shed no beneficent rain (v. 12), to wandering stars which have turned from their true course (v. 13). They were long ago marked down for judgment (v. 4) and they will be punished like the rebellious Israelites in the desert, like the guilty angels or like the inhabitants of Sodom and Gomorrah (vv. 5-7). According to the word of Enoch, the Lord himself, surrounded by his heavenly court, will come to judge them (vv. 14 f.).

Jude castigates them for immorality. They walk according to their passion (v. 16) and ungodly desires (v. 18), giving themselves to debauchery (v. 4) and perhaps unnatural lust (v. 7), and defiling the flesh (v. 23). They disseminate their false teaching for gain and court the favor of the wealthy (v. 16). And all the while they justify their conduct by appealing to the grace which God has given them (v. 4). These false teachers bear a marked resemblance to the Nicolaitans of Ap. 2:6, 14 f., 20-23.

It does not seem likely that they — or for that matter the addressees — were former Jews. The emphasis is on moral misconduct, especially in sexual matters; this would have been a greater danger for Gentiles than for Jews with their rather puritanical background. The error seems to have been a gnostic type of antinomianism (that is, the view that the moral law was not binding on Christians, who had been liberated by grace).

AUTHORSHIP   The author of the epistle names himself 'Jude,' a servant of Jesus Christ and brother of James' (v. 1). The most likely identification is with the Jude named together with James in Lk. 6:3 and Mt. 13:55 as brothers of the Lord. The author of

Jude (v. 1) does not name himself an apostle and in v. 17 he seems to distinguish himself from 'the apostles of our Lord Jesus Christ.' Jude is written in good Greek, although it is not without Semitisms. Verse 17 gives the impression that the first generation of Christians has passed away, and v. 3 speaks of the christian faith as a traditional and unchangeable deposit. Consequently, many hold that the letter is pseudonymous and was written in the decade 80-90 A.D., or perhaps even later.

SUMMARY   The author was desirous to write to the faithful on the subject of Christian salvation; now, instead, he must appeal to them to contend for their traditional faith. He writes as he does because he has become aware that certain heretical teachers have found their way into the community (vv. 3 f.).

In verses 5-7, the author brings forward, as a threat to these false teachers, three Old Testament instances of sin and its punishment. The false teachers are blasphemers (vv. 8-11; cf. 2 Pt. 2:10-12). Their "dreamings" may be the alleged revelations of Gnostics. They "defile the flesh" by unnatural lust (cf. v. 7). They reject *kyriotēs* ("lordship," "authority"), either the lordship of their Master and Lord, Christ (v. 4), or authority as such. They revile the angels (cf. 2 Pt. 2:10 f.). Even their instinctive knowledge has been morally perverted (vv. 8-10). They are compared with traditional representatives of evil known to the Bible (Gn. 4:3-15; Nm. 16:22-24; Dt. 23:5) and in Judaeo-Christian tradition. The presence of the false teachers was a blemish on the *agapē* of the community, the common cultic meal which was accompanied or followed by the Eucharist. Their deceitful and useless character is illustrated by a series of examples. A catalogue of their vices closes this polemic against the false teachers (vv. 11-16).

The faithful must not be led astray by error, but should cling to the teaching of the Apostles (vv. 17-19). Verse 17 implies that the writer is not an Apostle; verse 18 is a summary of the warnings of the Apostles. The faithful must build themselves up on the sure foundation of the Christian religion they profess. By prayer in the Holy Spirit, they must maintain themselves in the love of God, looking to the mercy of Christ that leads to eternal life (vv. 20 f.). Their attitude toward the false teachers is outlined: some, the waverers (cf. Jas. 1:7; 4:8), they should seek to convince; they should seek to snatch others, as at the last moment, from the "fire," the eschatological punishment (cf. 2 Pt. 3:7; 10,12). They should look with eyes of mercy on those who have been won by the heresy, while abhorring the sin and entertaining a salutary fear of contamination (vv. 22 f.). The closing doxology (vv. 24 f.), which resumes the trinitarian formula of verses 20-21, resembles that of Rm. 16:25-27 (cf. 2 Pt. 3:14).

4. 2 PETER

PURPOSE   The author is concerned that his readers should not lose their promised entry into the eternal kingdom of Jesus Christ (2 Pt. 1:11) and he writes to strengthen them in the traditional faith (2 Pt. 1:12 f.; 3:2), in a special way taking issue with false teachers who might lead them astray. Especially in chapter 2 the antinomianism of these false teachers appears; in this respect they are quite like those envisaged in Jude. But 2 Pt., later than the other writing, gives us to understand that they have progressed in error and have now become deriders of the hope of the Parousia. From their fundamental error others flowed: the Lord of the Parousia is denied (2 Pt. 2:1, 10), and, ignoring the expectation of judgment, they also set the moral order aside (2 Pt. 3:3). Against these false views, 2 Pt. insists on the expectation of the Parousia (2 Pt. 1:4, 8, 11; 3:10, 14). It teaches the divine Lordship of Jesus (2 Pt. 1:2, 16 f.; 3:18) and insistently exhorts them to moral living (2 Pt. 1:4-11, 3:11, 14, 17).

AUTHORSHIP   The author of the Epistle names himself Symeon Peter (2 Pt. 1:1); he claims to have been present at the Transfiguration (2 Pt. 1:16-18); he refers to an earlier letter of his, meaning 1 Pt. (3:1); he recalls that Jesus had predicted the time of his death (1:14); and he speaks of Paul as his beloved brother (3:15). But, at the same time, we gather that the first christian generation has passed away – 'The fathers have fallen asleep' (3:4) – and the author can speak of the apostles as though he were not one of them (3:3). There was already a collection (not necessarily complete) of the Pauline writings (3:15 f.). And the author of 2 Pt. has freely adapted and incorporated the short writing of Jude.

Furthermore, there are notable differences between 1 Pt. and 2 Pt., differences of vocabulary, style, and thought. In 1 Pt., christology is a dominant theme and Christ is the model of Christians, while in 2 Pt. he is simply the object of christian profession. Although both epistles claim the proximity of the Day of the Lord, they use different terminology: 1 Pt. (1:7, 13; 4:13) speaks of *apokalypsis* ('revelation') and 2 Pt. (1:16; 3:4, 12) of *parousia*. Besides, in 1 Pt. the proximity of the Coming is unquestioned, while in 2 Pt. the hope faces grave opposition. Again, 1 Pt. frequently and confidently uses the Old Testament, while 2 Pt. has scant reference to scriptural texts.

It is of particular significance that in 3:15 f. the author sets the writings of Paul ('in all his letters') on a par with 'the other scriptures.' Already the canon is taking shape, and a collection of Pauline letters is regarded as canonical. This could scarcely have been before the end of the first century. On the whole, it would seem that 2 Pt. is not only among the later New Testament writings: it is the latest New Testament writing — perhaps about 120 A.D. The author, by identifying himself with Peter, shows that his intention is to transmit apostolic teaching. It is in the same spirit that he has made use of the letter of Jude and appealed to the authority of Paul.

SUMMARY   The address (2 Pt. 1:1 f.) names Symeon Peter as the writer of the Epistle; he is a "servant and apostle of Jesus Christ" (cf. Rm. 1:1; Ti. 1:1). Growth in the knowledge (*gnosis*) of Jesus Christ is a wish repeated in the conclusion (2 Pt. 3:18; cf. 1:5 f., 8; 2:20).

The first part of the writing (2 Pt. 1:3-11) reminds the readers of the wonderful gifts they have received along with God's call and the promises he has made them. The divine power of Christ has enabled him to give to Christians hope and the knowledge of him and entry into his kingdom, by making them partakers in the divine nature (2 Pt. 1:3 f.). In gratitude for this divine liberality, they must practice virtue (2 Pt. 1:5-11). In 2 Pt. 1:12-18, the author, in the name of Peter, makes a personal appeal. Verse 14 is a witness to the tradition that Peter's death was foretold by Jesus (cf. Jn. 21:18 f.). As in 2 Pt. 1:9, he warns against Gnostic errors by assuring them that he did not follow "cleverly devised myths" (2 Pt. 1:16), but recalls his presence as eyewitness on the Mount of Transfiguration; hence, he can bear testimony to Christ's power and to his Second Coming because he had seen the anticipated glory of his Parousia (cf. Mk. 9:2-8 parr.). Besides, there is the "prophetic word," the oracles of the Old Testament relative to the Parousia, and confirmed by the Transfiguration experience. The false teachers' interpretation of Scripture is arbitrary; God alone, by his Spirit, makes known the true sense of his Scripture (2 Pt. 1:20 f.).

2 Pt. 2 is very like Jude 4-16, which it has used as a source. Both passages condemn false teachers in similar terms and bring forward Old Testament examples of transgressors. False teachers are to be expected because false prophets arose even in Israel (for example, Dt. 13:1-6; Jer. 3:31). Many will be deceived by their immorality and the Christian way will be discredited because of them (2 Pt. 2:1-3). Inevitable judgment is illustrated by examples from the Old Testament which show that the Lord knows not only how to punish the wicked but how to rescue the godly (2 Pt. 2:4-10a; cf. Jude 6-8).

These false teachers do not hesitate to revile the fallen angels, whereas the superior angels do nothing of the kind (2 Pt. 2:10b-11; cf. Jude 9 f.). They are like brute beasts, given over to debauchery and avarice; they follow the way of Balaam (2 Pt. 2:2-16; cf. Jude 11 f.). They are waterless springs or useless mists (2 Pt. 2:17; cf. Jude 12 f.). Their immorality seduces the weak, "unsteady souls" (cf. 2 Pt. 2:14), by promising a freedom from the moral law (cf. Jude 4), while they themselves are slaves of sin (cf. Jn. 8:34; Rm. 6:16 f.) (2 Pt. 2:18 f.). The warning of 2 Pt. 2:20 f. is in the line of Heb. 6:4-8; 10:26 (cf. 1 Tm. 6:3-5, 2 Tm. 14-18). The first proverb in 2 Pt. 2:22 is from Prv. 26:11.

The author returns to his vindication of hope in the Parousia. In this second letter (a deliberate reference to 1 Pt.), he again reminds his readers of the prophecies referring to the Coming and of the apostolic teaching founded on the authority of Christ (2 Pt. 3:1 f.; cf. 1 Pt. 1:12-21; Jude 17 f.). The skepticism of the false teachers is refuted (2 Pt. 3:3-7); and the nature of the Parousia, with its implications for Christian living, is explained for the faithful (2 Pt. 3:8-13). In 2 Pt. 3:15 f., the author refers to a collection of Pauline letters regarded as authoritative (the "other scriptures"); the heretics had misinterpreted the difficult Pauline texts relative to the Second Coming. The closing admonition sets the faithful on their guard, and the final doxology (2 Pt. 3:18) is a condensed form of Jude 25.

| *The Johannine Writings*

THE FOURTH GOSPEL

THE THREE EPISTLES OF JOHN

THE APOCALYPSE OF JOHN

1. THE FOURTH GOSPEL

1) Authorship

The problem of the authorship of the Fourth Gospel is very involved. According to the main stream of early Church tradition, John the Apostle, the son of Zebedee and brother of James, wrote, in his old age, the fourth gospel, at Ephesus. But the tradition is not quite unanimous. And, more significantly, there is the impression that the gospel was slowly built up, over a lengthy period of time and that, in its final form, it dates from the close of the first century. It is felt that Raymond E. Brown, in his hypothetical reconstruction of the formation of the gospel, has drawn attention to the complexity of the matter, and has given a plausible outline of the growth of this gospel.[1]

STAGE 1.   Brown posits five stages in the composition of the gospel: The existence of a body of traditional material pertaining to the words and works of Jesus — material similar to what has gone into the synoptic gospels, but material whose origins were independent of the synoptic tradition.

STAGE 2.   The development of this material in Johannine patterns. Over a period lasting perhaps several decades, the traditional material was sifted, selected, thought over, and moulded into the form and style of the individual stories and discourses that became part of the Fourth Gospel. This process was probably accomplished through oral preaching and teaching; but towards the end of this second stage, written forms of what was preached and taught took shape. This stage was decisively formative for the material that ultimately went into the Gospel. That this stage was the work of more than one man is suggested by the existence of units of Johannine material, like chap. 21, that are different in style from the main body of material. However, what has gone into the gospel seems to stem in large part from one dominant source. We should probably think of a close-knit school of thought and expression. In this school the principal preacher was the one responsible for the main body of gospel material.

STAGE 3. The organization of this material from Stage 2 into a consecutive gospel: the first edition of the Fourth Gospel as a distinct work. It is logical to suppose that the dominant preacher of Stage 2 was he who organized the first edition of the gospel – for Brown he is the 'evangelist.' There is a cohesiveness in the overall plan of the gospel as it has come down to us; we suspect that this basic cohesiveness was present in the first edition of the gospel. The organization of the first edition meant selection – not all Johannine material would have been included.

STAGE 4. Secondary edition by the evangelist. The Fourth Gospel was intended to answer the objections or difficulties of different groups; the suggestion is that the adaptation of the gospel to different goals meant the introduction of new material designed to meet new problems.

STAGE 5. A final editing or redaction by someone other than the evangelist and whom we may call the 'redactor' – a close friend or disciple of the evangelist. One of the principal contributions of the redactor was to preserve all the available Johannine material from Stage 2 that had not been previously inserted into the editions of the gospel. This material is no less ancient than the material which found its way into the earlier editions; age of material is not a criterion that will disclose the additions of the redactor. Reliable criteria are the awkwardness of an intrusive passage in the sequence of the gospel, and the fact that some of this material represents a variant duplicate of material (a doublet) already in the gospel (e.g. 6:51-58 and 6:35-50).

'To sum up, although we have spelled out this theory of the five stages of the composition of the Gospel at some length, we should stress that in its basic outlines the theory is not really

complicated and fits in rather plausibly with what is thought about
the composition of the other gospels. A distinctive figure in the
primitive Church preached and taught about Jesus, using the raw
material of a tradition of Jesus' works and words, but shaping this
material to a particular theological cast and expression. Eventually
he gathered the substance of his preaching and teaching into a
Gospel, following the traditional pattern of the baptism, the
ministry, and the passion, death, and resurrection of Jesus. Since
he continued to preach and teach after the edition of the Gospel,
he subsequently made a second edition of his Gospel, adding more
material and adapting the Gospel to answer new problems. After
his death a disciple made a final redaction of the Gospel, incorporating other material that the evangelist had preached and
taught, and even some of the material of the evangelist's co-
workers.'[2]

It is not unreasonable to suppose that the source of the historical tradition underlying the gospel is John, son of Zebedee. But
we cannot name the dominant figure who put his stamp on the
gospel and, more than any other, is entitled to be regarded as its
author. As for place of origin and date: Ephesus remains the
primary contender for identification as the place where Jn. was
composed, and its date 90-100 A.D.

2) The Special Character of John

John may have used special material to develop a valuable historical tradition. He likely used a foundation of good historical and
topographical knowledge on which to develop a profounder
theological vision of the 'history' of Jesus, which uses the eyes of
faith to go to the root of the historical events and external things.
It strives to reveal the secret divine thoughts which they enshrine.
That Jn. did not aim at a 'historical' presentation in the modern
sense may be seen from his rendering of Jesus' words. When we
compare the simple, vivid language of Jesus in the Synoptics, full
of images and parables, with the profoundly theological discourses
in Jn., we feel ourselves in another world with the latter. The
diction is raised to a higher plane; this even includes the repetition
of ambiguous expressions. The subject matter, too, of John's words
of Jesus reveals their uniqueness. The Johannine Jesus is the
bringer of a revelation which apparently retains little contact with
the proclamation of the kingdom of God on the lips of the Jesus
of the Synoptics. What the Johannine Jesus reveals, constantly and

exclusively, is himself. The theological principle behind this procedure is disclosed with all desirable clarity in the discourse on the 'goal and the way' (14:4-11). Finally, sometimes the various matters treated in the Johannine discourses have no 'historical' coordinates. These examples suffice to prove that the discourses in John cannot and do not intend to be historical reporting or a word for word record.

What are they, then? Whatever one thinks of the 'historical' character of his words, it cannot be proved from the evangelist's presentation, from the tenses he uses and the subject matter, that Jesus *must* already be speaking as the risen and glorified Lord. It is more correct to say that, in the mind of the evangelist, the earthly Jesus speaks — though always conscious of his imminent 'exaltation' which begins with the Crucifixion. More precisely, he is conscious of his divine origin. He speaks in full consciousness of his unity with the Father, which does not cease on earth, but is merely presented otherwise in the incarnate Word. 'The deep faith of the writer moved him to clothe the thoughts and words of Jesus in their present dress, but his intention is to let the earthly Jesus speak and express his own thoughts.' He wishes Jesus to be heard — not himself. There is a vast difference between the approach which holds that the Johannine discourses have been freely, consciously invented as 'discourses of Christ,' and that which says they are discourses of Jesus which have passed through the medium of faith. In the Synoptics, too, tradition was permeated by and interpreted in the light of faith. The only difference in Jn. is that here this process has reached its climax, so that the fourth gospel is a presentation completely dominated by the vision of faith.[3]

3) Relationship to the Synoptics

The relationship of Jn. to the Synoptics, already mentioned, may be fairly expressed in the following conclusions:

a) A direct literary dependence of Jn. on the Synoptics is improbable.

b) The Johannine tradition is, on the whole, independent. Even where it deals with matters also found in the Synoptics, it does not seem to pass any judgment on them. The fourth evangelist has his own style of narration and formulation, and does not show any tendency to correct or replace the synoptics.

c) Whether Jn. had some knowledge of the traditional matter

behind the Synoptics is another question. When he supposes his
readers' knowledge of several matters known to us from the
synoptic tradition, such information may not be derived from the
synoptic gospels, but may have been available also in the oral tradition. Here we must certainly assume the existence of cross-currents
between the 'Johannine' and the 'synoptic' traditions.

d) As regards the number of external facts recorded, the
Johannine tradition is in many respects poorer than the synoptic.
But, it gives a considerable amount of extra information, which
merits respect even from the historical point of view.

e) John shows many traces of an old tradition in the words
and deeds of Jesus which seems to be as weighty as that of the
synoptics, and is even similar in style to it. This early stage or substratum of the Johannine tradition may be contemporaneous with
the synoptic tradition. What we have before us at present in Jn. is,
of course, a later stage of development, with a long evolution of
tradition behind it.

f) Jn. has a special aim in view of his presentation, and this is the
readiest explanation of the remarkable relationship which obtains
with regard to the synoptic tradition. Where he diverges from the
synoptic accounts, it is not merely because he has a different and
independent tradition at his disposal, but also because he is intent
above all on his own theological purpose.

His main interest is 'to delineate boldly the majestic figure of
the eschatological bringer of revelation and salvation, to display the
radiant glory of the Logos (Word) as he lives on earth and dwells
among us, to disclose the ever-present significance of the saving
events which lie in the past. The words once spoken by the Son of
God when he came into the world, are to become audible as his
unremitting and ever urgent interpellation. The earthly Jesus is
understood as the Christ who continues to be present in his
community; in its preaching, worship and sacraments he is the
Christus praesens. In other words, the evangelist desired, in the
Holy Spirit (16:13 f.), to link up the time of Jesus, the bearer of
the Spirit (1:33), with the time of the Spirit (7:39); but the Spirit
is imparted to the faithful in the words of Christ (6:63), in the
sacraments which realize and render fruitful the saving events (cf.
19:34; 1 Jn. 5:6 ff.), through the mediation of the Church, which
takes over with the mission of Jesus his preaching and his authority, for the salvation of mankind (cf. 20:22 f.).[4]

4) Outline of the Gospel[5]

THE PROLOGUE (1:1-18)

An early christian hymn, probably stemming from Johannine circles, which has been adapted to serve as an overture to the Gospel narrative of the career of the incarnate Word.

THE BOOK OF SIGNS (1:19 — 12:50)

The public ministry of Jesus where in sign and word he shows himself to his own people as the revelation of his Father, only to be rejected.

Part One:	The Opening Days of the Revelation of Jesus	1:19 — 51 + 2:1 11
Part Two:	From Cana to Cana — various responses to Jesus' ministry in the different sections of Palestine	2 — 4
Part Three:	Jesus and the principal feasts of the Jews	4:46 — 10:42
	Introduction	4:46-54

A. 5:1-47   *The Sabbath* — Jesus performs works that only God can do on the sabbath.

B. 6:1-71   *Passover* — Jesus gives bread replacing the manna of the Exodus.

C. 7:1-8:59   *Tabernacles* — Jesus replaces the water and light ceremonies.

    9:1-10:21   Aftermath of Tabernacles.

D. 10:22-39   *Dedication* — Jesus the Messiah and Son of God is consecrated in place of the temple altar.

    10:40-42   Apparent conclusion to the public ministry.

Part Four:		Jesus moves towards the hour of death and glory	11-12
A.	11:1-54	Jesus gives men life; men condemn Jesus to death.	
	11:55-57	Transition.	
B.	12:1-36	Scenes preparatory to Passover and death.	
		Conclusion: Evaluation and summation of Jesus' ministry.	12:37-50

THE BOOK OF GLORY 13-20

To those who accept him Jesus shows his glory by returning to the Father in 'the hour' of his crucifixion, resurrection and ascension. Fully glorified, he communicates the Spirit of life.

Part One:		The Last Supper	13-17
A.	13:1-30	The Meal	
B.	13:31–17:26	The Last Discourse	
	Division I:	The departure of Jesus and the future of the disciples.	
	Division II:	The life of the disciples and their encounter with the world after Jesus' departure.	
	Division III:	The concluding prayer of Jesus.	

Part Two:		The Passion Narrative	18-19
A.	18:1-27	The Arrest and Interrogation of Jesus.	
B.	18:28–19:16a	The Trial of Jesus before Pilate.	
C.	19:16b-42	The Execution of Jesus on the Cross and His Burial.	

Part Three		The Risen Jesus	20:1-29
A.	20:1-18	At the Tomb.	
B.	20:19-29	Where the Disciples are Gathered.	
	Conclusion:	A Statement of the Author's Purpose.	20:30-31 20:33-31

THE EPILOGUE 21.

An added series of post-resurrection appearances in Galilee.

A.	21:1-14	The Risen Jesus Appears to the disciples at the Sea of Tiberias.
B.	21:15-23	The Risen Jesus speaks to Peter.
C.	21:24-25	The (Second) Conclusion.

5) The Movement of Thought

In the narrative matter, the structure of the gospel as a whole displays a notably dramatic element. This skilfulness of presentation is also present in the longer individual episodes, such as the Samaritan woman, the cure of the blind man, the raising of Lazarus. In these episodes the reader is brought stage by stage to the full self-revelation of Jesus. And the reader, too, comes to an increasing certainty of his faith. The longer narrative complexes illustrate the conflicts of opinion, the antagonism between belief and unbelief. At the same time, these episodes serve to present the great struggle between light and darkness, a struggle in which, seen from the outside, the powers of darkness and unbelief appear to be gaining the upper hand. Even in the shorter passages such as the marriage at Cana, the cleansing of the temple, and the healing of the official's son, dramatic presentation is not lacking. Here, too, one finds the moment of suspense before the liberating vision of faith.

An aspect of the dramatic in Jn. is present in the emphasis placed on 'signs'; the signs are mighty works, performed in the sight of Jesus' disciples, miracles. Still, it is by contrasting 'miracle' and 'sign' that we can best understand John's intention. The restoring of sight to a blind man at Siloam (9:1-12) is indeed a miracle, just like similar miracles in the synoptics (cf. Mt. 9:27-31). But John is not interested in this or other miracles as such; his interest is in their symbolism, their signification. For him, the giving of sight to a blind man is a sign of the spiritual light that Christ, who is Light, can give, because he viewed such actions of Jesus as pointers to a deeper, spiritual truth. We are not always left to work out these hidden meanings for ourselves, for, in many cases, they are brought out in the discourses that accompany the signs; we are also thereby provided with a criterion for judging other passages where such comment is lacking. The signs are closely linked to the work of Jesus on earth; their purpose is to bring out the deeper dimension of his works, to reveal the glory of the Incarnate One.

Nowhere does the difference between John and the synoptic gospels strike one more forcefully than in the discourses of Jesus: the discourses of the fourth gospel are quite distinctive. John does not reason in our western manner: he testifies, he affirms. He does not set out to prove a thesis by building up consecutive arguments until the conclusion is reached. Instead, his thought moves around a central point. Jn. 14:1-24 can be taken as an example of how the thought 'circles,' repeating and insisting, while, at the same time, moving forward and upward to a higher level. Again, one may instance the two great 'parabolic discourses' in Jn. — the Shepherd and the flock (10:1-18) and the Vine and the branches (15:1-10). Both passages are built on similar lines: first a presentation of the matter, the 'parable' (10:1-5; 15:1-2), followed by the strictly Johannine development: a method of concentric thinking which progresses in new circles. It is a meditative way of thought which, instead of proceeding by arguments delves deeper into its subject to gain a deeper and higher understanding of it. This distinctive Johannine movement of thought seems to have no direct parallels. 'It is a personal style, achieved by meditation on the revelation of Jesus Christ and used to clarify this revelation.'[6]

Another notable feature of Jn. is the frequent use of double or ambiguous expressions; this practice involves a whole technique. Such expressions, when spoken by Jesus, are first understood by his interlocutors in the obvious or natural sense, and he then goes on to explain the deeper spiritual meaning. For example, in 2:19, the 'temple' of which Jesus speaks is not the building — as the Jews believed — but the temple of his body (2:21).

More characteristic, however, are such words as the adverb *anōthen* (3:3, 7) which means 'again' (and was so understood by Nicodemus) and also 'from above' (the meaning really intended by Jesus). The rendering of the adverb qualifies the meaning of 'birth' (3:3, 7) and this is also misunderstood by Nicodemus. In 3:14 we read of the Son of Man being 'lifted up'. The same expression occurs in 8:28 and 12:32 f.; in the latter case, a note makes it clear that crucifixion is meant. The evangelist regards the 'elevation' of Christ on the cross as a symbol of his 'elevation' to heaven by his resurrection and ascension. In John's eyes, the death, resurrection, and exaltation of Christ are all aspects of one and the same mystery; hence, he can regard the exaltation on the cross and the exaltation in glory as one movement.

In interpreting the Fourth Gospel, we must be careful to give full weight to this technique of the evangelist. We should realize that he has chosen these expressions precisely because they have more than one signification, and that he clearly intends the two (or more) significations of each expression. We should not be true to his mind if we were to narrow his meaning to one or other alternative. If John uses ambiguous words, it is not because he wants to be obscure or wishes to hide something. Quite the opposite is true, because what he does is to look beyond the superficial signification of an expression to a deeper, spiritual meaning. This method is to be understood in much the same way as his presentation of signs; not only the actions of Jesus, but his words too are 'signs.' It is because they are words of Christ — 'words of eternal life' (6:68) — that they have a deeper meaning, and this truth can be effectively symbolized by the use of double expressions.

6) *The Johannine Tradition*

Already, in comparing Jn. and the synoptics, we have acknowledged the existence of a Johannine tradition, in part parallel to the synoptic tradition and in part complementary. We may indicate briefly the character and content of the Johannine tradition. The Aramaic coloring of the fourth gospel is relevant here, for a tradition that purports to go back to the beginnings of Christianity would reasonably show traces of Aramaic idiom. So, too, certain features of the pre-gospel tradition point to a Jewish-Christian setting — for instance, an allusion to the belief that the Messiah would remain unknown until Elijah had pointed him out (cf. 1:26 f.) and the belief in the high priest's gift of prophecy (11:51). The curious expression, 'when you were under the fig tree' (1:48), would seem to have point only in a Jewish environment (cf. Dn. 13:51-60 and some rabbinical evidence). And there are other contacts with Jewish tradition. John's date for the crucifixion, the eve of the Passover, while differing from the synoptic dating, agrees with that of rabbinical tradition: 'Jesus was hanged on the Eve of the Passover.' The discussion of the sabbath in 7.22-24, like similar discussions in the Synoptics, clearly points to a Jewish environment; while, in forecasts of persecution for the disciples, the threat of excommunication from the synagogue (16:2) would hold terrors for none but a Jewish-Christian community. We may note, too, that the political situation reflected by the Johannine tradition fits the years before the outbreak of the Jewish rebellion in 66 A.D., a situation that had passed away when the gospel itself was written.

So much for the Jewish-Christian character and setting of the tradition; now we may consider its contents, at least the salient points. The ministry of John the Baptist is treated more fully than in the synoptics and his importance in preparing the way for Jesus is more in evidence. Yet, in his handling of the tradition, it does seem that the evangelist had in mind a false evaluation of John the Baptist by the 'disciples of the Baptist.' The existence at Ephesus of a group so designated is attested by Acts 19:1-8, and we know that some of them were still there in the third century. Thus, the fourth gospel is silent about the repentance preaching of the Baptist and presents him exclusively in his role as Precursor. He is not the light, but bears witness to the Light (1:6-8); he is not the Messiah or Elijah or the Prophet (1:20); he is only the friend of the Bridegroom, who must decrease while the Bridegroom must increase (3:28-30). His great glory is that he had recognized the Lamb of God (1:29). The evangelist was able to select material that suited his polemical purpose.

We learn of an early ministry of Jesus in Judaea, parallel to that of the Baptist. The tradition preserved much topographical information; in particular, it contained many placenames of Judaea and Transjordan not found in the other gospels. It is likely that the tradition, in great part – and not the evangelist only – is responsible for an overwhelming interest in the Judaean ministry. On the other hand, we learn from this gospel of a threatened messianic rising in Galilee, followed by a widespread desertion of followers and the loyal adherence of the Twelve (6:14 f., 66-69). The Passion-narrative is full and detailed, supplementing the synoptic accounts and even deviating from them. It stresses the political aspect of the charges against Jesus. It is difficult to define the content of the tradition in regard to the sayings of Jesus because the evangelist has consistently recast the teaching. But it is still possible to point to sayings and parables obviously drawn from a reservoir common to the four gospels, and it is reasonable to believe that many more, now veiled in Johannine language, are from the same general source.

We may end this brief survey by noting that, in his introduction to his study of historical tradition in the fourth gospel, Professor Dodd asked the question: 'Can we in any measure recover and describe a strain of tradition lying behind the fourth gospel, distinctive of it, and independent of other strains of tradition known to us?' And at the close of the work, he asserts that his investigation had led him 'to the conclusion that, behind the fourth gospel, lies an ancient tradition independent of the other gospels, and meriting serious consideration as a contribution to our knowledge of the historical facts concerning Jesus Christ. For this conclusion I should claim a high degree of probability — certainly in such matters is seldom to be attained.'[7]

7) The Johannine Theology

John has indicated, quite firmly, the purpose of his gospel: 'These (signs) are written that you may believe that Jesus is the Christ, the Son of God, and that believing you may have life in his name' (20:31). Obviously, he has sought to stress faith in the person of Jesus Christ and in his salvific power. The foundation of that faith is his own presentation of the facts, his choice among many other signs which Jesus had wrought (20:30). His intent is to bring men to believe that this man of flesh and blood, Jesus of Nazareth, is the Messiah of Jewish expectation — and something far, far more than that. He is 'Son of God' in the sense of the christian profession of faith which surpasses all Jewish expectations. 'That you may believe' is not only addressed to potential converts; it also envisages those who already believe, inviting them to 'go on believing,' to attain to a more profound and stable faith. This faith is directed to the living and glorified Lord, preached by the Church, living in the Church. He is the Savior, the Lord of glory . . . and none other than the Jesus of the gospel. Faith in him has power to bestow salvation, life, 'in his name.' Faith is faith in the person of Christ, a Christ who is Savior.

The Johannine world is characterised by a division into light and darkness, life and death. Yet, it is clear that John's dualism has nothing to do with a philosophical speculation on good and evil, but is a component of salvation history. The warfare between light and darkness in this world is not cosmic, but is a struggle within man in his search for truth and light. In the Johannine view, truth has come, whole and entire, with the coming of the Son of man. In him the meeting of God with man takes place: he is the communication of divine life. John stresses equally the divinity and the humanity of the Savior: the truth, light and life which men need have been brought from above by the Son, but they are given because he is one with mankind, who through him can enter into the divine sphere.

For John the story of Jesus is that place in history where the ultimate truths about God are to be found. More than the synoptists, it is he who gives us an awareness of this through his theme of *life*. John had more to tell about Jesus than any gospel could hold. This is why he emphasized the coming of the Spirit – promised not so much to supply for Jesus' absence as to complete his presence. This Spirit had matured John himself, and his work is characterized by his experience of the Spirit. He saw the divine light which all along had irradiated the human Teacher from Nazareth.

THE WORD   When he identifies Jesus as the creative Word of God, source of the light that is man's life, John presents him as the revealer of God. But his conception of revelation is dynamic – the idea of the Word is eminently soteriological. The revelation made by the Word gives knowledge of God; the revelation is found in the example and invitation of a life that has been lived, the life of the Son of Man. Because the incarnation is the supreme grace of God, the Word is preeminently the revelation of God's love – hence John's stress on love. It is the essence of discipleship, of what it means to be a Christian.

The incarnation is a beginning. It has to be fulfilled in the work for which the Son has been sent into the world: the glorification of the Father that in turn is his own glorification. The 'hour' of Jesus, the hour of his suffering and death, is one phase of his 'glorification,' the other phase being his resurrection and return to the Father. In contrast to the synoptists, who reflect the common tradition, John has underlined the glorification aspect of the passion story. It is an hour of triumph because, despite appearances, it is the world that stands judged and the power of evil broken. The incarnate Word has glorified God by his words and deeds; God in turn has glorified him by the same words and deeds. The 'signs' of Jesus comprise his words and works – the words give determination to his works and show them to be the works of God. The 'signs' of Jesus are the communication of God to men, and so they are truth and life; they are abiding realities. The glory of Jesus is something that has been seen by men and in him they have found the glory of God.

The pre-existence of the Johannine Christ is affirmed in the Prologue (1:1 f.) and in the testimony of the Baptist (1:30). It is asserted by Jesus himself ('where he was before,' 6:62), ('before Abraham was, I am,' 8:58), in the great prayer to the Father (17:5, 24), and indirectly in many other texts where his pre-existence is assumed. It is present in the *ego eimi* ('I am') sayings. Indeed, the strongest expression of Jesus' claim to be the divine redeemer in the strict sense is found in the absolute usage of *ego eimi*: 'You will die in your sins unless you believe that I AM' (8:24); 'I tell you this now, before it takes place, that when it does take place you may believe that I AM' (13:19). The source of these confident assertions of pre-existence lies in the Christology of the primitive Church previous to John. Only an acceptance of pre-existence can explain Paul's identification of the legendary Rock, which accompanied the Israelites in the desert, with Christ (1 Cor. 10:4). Only this can account, too, for his assertions in 1 Cor. 8:6; Gal 4:4, Rm. 10:6 f. John is not introducing a wholly new idea, but is developing an aspect of the christology of the early Church.

FAITH   Faith plays a supremely important part in John's theology. Faith, of course, is equally emphasized by Paul, but the accent is different. For one thing, John prefers the verb 'to believe' while Paul favors the noun 'faith.' Perhaps John wants to stress that faith is less an internal disposition than an active commitment, but surely Paul would fully concur in this. More significant is the fact that, for Paul, faith in the crucified and risen Lord is all-important. John projects this faith into his account of the earthly work of Jesus and shows it unfolding in personal encounter with the redeemer during his life in the world. However, John is careful to bring out its bearing on the time after Easter in Jesus' concluding statement (20:29). But by thus projecting christian faith into the time of the ministry, John can strikingly and effectively describe exactly the beginning and the growth of faith, the motives that inspire it, the dangers it runs. He can show that Jesus himself demands faith as the one thing necessary for salvation, and can make it clear that faith is faith in Jesus as the one in whom God has revealed himself. And he also brings out that faith is rooted in this historical and incarnational revelation. It is precisely because of this incarnational aspect that Paul and John are at one in asserting that faith must become effective in love. 'For in Christ Jesus neither circumcision nor incircumcision is of any avail, but faith working through love' (Gal. 5:6). And, in John, fraternal charity becomes the 'new commandment' of Christ (13:34 f.).

The most distinctive, and the most frequent, Johannine expression is *pisteuin eis*, 'to believe in.' The usage brings out the most marked characteristic of Johannine faith – faith is directed exclusively to the person of Jesus. To believe means to receive and accept Jesus' self-revelation; it means to attach oneself to him, in personal union, in order to receive from him eternal life; it means a total commitment to him. It is so much more than trust or confidence in him. The believer can have the fullest assurance as he finds, in the very object of his faith, the deepest motive and the surest foundation of his faith. For, this Son is attested by the Father, attests himself in God, and is continually attested in the apostolic testimony.

The personal union of the believer with Christ is also expressed by other terms which can stand for the Johannine faith. It emerges clearly in the parallelism of 6:35 that 'to believe' in Jesus is *to come to* him: 'I am the bread of life; he who comes to me shall not hunger, and he who believes in me shall never thirst.' Faith can also be described as 'hearing' the voice or the words of Jesus – hearing and obeying. The believer *abides* in the word – and in Jesus himself (8:31). Believing is also seeing. More than any other New Testament writer John has laid stress on faith as vision; it is a true vision of God, of Truth. Faith and knowledge are often associated, but they are not identical. 'Faith,' whose object is a Person, can certainly grow into 'knowledge' for, in biblical thought, 'to know' is always an act which institutes or reinforces fellowship. Knowledge comes through faith, and faith should grow into knowledge – more intimate fellowship with Father and Son. And because the revelation of God in Christ is pre-eminently the revelation of his love, there is the closest possible connection between faith and love.

THE SPIRIT   In John, the Spirit is presented as the divine power that continues and completes Jesus' ministry; the Spirit is the perpetuation of Jesus' presence among his followers. The Spirit is the principle of the divine sonship that Jesus has made possible for men; John's emphasis is on the Spirit as sanctifier and as principle of the life of the Christian. The activity of the Paraclete (John's designation of the Spirit) is to reveal the mind of Christ. We live not by the words of the 'historical' Jesus, but by the words of

Jesus as made known through the Church enlightened by the Spirit.

All this becomes more obvious and, indeed, self-evident, if we accept that, for John, the Paraclete is 'the personal presence of Jesus in the Christian while Jesus is with the Father.'[8] Thus, the one whom Jesus calls 'another Paraclete' is another Jesus. 'As yet the Spirit had not been given, because Jesus was not yet glorified' (7:39) – if, then, the Spirit can only come when Jesus departs, the Spirit/Paraclete is the presence of the 'absent' Jesus. As Paraclete, the glorified Lord is abidingly present in his Church. In this way, the later Christian is assured that he is no further removed from the ministry of Jesus than the earlier Christian, for the Paraclete dwells within him as fully as Jesus 'abode' in his disciples. John's theology of the Spirit meant that his eschatology could hardly be other than 'realized.' Hence it appears that it is not so much the 'delay' of the Parousia as the Church's consciousness and experience of the presence of the Holy Spirit that was responsible for the development of 'realized eschatology' – the possession of eternal life here and now.

Men find in the Church not only the words of Jesus but also his works of salvation; and the works of Christ perpetuated in the Church by the Spirit are chiefly the sacraments, which draw their efficacy from the Christ-event. The presence of the Spirit is manifested in christian life, specifically in fraternal love. John's concept of judgment is in line with his realized eschatology: while not denying a final 'judgment' he insists on the present reality of judgment, on the importance of the existential moment of decision. The coming of Jesus is, and remains, an occasion of judgment; men must decide whether to accept him or reject him. In making this decision, man judges himself. The 'division' caused by the appearance of the Light continues into John's Church and into the Church of our day.

2. THE THREE EPISTLES OF JOHN

1. The First Epistle of John

In the early Church this epistle – like the Fourth Gospel – was attributed to John the Apostle; indeed, the writings are so closely related that their attribution to the same author is natural. Resemblances between gospel and letter are marked and constant; yet there are, too, notable differences between them. The latter cannot

PROLOGUE 1:1-4

Part I: The Demands of the Fellowship with God is Light	1:5 — 2:29	
Principle: To Walk in the Light	1:5-7	A
1) To break with sin	1:8 — 2:2	A
2) To keep the commandments — especially that of love	2:3-11	B
3) To keep oneself from the world	2:12-17	A'
4) To be on guard against antichrists	2:18-29	B'

In Part I the four small literary units present a dual alternating rhythm:

A. A prevailingly negative aspect:
   break with sin

B. A prevailingly positive aspect:
   keep the commandments

A'. A prevailingly negative aspect:
   no love for the world

B'. A prevailingly positive aspect:
   faithful to doctrine received

Part II: The Conduct of the Authentic Children of God	3: — 5:12	
Principle: To Live as Children of God	3:1-2	
1) Children of God and children of the devil	3:3-10	A
2) Brotherly love	3-11-18	B
3) Faith, love, confidence	3:19-24	C
4) True Christians and false prophets	4:1-6	A'
5) Brotherly love	4:7-21	B'
6) Love and faith	5:1-12	C'

EPILOGUE 5:13

APPENDIX 5:14-21

In Part II there is a ternary alternating rhythm:
A B C — A' B' C'

outweigh the impressive contacts between the writings, and may be explained by the complex history of the Johannine literature. The dominant figure who put his stamp on the gospel is the main author of the epistle too; the differences are due to the hand of a redactor.

In spite of the close relationship between the gospel and the epistle, it is not easy to say which preceded the other. The epistle presupposes the main themes of the gospel, but we have seen that the gospel took shape gradually. Something the same may be said of the epistle. While it does seem that the fourth gospel, in its final form, is the later writing, it does not appear that the epistle can be much earlier. A date toward the end of the last decade of the first century is reasonable.

PLAN[9] First John has fundamentally the same structure as the fourth gospel: a Prologue (1:1-4), two parts firmly bound together, of which the second completes the first (1:5-2:29 and 3:1-5:32), and finally an Epilogue closely related to that of the Gospel (5:13) and similarly a long additional note (5:14-21).

The marked similarity in structure between 1 Jn. and the fourth gospel follows a suggestive doctrinal similarity: although they pursue different ends, the two writings are in total agreement on the nature and quality of Christian life.

'First John is principally the attestation of what an authentic Christian experience is, just as the fourth gospel is principally the proclamation of the great divine revelation which conditions this experience. In both cases the Christian experience is presented as being essentially communion in divine life, and more precisely in Trinitarian life. this communion springs in fact from the love of the Father who gives us the Son and the Holy Spirit, and it has for object the mutual immanence, thanks to the Spirit's anointing, of the Father and the Son, on the one hand, and of the Christian on the other.

In the gospel it is first by faith that man opens himself to the light which emanates from Christ the Revealer, but in the second part, starting with chap. 13, Christ pleads insistently for brotherly love on the part of those who have given themselves to him by faith: *believe and love*, these are the two fundamental demands of Christ in the fourth gospel. To live in the light of faith, by reject ing error and sin, and to love one's neighbor, these are, in the epistle also, the two essential conditions of an authentic communion with God. The various themes presented in 1 Jn. gravitate, we believe, around the two basic motifs of divine light and divine love, as well as around the two corresponding human attitudes: faith and charity.'[10]

PURPOSE   The occasion of the letter is the activity of false teachers: John has written to counteract it. Since, however, he is aware that his readers know the truth and have, in fact, effectively repulsed the false prophets (2:20, 27; 4:4), his message is essentially positive. True, he does denounce the false teachers (2:18, 28; 4:1, 6), men who had belonged to the Christian community — although they had never known its spirit (2:19, 22 f.; 4:1) — and his tone can be polemical at times (1:6-10; 2:3-6:9). Yet, the conclusion (5:13) states unequivocally the purpose he had in mind: 'I write this to you who believe in the name of the Son of God, that you may know that you have eternal life.' He, conscious of his fellowship with the Word of life (1:1), desires to share that experience. He is a witness, and he bears witness. This epistle is his testament to his disciples. And if he does point to certain dangers, and if there is an element of exhortation, we learn once again — what the author of Hebrews has so effectively taught us — that the only effective way to counter error is to give men an ideal to live by, to hold up before them the Incarnate Son of God.

Who were the false teachers John had in view? It can scarcely be doubted that they were Gnostics of some sort (those who claimed a special *gnosis* — knowledge or wisdom — which often went hand-in-hand with an indifference to moral conduct). From the epistle we learn that the false teachers claim a knowledge of God (2:4; 4:8), love of God (4:20), and a fellowship with God (1:6; 2:6, 9) superior to those of ordinary Christians. They deny that Jesus is the Messiah (2:22), the Son of God (4:15; 5:5), and that he has come in the flesh (4:2). The assertion of 5:6: 'This is he who came by water and blood, Jesus Christ, not with the water only but with the water and the blood,' which refers to the baptism and death of Jesus and demonstrates that he is no phantom but was baptized in the Jordan and died on the cross, is probably aimed at a denial of the reality of the Incarnation. The antichrists held that the Son of God dwelt in Jesus only from the moment of baptism and, before the passion, departed to the Father. The author's emphasis on the need of breaking with sin and his insistence on practical christian living would have in mind the Gnostic view that sin is of no account in one who possesses the perfect knowledge of God – it does not touch that deepest reach of the spirit where one loves the Father. Similarly, they felt that, when one is occupied with God, one has no concern with others. John deals with both errors in a characteristic statement of devastating simplicity: 'Whoever does not do right is not of God, nor he who does not love his brother' (3:10).

THE MESSAGE   The author's primary purpose is not to exhort his readers to practise virtue or to fly sin, but to make them understand the sublimity of their condition as Christians. Christian existence is defined as a vital relationship to God. It is a matter of birth to the life of God, of fellowship with Father and Son: the faithful are born of God, they abide in God, they know God. In short, they have 'eternal life'; and, for John, eternal life is the very life of God. This life, possessed by the Christian, is a reality, but it is mysterious: what the faithful are now, as well as what they will be hereafter, is attested only by faith. Therefore, the author multiplies the criteria by which the believer may judge the genuineness of his Christian life; hence, the frequency of 'by this' and the verb 'recognize' (2:3, 5; 3:10, 14, 19, 24; 4:2, 6, 13, 18, 20). Since it is a participation in the divine life, Christian life must reflect the very qualities of God; if we are children of God, in fellowship with him, it is impossible that we should not be conformed to him.

God is Light (1:5) and Love (4:8): *Light* because he is the absolute good and because our moral conduct should be modeled on his justice and holiness (2:20; 3:7); *Love* because he is the source of all the tenderness and generosity that the verb 'to love' suggests. The Christian is called to walk in the Light (1:6 f.) and to abide in Love (4:16) by observing the commandments (2:3-7; 3:22-24; 5:2 f.), summed up in the two precepts of faith in the name of Jesus and of fraternal charity (3:23). To believe in the divine Love which is incarnate in Jesus and, in turn, to love their brethren – such is the message addressed by John to Christians.

But the Apostle does also intend to recall – by implication at least – the fundamental norms of the Christian life. In the realm of faith, his readers must readily accept the apostolic witness (1:5; 2:21-24), as well as the testimony of God (4:6, 9, 13) and the intimate word of the Spirit (2:20, 27). Their relationship to their brethren is colored by their care to observe the commandments, centered in the precept of charity (2:3-11; 3:11-24; 4:7-5:4). They must take their stand against the unbelieving world and face up resolutely to its allurements (2:12-17; 3:13; 4:1); similarly, they must adhere to the truth and combat the errors that are propagated around them (2:18-23; 4:1-4). Their personal attitude must be characterized by the candid avowal of sin (1:8-10; 2:1; 3:3 f.) and by confidence in the person of the Savior (2:1 f.; 3:5, 8; 5:6 f.). The Christian life makes demands, and its sublimity is matched by a practicality that calmly accepts the realities of human existence.

John combats Gnostic tendencies, but it is true to say that the first epistle is the fruit of an authentically Christian *gnosis*, at once knowledge and fellowship. Its spiritual teaching is basically the same as that of Paul, but it is more theocentric than Paul, and goes to the Father. Here the ideal is not to live 'in Christ,' but to 'abide in God,' in the 'Father and Son.' But this does not prevent John from emphasizing, just as strongly as Paul, the indispensable mediation of the Incarnate Son of God: it is through the Son that the believer receives the very life of God. All the while, let it be said again, a writing of such elevated spirituality, cast in the realm of Father and Son, keeps a close and constant grip on the world of men and testifies to a simple and demanding moral realism: fellowship with God, participation in the divine life, is impossible without absolute fidelity to the Commandment. This short writing has an abiding message for those far advanced in Christian perfection – and for all Christians.

2) The Second and Third Epistles of John

Unlike 1 Jn., which has something of the character of an encyclical, 2, 3 Jn. are addressed, respectively, to a single church and to an individual. Again, the first epistle is anonymous, but the others are written to 'the elder' – in the context one whom the title sufficiently identifies to his readers.

The *Second Epistle* is addressed to the 'Elect Lady' and her children.' There is little doubt that the title designates a church (vv. 1, 14, 13), probably a church of Asia Minor. This community, still faithful, is threatened by deceivers 'who will not acknowledge the coming of Jesus Christ in the flesh' (v. 7). Hence, the Elder puts the faithful on their guard against the false prophets (vv. 7; 10); he assures them that to abide in the doctrine of Christ (that is, the doctrine of the Incarnation [v. 7]) is to have fellowship with the Father and the Son (v. 9) and he forbids them to associate with the false teachers (v. 10). Typically, he insists on the love of one another in fulfillment of the new commandment of Christ (vv. 5 f.). This short letter is, in fact, a summary of 1 Jn., and may be regarded either as a first outline of it or as a brief résumé. In both writings, circumstances are similar and the purpose is the same.

Very likely, the *Third Epistle* was written earlier than the others, before the emergence of the false teachers. The letter is addressed to Gaius, a faithful disciple of John (vv. 1 f.). His conduct is beyond reproach, and he is especially conspicuous for his generous hospitality to the brethren who visit his community. These are probably itinerant preachers (like Demetrius [v. 12]) sent out by John. On principle, they accepted nothing from the pagans to whom they preached (v. 7) and so were altogether dependent on the generosity of the faithful. Indeed, it was the duty of Christians to support such men (v. 8).

However, the Epistle is more directly concerned with a conflict between the Elder and Diotrephes, the head of a community (most likely that to which Gaius belongs). The authority of the Elder is being challenged: in practice, by refusal to accept the Elder's envoys and by the expulsion of those Christians who do receive them. Some, however, like Gaius, were not cowed by Diotrephes, and the Elder counted on them to have his orders carried out. Demetrius is obviously a trusted emissary. His commission may have been to replace Diotrephes as head of the community, or to install Gaius in that office.

From both epistles it emerges that the Elder claims considerable authority; his attitude to the churches is quite like that of Paul.

3. The Apocalypse of John

I. AUTHORSHIP   Four times (1:1, 4, 9; 22:8) the author of Apocalypse names himself John, and christian tradition has, on the whole, identified him with the Apostle John. We have noted that the fourth gospel and the three epistles have also been traditionally attributed to John the Apostle – though he is not the author of them. It is clear that Ap. and they cannot have been written by the same hand; perhaps, then, the author of Ap. is, after all, the apostle? Yet, Ap., in its final form at least, appears to date from the close of Domitian's reign, from the last decade of the first century – too late for John. The traditional attribution of the Johannine corpus to John finds its justification in the probable existence of a 'Johannine school' – a group of disciples of the apostle – within which the rich Johannine tradition grew and developed.

2. LITERARY FORM   The word 'apocalypse' – from the Greek *apokalypsis* – means 'revelation'. An apocalypse is a revelation, or a series of revelations, made to a seer, by God, or by an angel acting in his name. The revelation is almost always concerned with the development of history, culminating in the end of this world and pointing to the mysteries of the future. As a literary form the apocalyptic is closely related to the prophetical – it is, in fact, a child of prophecy. Already the visions of Ezekiel, for instance, have something of the fantasy and exuberance of the apocalyptist's visions. Besides, many passages in the prophetical books deal with the far horizons of time; they have the eschatological interest that is a marked feature of apocalypse.

While pseudonymity is not an essential feature of apocalypse, an apocalyptic work is almost always attributed to an venerated figure of the past. The reputed author is supposed to receive, in a series of visions, a revelation of God's plan working out in the world's events – and this revelation is represented as having been hidden for many years, laid up in a 'sealed book.' History is unfolded in symbols and finds its term in the epoch of the true author. The language is regularly designedly vague – this in accordance with the literary fiction since it is supposed to be prophecy. The apocalypse closes with a prediction of the imminent eschatological judgment and the advent of unending happiness; in other words, with the advent of the messianic age. A notable feature is the frequent intervention of angels; it is they who usually explain the mysterious symbols.

The object of apocalypse is to show the providence of God at work in history; born in times of crisis, it inspired the readers with hope and confidence. As a literary form, it flourished in the last two centuries B.C. and in the first two centuries A.D.: the book of Daniel (more precisely Dn. 7-12) is the earliest Jewish apocalypse. The form was also cultivated in the early church but never to the same extent as among the Jews; and the Apocalypse is the only New Testament apocalyptic work. The popularity of the form should be taken into account when interpreting Apocalypse: features that appear very strange to us were part of a widespread and familiar literary convention. This fact alone would, for people of those centuries, dispel much of the mystery we attach to the form.

In general, we may say that the purpose of apocalyptic was to keep alive hope in God and to remind men that God is in final control of history. This is reinforced by the thought of the future life, though, in the different Jewish apocalypses, this is presented in a great variety of ideas. Some think of a resurrection of the good to life on earth, while others think of a blissful hereafter. All are agreed that the triumph of God's will is paramount, for only in a world in which his will is perfectly done – the kingdom of God – can happiness be perfected.

A characteristic of these works, variously expressed, is the recognition that the golden age will not come of itself nor be ushered in by men, but is God's gift. Men could play their part and serve God's purpose only by obedience to his will; and their faithfulness could entail anguish and distress. The thought of the final judgment was in keeping with this outlook, because it was seen that bliss lay in obedience to God in a world that was obedient to him; it could not be shared by those who set themselves against God.

The revelations of an apocalypse are made through the medium of visions which the seer describes in conventional language; thus we have images, symbols and numbers. Everything, or nearly everything, in an apocalypse is symbolic, although the details of the symbols are not always significant and should not be unduly pressed. It is imperative that the procedure should be correctly understood.

When the seer describes a vision, he translates into symbols the ideas which God had suggested to him; he accumulates things and colors and symbolic numbers without worrying about the form of his picture. His primary purpose is to convey the ideas he has received from God, not to describe a coherent vision, and *imaginable* vision. If we are to follow, without discouragement, the way he has traced, we must accept his terms, and translate into ideas the symbols which he describes, and not be disturbed by their lack of coherence. Thus, it would be wrong to strive to imagine *visually* the Lamb with seven horns and seven eyes (5:6), and the Beast with seven heads and ten horns (13:1), and to wonder how the ten horns should be shared among the seven heads. These visions are not plastically conceivable, but that fact should not disturb. One must be satisfied with understanding the symbols *intellectually* without lingering over their more or less surprising details: the Lamb enjoys the fulness of power and knowledge; the beasts represent the Roman Empire with its emperors (the heads) and vassal kings (the horns). If one does not take full account of such procedure – often disconcerting – it is impossible for one to understand the Apocalypse. [11]

The author of an apocalypse looks to the future not only when he describes the time of the end but also when he unrolls the course of history. His vantage point is in the past – an apocalypse is almost always pseudonymous – and he speaks as a prophet. Apocalyptic flourished in times of crisis and was designed to console and to encourage those undergoing affliction and distress, to fill them with confidence in God, who guided human destiny and was master of history. Here the Apocalypse is at one with the other apocalyptic writings.

When we describe John's work as an apocalypse, taking that word in its proper sense, we leave aside the first three chapters, the 'letters to the seven churches.' Although an integral part of the whole book, these are not apocalyptic in form. Even though we call them 'letters,' they are not, strictly speaking, letters, but prophetic messages. Primarily, they are judgments on the spiritual state of the churches and they stress the necessity of keeping faith; hence, they are closer to the prophetical form than to the apocalyptic.

3. THE PURPOSE   Like the book of Daniel, Ap. was written in a troubled time and for a special purpose; like Dn. too, it carries a message that goes beyond the immediate crisis. Ap. is at once a declaration of christian faith and hope and a manifesto against the official paganism of Rome. The author is a witness, and he speaks with the authority of the former prophets sent by God, echoing their words and images. His book is a commentary on the words of Jesus to his disciples: 'In the world you have tribulation; but be of good cheer, I have overcome the world' (Jn. 16:33). Just as Dn. was aimed at rekindling the spiritual energy of the Jewish nation at a time when monotheism was menaced by pagan hellenism (Dn. 7-12), so also Ap. was written to console and to strengthen Christians in the midst of persecution (Ap. 2:8-10, 12 f.; 6:9-11; 7:14; 13:11; 17:6; 20:4). In both cases, the intention and the method employed are the same.

In the time of John the persecutor was the Roman Empire, and the most pressing danger to the faithful of the province of Asia was the cult of Rome and of the emperor. The notion of the divinity of kings was an ancient and common one in the East. Alexander the Great found that his Eastern (and Egyptian) subjects regarded him as a god; his successors, both Seleucids and Ptolemies, complacently assumed divine titles – for instance, Antiochus IV was 'Epiphanes' ('God manifest'). The practice was slower to find a foothold in Rome, but was eventually seized upon as a valuable political factor. In the hellenistic age, Rome itself had attained the status of a deity, and the cult of the *Dea Roma* (the goddess Rome) had grown up. In the East it was soon accompanied by the cult of the emperor.

After his death in 44 B.C. Julius Caesar, by decree of the senate, was declared one of the divine protectors of the state. Augustus did not claim divine honors in Rome, but he was worshipped as a divinity in the East where temples were raised to him (like the temple of Augustus built by Herod the Great in Sebaste, the restored Samaria). Later emperors (notably Domitian) openly claimed divine honors during their lifetime. The imperial cult had secured a firm grip in Asia Minor and was nowhere more enthusiastically propagated.

Emperor-worship demanded that sacrifice should be offered (or incense burned) before an image of Caesar, with the declaration: *Kyrios Kaisar* – 'Caesar is Lord,' that is, divine – sheer blasphemy in Christian eyes. For Christians, Jesus Christ was *Kyrios*, and they must 'hold fast his name' (2:13), reserving that title for him alone. The readers of Ap. who were contemporaries of John, and to whom the book was addressed in the first place, were well able to understand its purpose and its veiled allusions to the contemporary situation and its polemic against the state religion.

A constant preoccupation of Ap. is the fate of the martyrs, readily understandable in the historical circumstances of the book. The readers are being encouraged to face a violent persecution in which many of them may well find death. Thus, John, time and time again, refers to the blessedness of the martyrs, and he becomes more and more explicit. In 6:9-11, the souls of those who had been slain for the witness they had borne – sacrificial victims – rest under the alter of holocausts, but they wear the white robes of victory. Then (7:9-17) they are represented as celebrating, in heaven, an everlasting Feast of Tabernacles (the most joyous of Jewish feasts). Satan has no power over them; they are in heaven and he has been cast out (12:7-11). They are the close companions of the Lamb (14:1 5); a few verses on their situation is stated in explicit terms: 'Blessed are the dead who die in the Lord! Henceforth, says the Spirit, they can rest for ever from their labors'

(14:13). Before the throne of God they sing the song of Moses, the song of a new deliverance (15:2-4). They are privileged guests at the marriage supper of the Lamb (19:9). Finally, they are those who reign with Christ for a thousand years, beyond the power of Satan (20:4-6). But, always, they are seen as 'first fruits for God and the Lamb' (14:14); they are the consecrated offerings of a mighty harvest, of the multitude of those whose names are written in the Lamb's book of life (13:8; 20:12).

4. THE PLAN   Although the unity of Ap. has often been called into question, it does seem that it really is a single work. Even the letters to the seven churches (chap. 1-3), written in a different literary form, are an integral part of the book; the whole bears the stamp of one hand. At the same time, there is an unevenness which may be accounted for, in part at any rate, by the apocalyptic form – where a strictly logical arrangement is not to be sought. In short, one may say that Ap. is structured on a plan which is discernible in its broad lines, but which is quite flexible in its details. Attempts have been made to trace an elaborate sequence within the book – to find in it, for instance, an intricate system of septets. But nothing is to be gained by imposing, from without, a strictly logical plan on a work of such imaginative power and of such deep religious feeling. Ap. has the freedom of great art.

PROLOGUE 1:1-3

A. THE LETTERS TO THE SEVEN CHURCHES 1:4 – 3:22

Introduction	1:4-8
The vision of the Son of Man	1:9-20
The Letters to the seven churches:	
I. Letter to Ephesus	2:1-7
II. Letter to Smyrna	2:8-11
III. Letter to Pergamum	2:12-17
IV. Letter to Thyatira	2:18-29
V. Letter to Sardis	3:1-6
VI. Letter to Philadelphia	3:7-13
VII. Letter to Laodicea	3:14-22

B. THE PROPHETICAL VISIONS AND EPILOGUE 4:1 – 22:21

The Church and Israel 4-11	
I. *God transmits the sealed scroll to the Lamb*	4-5
Vision of the throne of God	4
The Lamb receives the sealed scroll	5
II. *The opening of the seven seals*	6:1 – 8:1
The first four seals	6:1-8
The last three seals	6:9 – 8:1
The fifth seal	6:9-11
The sixth seal	6:12-17
The Christian martyrs	7:9-17
The seventh seal	8:1;
III. *The seven trumpets*	8:2 – 11:19
The first four trumpets	8:2-12
The prelude	8:2-6
The four trumpets	8:7-12
The three woes	8:13 – 11:19
The prelude	8:13
The first woe (fifth trumpet)	9:1-12
The second woe (sixth trumpet)	9:13-21
The little scroll	10
The Temple measured	11:1 f.
The two witnesses	11:3-13
The last woe (seventh trumpet)	11:14-19
Part II. The Church and pagan Rome 12:1 – 20:15	
I. *The dramatis personae*	12:1 – 14:5
The woman and the dragon	12
The woman and the dragon	12:1-4a
The Victory of Christ	12:4b-12
Persecution of the Church	12:13-18
The two beasts	13
The first beast	13:1-10
The false prophet	13:11-18
The companions of the Lamb	14:1-5
II. *The hour of judgment*	14:6 – 16:21
Proclamation of the hour of judgment	14:6-13
Harvest and vintage of the earth	14:14-20

	Preparatory vision of the seven last plagues	15
	The last plagues: the seven bowls	16
	The fifth bowl	16:10f
	The sixth bowl	16:12-16
	The seventh bowl	16:17-21
III.	*The chastisement of Babylon (Rome)*	17:1 – 19:10
	The great harlot	17:1-6
	Interpretation of the vision	17:7-18
	Proclamation of the fall of Babylon	18:1-8
	Dirges over Babylon	18:9-24
	The kings' lament	18:9f
	The merchants' lament	18:11-16
	The seafarers' lament	18:17-19
	The heavenly dirge	18:20-24
	Triumph in heaven	19:1-10
IV.	*The end*	19:11 – 20:15
	Victory over the beasts	19:11-21
	Blessedness of the martyrs:	
	The reign of a thousand years	20:1-6
	Victory over the dragon	20:7-10
	The last judgment	20:11-15
Part III.	The new Jerusalem 21:1 – 22:5	
	The new Jerusalem	21:1-8
	The glory of the new Jerusalem	21:9-27
	Within the new Jerusalem	22:1-5
	EPILOGUE 22:6-21	

5. THE INTERPRETATION   When the literary form of Ap. is taken into account, as it must be, a certain line of interpretation necessarily opens up – if violence is not to be done to the work. For, as an apocalypse, the book was written in view of a crisis, and it is concerned with concrete historical events. The author may well have been aware that his book would live and speak to ages yet to come, but he wrote primarily for the Christians of his own day, the communities of Asia Minor. This must be our starting-point, and to ignore the historical milieu of Ap. is to invite inevitable misinterpretation. Even granted this approach, however, there is

much that we do not fully understand and there is scope for different interpretations of the writing. Yet Ap. is one of the most fascinating books of the New Testament; and although its literary form is strange to us and although parts of it remain obscure, the book itself can be made intelligible to the modern reader. We attempt, then, to break the seven seals and open up a writing that is indeed a closed book to one who may come upon it without some explanation of its nature, its purpose and its meaning.

A. The Letters

The letters to the seven churches (chap. 1-3) have the same literary characteristics as the properly apocalyptic part of Ap. and are the work of the same author. Originally, they may have been independent of the rest, to be joined later to the apocalypse proper; as such they form an integral part of the work as we know it. But the links between the letters and the rest are so close that the independent existence of the former seems unlikely

The prologue (1:1-3) introduces Ap. as a letter of the prophet John, a letter destined to be read at the liturgical ceremonies; but the author is conscious that it is, in effect, a message from the supreme pastor of the church. The introduction (1:4-8) addresses the christian congregations to which John had ministered; it is notable for a trinitarian formula which, in christian fashion, lingers over the Son: his incarnation, death, and glory.

In a striking vision (1:9-20), John is commissioned by the glorified Son of Man to write what is to be revealed to him and to send the message to seven churches of Asia. The Messiah appears as judge (as in Dn. 7:13) and here the details of the vision have a symbolical value: he wears the long robe of priesthood, the golden cincture of royalty, the white hair of eternity. Eyes like a flame of fire represent his divine knowledge, and feet of bronze indicate stability. He holds in his right hand (that is, in his power) the seven lampstands representing the seven churches, and the stars, the angel guardians or protectors of the churches. The overall effect is one of terrifying majesty. The vision of the Son of Man effectively brings out the oracular character of the first part of Ap., for it is closely parallel to the inaugural visions of the prophets (cf. Is. 6; Jer.; Ezek. 1). But where the latter proceeded to speak in the name of Yahweh ('thus says Yahweh') John will make known the 'revelation of Jesus Christ.' And since, in the eyes of the inspired writer, the seven churches represent the universal

church, his message — the message of the Lord — has meaning for
the church until the end of time.

The seven churches are not listed haphazardly, but in order.
They were linked by a circular road that, from Ephesus, went
north to Smyrna and Pergamum and then swung southwards to
take in the others. Each church receives a judgment which is based
upon a full knowledge of its condition, both external (there are
several topical references) and spiritual. The churches receive praise
or blame (or both), usually with some qualifications, and in this
there seems to be a definite plan and progression. Ephesus receives
censure and commendation; then Smyrna, Thyatira, and Philadelphia (the even numbers) are praised — the latter with marked
warmth, while Pergamum, Sardis, and Laodicea are censured — the
latter very severely. Their chief faults are a cooling in first fervor
and a decline in charity, together with indulgence of or concessions
to Nicolaitanism, an heretical trend not easy to identify but which
seems to have some affinity with Gnosticism.

B. *The Prophetical Visions*

Ap. is certainly not concerned with the 'seven ages of the world' —
a theory popular in the Middle Ages; nor does it regard, in any
detailed manner, the future of the Church. On the other hand, certain capital stages of human history are in view. John is concerned
with the meaning of events rather then with the events themselves.
Thus he brings out the significance of the destruction of Jerusalem
in 70 A.D. and then goes on to point to the inevitable issue of the
persecution that had just begun.

A consideration of Dn. 7-12 can help us to understand Ap.
Daniel was written in the Maccabean Age; hence, it is largely concerned with events of the past. Yet, the succession of empires is
seen in relation to the purpose of the divine plan: the final establishment of the kingdom of God. That future event is not treated
in detail; it is simply foretold that the persecution will end in failure and that God will have the last word. The perspective of Ap. is
no different.

Part I *The Church and Israel* (4-11)

We may divide the central section of Ap. into two parts: 4-11 and
12:1-20:15. Though chaps. 4-11 fit into the integral plan of the
whole work, they can, in a true sense, be regarded as forming a
complete apocalypse. In 12:1 the author makes a fresh beginning

for which the reader had been prepared in 10:11; and, again, we come to an ending at 20:15. We have, then, two apocalypses, each of which stretches to an end. From chap. 12 onwards the author is concerned with the church and pagan Rome, while in chaps. 4-11 he is preoccupied with the church's relation to the chosen people. His work has about it something of the structure of the Old Testament prophetical books: first oracles against Israel and then oracles against the nations.

The opening vision of the throne of God (chap. 4) is manifestly inspired by several prophetical texts (Is. 6:1-5; Ezek. 1:4-10, 25-27; Dn. 7:9 f.). Before the throne, the 'twenty-four elders' represent the saints of Israel and the 'four living creatures' represent the created world. Then (chap. 5), 'he who was seated on the throne' – a designation of God throughout Ap. – gave to the Lamb the sealed scroll which he held in his right hand (a transfer of power). The chapter ends with the first of the heavenly liturgies that recur so frequently in the book; these are either early christian hymns or were modeled on them. The scroll contained the divine decree against an Israel that had not believed in Christ. As a sealed book it may well be the Old Testament: 'To this day whenever Moses is read a veil hangs over their minds' (2 Cor. 3:15).

The breaking of the seals unleashes a series of plagues (6:1-8:1), a series which follows the pattern of events in the synoptic apocalypse (Mk. 13 parr.): war, strife among nations, famine, pestilence, persecution, cosmic phenomena (earthquakes, eclipses, etc.). The description of the first four, war and its attendant evils (6:1 8), is inspired by the visions of the four horsemen and the four chariots of Zech. 1:8-11; 6:1-8. At the breaking of the fifth seal, the martyrs appear – here the martyrs of the Old Law (6:9-11); and the cosmic phenomena appear at the opening of the sixth seal. Before the last seal is broken, the servants of God are signed with the seal of the living God – one hundred and forty-four thousand of them (7:1-8): the saved remnant of Israel. The great multitude from all nations, celebrating a Feast of Tabernacles in heaven (7:9-17), seem to be christian martyrs, the 'fellow servants and brethren' of the Jewish martyrs of 6:9-11. A solemn silence precedes the second series of plagues (8:1).

The opening of the seventh seal marks a beginning rather than an end; it heralds a fresh series of plagues. The trumpets are presented in much the same way as the seals: the first four (8:7-12) are described in a few verses, while the others unfold at greater length, interspersed with other visions. The plagues of 8:7-12 strike only *one-third* of the earth and of the heavenly bodies, and again in 9:15 only one-third of mankind is stricken by the sixth plague, just as the seals struck 'a fourth of the earth' (6:8); there is no such qualification in the parallel plagues of bowls which are aimed at the pagan world. We may seek the reason for this difference in the prophetic doctrine of the remnant (compare the 'third' of Ezek. 5:1-4; Zech. 13:8 f.). It follows that the plagues of bowls are not a doublet of the plagues of trumpets: the former are inflicted on the adorers of the beast, while the latter are closely related to the judgment of God on an unbelieving Israel executed through the destruction of Jerusalem. Since the seals are the prelude and preparation of trumpets, they must be understood in the same context. The first two 'woes' (fifth and sixth trumpets) are a highly-colored development of the plague of locusts (Ex. 10:12-15), already utilized in striking fashion by Joel (1:6-2:11) — a passage that immediately influenced John.

Chapter 10 opens with a vision of a mighty angel coming down from heaven wrapped in a cloud and with a rainbow over his head. He had a little scroll open in his hand and he set his right foot in the sea and his left foot on the land (vv. 1 f.). In 5:2, the invitation of a 'strong angel' led to the opening of the sealed scroll: there is a parallel between angels and scrolls. The angel of chap. 10, with traits of the Son of Man of Daniel (Dn. 7:14), is more majestic than the other; of giant stature, he stands on sea and land because his message is for all mankind. This is in contrast to Ap. 5:1-12 where the title given to Christ (the lion of the tribe of Judah, the root of David), and the role of the twenty-four elders (the saints of the Old Law), point to the chosen people. The sealed book is the Old Testament, especially the prophetic oracles, to which Christ has supplied the key. The little book (less extensive than the Old Testament, but open and universalist in scope) is the message of Jesus.

In 10:3-7, two antithetical scenes are followed by a new prophetic investiture (parallel to that of 1:9-20), patently based on the investiture of Ezekiel (Ap. 10:8-10; cf. Ezek. 3:1-3). Then (Ap. 10:11), John is told: 'You must again prophesy about many peoples and nations and tongues and kings.' In the context of these chapters, this means that he is called to a new mission: he must prophesy as he had not done up to now. The message of the sealed scroll bears directly on the chosen people (cf. 7:4-8), and it is only from chapter 12 onward that there is question of 'peoples and nations and tongues' (cf. 12:5; 13:7; 14:6, 8; 15:4; 17:12). It seems that the purpose of chapter 10 is to introduce the period of preaching to the gentiles and to bring out the paradox of the gospel: the end is near (we live in the last age), and yet the final episode may be long delayed.

A study of chapter 11 appears to confirm the interpretation of Ap. 4-11 in terms of Israel and the Church. John received a measuring rod and was bidden to measure the temple and the altar and the worshippers – what is thus measured is under God's special protection. But he must 'cast out the court that is outside' the temple for 'it is given over to the nations, and they will trample over the holy city for forty-two months' (11:1 f.). Lk. 21:24 springs to mind at once: unbelieving Jerusalem 'will be trodden down by the gentiles, until the times of the gentiles are fulfilled.' The measured temple represents the Church, and the outer court is the rejected synagogue; John refers to the final break between Church and synagogue brought about by the catastrophe of A.D. 70. The true temple of God, which Titus could not destroy, was constituted in the first place by the Jews faithful to Christ, the messianic remnant. The unbelieving Jews, until then rather like the outer court of the true temple, were now no longer part of it. However, the prospect is not one of unrelieved gloom: the court will be trampled for 'forty-two months'; this is nothing else than the 'time, two times, and half a time' of Dn. 7:25. In Ap., the expression, or its equivalent, is a symbolic designation of the temporary time of persecution which separates Christians from the perfect establishment of the kingdom of God. The sufferings of the unconverted Jewish world will last just so long – 'until the times of the gentiles are fulfilled' (Lk. 21:24). Then, with Paul (Rm. 11:25 f.), we can look to the salvation of Israel.

The two witnesses (Ap. 11:3-13) are modeled on Elijah (power to bring about drought: v. 6) and Moses (power to turn water into blood and to smite the earth with every plague: v. 6). Their ministry lasts for 1,260 days, that is to say, the forty-two months of v. 3 – the whole time of the Church. It appears that the witnesses are the incarnation of the testimony – from the Law and the prophets – which the church bears to Christ in the Jewish world. Verse 7, which abruptly introduces the beast, is best understood in terms of the final assault on the church. For, indeed, the death and speedy resurrection of the witnesses will happen at the end of the forty-two months – they are to testify for 1,260 days (v. 3), and they are slain only 'when they have finished their testimony' (v. 7) – and the victory of the beast is ephemeral. One tenth of the city (Jerusalem) was destroyed and seven thousand were killed (v. 13), but the rest 'gave glory to God.' This typically Jewish expression signifies the conversion of Israel at the end of 'the times of the gentiles.'

In Rm. 11:25 f., the conversion of Israel, coming after that of the gentiles, seems to mark the culminating point of the divine plan. The same is true here. Now is the end: then the seventh trumpet can sound to announce the end of the world and the inauguration of the kingdom of God and of his Christ. Significantly, the canticle (Ap. 11:17 f.) is put in the mouths of the twenty-four elders, for its language is thoroughly Jewish. Finally, God's temple was opened and the heavenly ark of the covenant was seen within it (11:19). It seems, then, that the historical background of Ap. 11 is the catastrophe of 70 A.D. which brought about the final separation of church and synagogue. This explains the artificial antedating of Ap.; for in 17:10 f., the sixth of a list of seven emperors in whose reign the writing is set is, most probably, Vespasian. By using the customary apocalyptic procedure, John could thus place himself before the destruction of Jerusalem and from that vantage point bring out the theological significance of the event.

We may regard chaps. 4-11 of Ap., with their series of seals and of trumpets, as no more than a development of the data of the synoptic apocalypse. It is an explanation based on the history of the events foretold in the synoptics: the Jewish war and the destruction of Jerusalem which, when Ap. was written, were events of the past, events of great significance. Luke, we have seen, has distinguished two periods of salvation history: the time of Israel; the time of Christ and of his Church. The Apocalypse is not a gospel, and the author does not insist on the time of Christ; but he does discern the time of Israel and the time of the church, each period closing with a divine judgment.

Part II *The Church and Pagan Rome*
(12:1 – 20:15)

This second part, although it offers its own particular problems, has met with a greater measure of agreement in its general interpretation than the preceding part. The historical background is undoubtedly the persecution of the church by Rome, and the precise occasion of the persecution is the Church's refusal to countenance Caesar-worship; the two beasts of chap. 13 represent Rome and the religion of Rome. Here is John's answer to the blasphemous pretentions of the emperors, which must end in disaster: Rome will go the way of Babylon.

Chapter 12 falls into three parts: (1) a diptych which introduces the two symbolical figures, the woman and the dragon (vv. 1-4a); (2) the assault on Christ and his victory (vv. 4b-12); (3) the persecution of Christians (vv. 13-17). The woman symbolizes the people of God which brings forth the messianic age and the Messiah. The dragon is the 'ancient serpent' of Gn. 3: once again the woman and Satan are face-to-face. The dragon seeks to destroy her son, but the child was snatched out of his power to the throne of God – a reference to the ascension and the triumph of Christ, which will bring about the fall of the dragon. Meanwhile, the woman (the people of God of the Old Testament which, having given Christ to the world, thereby became the Christian church) finds refuge in the desert where she is cared for by God for 1,260 days, that is the equivalent of forty-two months or three and a half years – the whole earthly duration of the Church. The fall of the dragon is dramatized in 12:7-12; and although Michael has cast Satan out of heaven, it really is the victory of Christ (vv. 10 f.). The martyrs (who represent all Christians) share in the victory of Christ; death has set them free from the devil's power. Thus, in heaven there is a great rejoicing; but, on earth, Satan can still, for a little while, give vent to his wrath.

The dragon's attempt to destroy the woman, implicit in 12:6, is described in 12:13-16. She is protected for 'a time, two times, and half a time.' (cf. 12:6); the Church, as such, is under God's special care all the time of its historical duration. However, the faithful on earth are vulnerable: Satan, through his instruments, can make war on them; they will be persecuted and put to death. But the message of Ap. is precisely that those who are steadfast to the end share in the glorious victory of the Lamb.

The two beasts of chap. 13, instruments of Satan, are Rome and the imperial religion in the service of Rome. The latter induces 'the inhabitants of the earth' (a term that corresponds to the *kosmos* of the Fourth Gospel and the Johannine Epistles: the unbelieving world) to worship the beast and to bear its mark. The number of the beast (13:18) stands for its name which can be discovered by the process of gematria (that is, by addition of the numerical value of the letters of his name – in Hebrew and Greek, in place of numerals, the letters of the alphabet have a numerical value). In Hebrew, Nero Caesar (*nrwn qsr*) gives 666, the identification is probable, but not certain.

In deliberate and striking antithesis to the beast and his followers stand the Lamb and his companions, bearing on their foreheads the name of the Lamb and of his Father (14:1-5). The 144,000 are not those of 7:4-8, the remnant of Israel; they are instead the faithful remnant of the new Israel – the martyrs. The designation 'virgins' must be understood in a metaphorical sense. The Old Testament prophets, especially Hosea, Jeremiah and Ezekiel, frequently represented the covenant of Sinai as a marriage of God with his people; therefore all idolatry was regarded as adultery or fornication. In Ap. the 144,000 are contrasted with the followers of the beast precisely because they have not adored the beast but have remained faithful to the Lamb. They have remained virgins because they have not given themselves to the cult of the beast but have clung to God.

Satan, the two beasts and their followers the 'inhabitants of the earth,' the woman and her children, the Lamb and his companions – the dramatis personae of the great eschatological struggle – have been introduced. Now comes the proclamation of the hour of judgment (14:6-13) followed by the harvest and vintage of the earth (14:14-20). The whole passage is proleptic; it anticipates events yet to come and summarizes the coming judgments.

The seven plagues *which are the last* (15:1) – and hence distinct from the plagues of the trumpets – are announced in chap. 15; the following chapter shows their execution. The bowls (like the trumpets) are based on the plagues of Egypt, but this time the chastisement is universal and definitive: all the worshippers of the beast and the persecutors of Christians are stricken. Moreover, they are already gathered at Armageddon ('the mountain of Megiddo': ever since the defeat of Josiah at Megiddo, 2 Kg. 23:29 f., it had remained a symbol of disaster) to await their destruction (19:17-21).

Although in 16:19 – 'The great city was split into three parts' – the fall of Rome is indicated, the end of that city cannot be treated so casually. The whole of chap. 17 is given over to a description of Babylon – the goddess Rome – seated on the satanic beast; the fall of Rome is solemnly proclaimed in 18:1-8.

Then follows a series of dirges (18:9 24) and a triumphal liturgy in heaven (19:1-10). After the fall of Rome, the end comes swiftly. The rider on the white horse leads out the armies of heaven (19:11-16) against the two beasts and their followers. Victory is complete: the two beasts are cast into the 'lake of fire' – the place of final punishment – and their followers are slain with the sword (19:17-21). Now Satan alone is left.

In 20:1-10 we find that two events are juxtaposed: on the one hand is the overthrow of Satan, in two phases; on the other hand there is the reign of a thousand years. Chapter 7 of Daniel furnishes the background of the vision. The first condemnation of the dragon coincides with the moment of judgment when dominion is given to the Son of Man (Dn. 7.9-14); henceforth the power is taken from the beast and belongs to the saints of the Most High. Thus, in Ap., while Christ and his faithful reign, the devil will remain powerless in their regard, imprisoned in the abyss, his 'place.' The binding of Satan for a thousand years also coincides with his downfall described in the parallel passage Ap. 12:7-12 – Satan, the 'accuser of our brethren,' is cast out of heaven by the victory of Christ; he can no longer accuse or harm the faithful ones who are in heaven with Christ.

John has made use of the Jewish tradition of a temporary messianic reign (his 'thousand years') to symbolize the truth that the martyrs already reign with Christ. The thousand years, then, is a symbol – it has no time value. It must be interpreted as a symbol, and the reality which it typifies must be sought out. The reign of a thousand years signifies the reign of the martyrs with Christ, who has won the final victory for them. Satan is bound for a thousand years: he cannot touch the martyrs, those who 'have conquered him by the blood of the Lamb' (12:11). If he is represented as being set loose at the end of the thousand years, this is due to the literary construction of the passage and to the image employed; and he is loosed not to take effective action against the elect, but to hasten his own doom. The conquest of all the powers hostile to God is followed by the general resurrection of the dead and the last judgment (20:11-15). With the conquest of Satan, 'the prince of this world' (Jn. 12:31), the present world order has come to an end.

Part III *The New Jerusalem* (21:1 – 22:5)

The central part of Ap. ends with the vision of a new heaven and a new earth, the setting of the new Jerusalem. The apocalyptic drama nears its end. The former creation has passed away and all evil has been destroyed; now is the final phase of God's plan. The book closes with a magnificent vision of the new Jerusalem, the heavenly city, the veritable kingdom of God. Certain details in Ap. 21:24-27, which seem rather to refer to the historical stage of the church (and not to the heavenly Jerusalem), may be explained, in their present context, by the fact that the author is echoing traditional concepts and imagery. One of the seven angels of the bowls had shown John the great harlot (17:1); one of the seven now steps forward to show him the bride. The bride image, however, is not developed but yields to that of the holy city. We might expect the glowing description of the city (21:16-21) to be followed by a particularly striking description of its temple (the Temple was the glory of the earthly Jerusalem). Instead — a brilliant touch — we learn that there is no temple, nor any need of one: God himself dwells there, and the Lamb (21:22). Consistently, the waters which in Ezek. 47 flow from the temple, here flow from 'the throne of God and of the Lamb' (22:1). It is the river of the first paradise and the tree of life is found again (22:2). There, the elect shall look upon the face of God and of the Lamb and shall reign for ever and ever.

Like the Fourth Gospel and 1 John, this book also closes with an appendix or epilogue (22:6-21), which gives the last words of the angel, the seer, and Lord. John ends his work with the prayer of the early Christians: *Marana tha* ('our Lord, come! ') and a final blessing on the saints, the faithful of Christ.

---

[1] R. E. Brown, *The Gospel According to St. John* 2 vols. (New York: Doubleday 1966), XXXIV-XXXIX

[2] R. E. Brown, Op. cit., XXXVIIIF.

[3] R. Schnackenburg, *The Gospel According to St. John*, Vol. 1 (New York: Herder & Herder 1968), 19-25.

[4] R. Schnackenburg, *op. cit.*, 41-43.

[5] R. E. Brown, op. cit., CXXXVIII-CXLIV, 545-547.

[6] R. Schnackenburg, *op. cit.*, 114-118.

[7] C. H. Dodd, *Historical Tradition in the Fourth Gospel* (New York: Cambridge University Press 1963), 8, 423.

[8] R. E. Brown, *Op. cit.*, 1139.

[9] A. Feuillet, 'The Structure of First John,' *Biblical Theology Bulletin* 3(1973), 194-216.

[10] A. Feuillet, *art. cit.*, 214f.

[11] M.-E. Boismard, *L'Apocalypse* (BJ), (Paris: Cerf 1959[3]), 8f.

Bibliography

This select bibliography has been restricted to works in English.

GENERAL

A. One-Volume Commentaries and Dictionaries of the Bible.

Bauer, J. B. (ed.), *Encyclopedia of Biblical Theology*, 3 vols., New York: Sheed & Ward, 1970.

Black, M. and Rowley, H. H., eds., *Peake's Commentary of the Bible*, London: Nelson, 1962.

Brown, R. E., Fitzmyer, J. A., Murphy, R. E., eds., *The Jerome Biblical Commentary*, Englewood Cliffs, N.J.: Prentice-Hall, 1968.

Buttrick, G. A., ed., *The Interpreter's Dictionary of the Bible*, 4 vols., Nashville: Abingdon, 1962.

, *The Interpreter's Bible*, 6 vols. Nashville: Abingdon, 1951-1957.

Fuller, R. C., ed., *A New Catholic Commentary on Holy Scripture*, London: Nelson, 1969.

Hartmann, L. F., *Encyclopedic Dictionary of the Bible*, New York: McGraw Hill, 1963.

Kittel, G., Friedrich, G., eds., *Theological Dictionary of the Bible*, 9 vols., Translated and edited by G. W. Bromiley, Grand Rapids: Eerdmans, 1969-1974.

Laymon, C. M., *The Interpreter's One-Volume Commentary on the Bible*, Nashville: Abingdon, 1971.

Léon-Dufour, X., ed., *Dictionary of Biblical Theology*, New York: Desclee, 1973².

McKenzie, J. L., *Dictionary of the Bible*, Milwaukee: Bruce, 1965,

The Power and the Wisdom. An Interpretation of the New Testament, Milwaukee: Bruce, 1965.

Richardson, A., ed., *A Theological Word Book of the Bible*, London: SCM, 1950.

B. Introductions

Bornkamm, G., *The New Testament: A Guide to Its Writings*, Philadelphia: Fortress Press, 1973.

Davies, W. D., *Invitation to the New Testament*, London: Darton, Longman & Todd, 1967.

Grant, R. M., *A Historical Introduction to the New Testament*, London: Collins, 1963.

Guthrie, D., *New Testament Introduction*, Downers Grove, Ill.: Inter-Varsity Press, 1970.

Harrington, W. J., *Record of the Fulfillment: The New Testament*, Chicago: The Priory Press, 1965.

Hunter, A. M., *Introducing the New Testament*, London: SCM, 1972[3].

Kee, H. C., Young, F. W., Froehlich, K, *Understanding the New Testament*, Englewood Cliffs, N.J.: Prentice-Hall, 1973[3].

Kümmel, W. G., *Introduction to the New Testament*, New York: Abingdon Press, 1966.

Marxsen, W., *Introduction to the New Testament*, Philadelphia: Fortress Press, 1968.

McNeile, A. H., *An Introduction to the Study of the New Testament* New York: Oxford University Press, 1953[2].

Moule, C. F. D., *The Birth of the New Testament*, London: A. & C. Black, 1966.

Robert, A., Feuillet, A., eds., *Introduction to the New Testament*, New York: Desclee, 1966.

Unnik, W. C. van, *The New Testament*, London: Collins, 1964.
Wikenhauser, A., *New Testament Introduction*, New York: Herder & Herder, 1958.

C. New Testament Theology

Bonsirven, J., *Theology of the New Testament*, London: Burns & Oates, 1963.

Brown, R. E., *Jesus, God and Man*, Milwaukee: Bruce, 1967.
Bruce, F. F., *The Message of the New Testament*, Grand Rapids: Eerdams, 1973.

Bultmann, R., *Theology of the New Testament*, 2 vols., London: SCM, 1952, 1955.

Conzelmann, H., *An Outline of the Theology of the New Testament*, London: SCM, 1969.

Cullmann, O., *Salvation in History*, London: SCM, 1967.
SCM, 1959. , *The Christology of the New Testament*, London,

Dodd, C. H., *The Apostolic Preaching and its Developments*, London: Hodder & Stoughton, 1963[3].

According to the Scriptures, London: Nisbet, 1952.

Fuller, R. H., *The Foundations of New Testament Theology*, New York: Scribner's, 1965.

Grant, F. C., *An Introduction to New Testament Thought*, New York: Abingdon Press, 1950.

Harrington, W. J., *The Path of Biblical Theology*, Dublin: Gill & Macmillan, 1973.

Hunter, A. M., *Introducing New Testament Theology*, London: SCM, 1957.

Jeremias, J., *New Testament Theology* I. The Proclamation of Jesus London: SCM, 1971.

Morgan, R., *The Nature of New Testament Theology*, London: SCM, 1973.

Richardson, A., *An Introduction to the Theology of the New Testament*, London: SCM, 1958.

Schelkle, K. H., *Theology of the New Testament* 3 vols., Collegeville, Minn. Liturgical Press, 1971-1973.

Schnackenburg, R., *New Testament Theology Today*, London: Chapman, 1963. , *The Moral Teaching of the New Testament*, New York: Herder & Herder, 1955.

Spicq. C., *Agape in the New Testament*, 3 vols. St. Louis: B. Herder, 1963, 1965, 1966.

Stauffer, E., *New Testament Theology*, London: SCM, 1955.

Taylor, V., *The Person of Jesus in New Testament Teaching*, London: Macmillan, 1959.

Vawter, B., *This Man Jesus*. An Essay Toward a New Testament Christology, Garden City, N.Y.: Doubleday, 1973.

D. General

Barrett, C. K., *New Testament Essays*, London: S.P.C.K., 1972.

Batey, R., ed., *New Testament Essays*, London: SCM, 1970.

Benoit, P., *Jesus and the Gospel* Vol. 1, N.Y., Herder & Herder, 1973.

Black, M., *An Aramaic Approach to the Gospel and Acts*, Oxford: University Press, 1954[2].

Bright, L., ed., *Scripture Discussion Commentary* (NT), London: Sheed & Ward, 1971.

Brown, R.E., *New Testament Essays*, Milwaukee: Bruce, 1965.

Derrett, J. D., *Law in the New Testament*, London: Darton, Longman & Todd, 1970.

Fitzmyer, J. A., *Essays on the Semitic Background of the New Testament*, London: Chapman, 1971.

Fuller, R. H., ed., *The New Testament in Current Study*, New York: Scribner's, 1971.

Jeremias, J., *The Central Message of the New Testament*, New York: Scribner's, 1965.

Leaney, A. R. C., *The New Testament*, London: Hodder & Stoughton, 1972.

Manson, T. W., *Studies in the Gospels and Epistles*, Philadelphia: Westminster Press 1962.

McKenzie, J. L., *New Testament for Spiritual Reading*, 25 vols, London: Sheed & Ward, 1971.

McNamara, M., *Targum and Testament*, Shannon: Irish University Press, 1972.

Neill, S., *The Interpretation of the New Testament* 1861-1961, Oxford: University Press, 1966.

Quesnell, Q., *This Good News*, Milwaukee: Bruce, 1964.

Taylor, V., *New Testament Essays*, London: Epworth Press, 1970.

CHAPTER ONE

Bammel, E., ed., *The Trial of Jesus*, London: SCM, 1970.

Benoit, P., *The Passion and Resurrection of Jesus Christ*, London: Darton, Longman & Todd, 1969.

Blinzler, J., *The Trial of Jesus*, Westminster: Newman, 1959.

Briggs, R. C., *Interpreting the New Testament Today*, Nashville: Abingdon, 1973.

Brown, R. E., *The Virginal Conception and Bodily Resurrection of Jesus*, New York: Paulist Press, 1973.

Bultmann, R., *The History of the Synoptic Tradition*, New York: Harper & Row, 1963.

Butler, B. C., *The Originality of St. Matthew*. A Critique of the Two-Document Hypothesis, Cambridge: University Press, 1951.

Dibelius, M., *From Tradition to Gospel*, Greenwood, S.C.: Attic, 1972.

Conzelmann, H., *Jesus*, Philadelphia, Fortress Press, 1973.

Dodd, C. H., *History and the Gospel*, London: Hodder & Stoughton, 1964[2].

    , *About the Gospels*, New York: Cambridge U.P., 1952.

    , *The Parables of the Kingdon*, New York: Scribner's, 1961.

    , *The Founder of Christianity*, London: Collins, 1971.

Evans, C. F., *Resurrection and the New Testament*, London: SCM, 1970.

Freyne, S., *The Twelve: Disciples and Apostles*, London: Sheed & Ward, 1968.

Fuller, R. H., *Interpreting the Miracles*, London: SCM, 1966.

    , *The Formation of the Resurrection Narratives*, London: S.P.C.K., 1972.

Harrington, W. J., *A Key to the Parables*, New York: Paulist Press, 1964.

    , *Stories Told By Jesus*, New York: Alba House, 1974.

Hunter, A. M., *The Works and Words of Jesus*, London: SCM, 1950.

    , *The Parables Then and Now*, London: SCM, 1971.

Jeremias, J., *The Parables of Jesus*, London: SCM, 1972[3].

    , *The Prayers of Jesus*, London: SCM, 1967.

Jones, G. V., *The Art and Truth of the Parables*, London: S.P.C.K., 1964.

Lightfoot, R. H., *History and Interpretation in the Gospels*, London: Hodder & Stoughton, 1935.

Linnemann, E., *Parables of Jesus*. Introduction and Exposition, London: S.P.C.K., 1969.

Manson, T.W., *The Sayings of Jesus*, London: SCM, 1949.

Montefiore, C. G., *The Synoptic Gospels*, 2 vols., New York: Ktav, 1968[3].

Nineham, D. E., *Studies in the Gospel*, Oxford: B. Blackwell, 1955.

O'Collins, G., *The Resurrection of Jesus Christ*, Valley Forge, Pa.: Judson, 1973.

Perrin, N., *What is Redaction Criticism?*, Philadelphia: Fortress Press, 1970.

    , *Rediscovering the Teaching of Jesus*, New York: Harper & Row, 1967.

Richardson, A., *The Miracle Stories of the Gospels*, London: SCM, 1941.

Robinson, J. M., *A New Quest of the Historical Jesus*, Naperville, Ill.: Allenson, 1959.

Rohde, J., *Rediscovering the Teaching of the Evangelists*, London: SCM, 1969.

Sloyan, G. S., *Jesus on Trial*. The development of the Passion Narratives, Philadelphia: Fortress Press, 1973.

Streeter, B. H., *The Four Gospels*, A Study of Origins, New York: St. Martin's Press, 1930[4].

Taylor, V., *The Formation of the Gospel Tradition*, New York: St. Martin's Press, 1933.

Trocmé, E., *Jesus as Seen by His Contemporaries*, Philadelphia: Westminster, 1973.

Vawter, B., *The Four Gospels*.   An Introduction, Garden City, N.Y.: Doubleday, 1967.

Via, D. O., *The Parables*. Their Literary and Existentialist Dimension, Philadelphia: Fortress Press, 1967.

CHAPTER TWO

Ambrozic, A. M., *The Hidden Kingdom*. A Redaction Critical Study of the references to the Kingdom of God in Mark's Gospel, Washington, D.C.: C.B.A., 1972.

Beasley-Murray, G. A., *A Commentary on Mark 13*, London: Macmillan, 1957.

Best, E., *The Temptation and the Passion*, Cambridge: U.P., 1965.

Burkill, T. A., *The Formation of St. Mark's Gospel*, Ithaca-London: Cornell U.P., 1972.

Freyne, S., Wansbrough, H., *Mark and Matthew*, London: Sheed & Ward, 1971.

Lightfoot, R. H., *The Gospel Message of St. Mark*, Oxford: U.P., 1950.

Martin, R., *Mark: Evangelist and Theologian*, Grand Rapids: Zondervan, 1973.

Marxsen, W., *Mark the Evangelist*, Nashville: Abingdon, 1969.

Neirynck, F., *Duality in Mark*. Contributions to a Study of the Markan Redaction, Leuven; U.P., 1972.

Nineham, D. E., *Saint Mark*, London: Pelican Books, 1963.

Rawlinson, A. E., *The Gospel According to St. Mark*, London: Methuen, 1925.

Robinson, J. M., *The Problem of History in Mark*, London: SCM, 1957.

Schmid, J., *The Gospel According to Mark*, Cork: Mercier Press, 1968.

Schnackenburg, R., *The Gospel according to St. Mark* 2 Vols., New York: Herder & Herder: 1971.

Schweizer, E., *The Good News According to Mark*, London: S.P.C.K., 1971.

Swete, H. D., *The Gospel According to St. Mark*, London: Macmillan, 1927[3].

Taylor, V., *The Gospel According to St. Mark*, London: Macmillan, 1966[2].

Weeden, T. J., *Mark. Traditions in Conflict*, Philadelphia: Fortress Press, 1971.

Wrede, W., *The Messianic Secret*, Greenwood, S. C.: Attic, 1971.

CHAPTER THREE

Albright, W. F., Mann, C. S., *Matthew*, Garden City, N.Y.: Doubleday, 1971.

Allen, W. C., *The Gospel According to St. Matthew*, Edinburgh: Clark, 1912[3].

Bornkamm, G., Barth, G., Held, H. J., *Tradition and Interpretation in Matthew*, London: SCM, 1963.

Davies, W. D., *The Setting of the Sermon on the Mount*, New York: Cambridge U.P., 1964.

Ellis, P. F., *Matthew – His Mind and His Message*, Collegeville, Minn.: Liturgical Press, 1974.

Fenton, J. C., *Saint Matthew*, London: Pelican Books, 1963.

Filson, F. V., *The Gospel according to St. Matthew*, New York: Harper & Row, 1971[2].

McNeile, A. H., *The Gospel according to St. Matthew*, London: Macmillan 1915.

Plummer, A., *An Exegetical Commentary on the Gospel according to St. Matthew*, Grand Rapids: Eerdmans, 1953

Schnackenburg, R., *God's Rule and Kingdom*, New York: Herder & Herder, 1963.

Stendahl, K., *The School of St. Matthew*, Uppsala: 1954.

Trilling W., *The Gospel according to St. Matthew* 2 vols., London: Shaeed & Ward, 1971.

CHAPTER FOUR

Barrett, C. K, *Luke the Historian in Recent Study*, London: Epworth Press, 1961.

Browning, W. R. E., *The Gospel according to St. Luke*, New York: Macmillan, 1960.

Cadbury, H. J., *The Making of Luke-Acts*, New York: Macmillan, 1927.

Caird, G. B., *Saint Luke*, London: Pelican Books, 1963.

Conzelmann, H., *The Theology of St. Luke*, New York: Harper & Row, 1960.

Creed, J. M., *The Gospel according to St. Luke*, New York: St. Martin's Press, 1965.

Drury, J., *The Gospel of Luke*, New York: Macmillan, 1973.

Flender, H., *St. Luke: Theologian of Redemptive History*, London: S.P.C.K., 1967.

Harrington, W. J., *The Gospel According to St. Luke*, Westminster: Newman, 1967.

Keck, L. E., Martyn, J. L., *Studies in Luke-Acts*, London: S.P.C.K., 1968.

Leaney, A. R. C., *A Commentary on the Gospel according to St. Luke*, New York: Harper & Row, 1958.

Plummer, A., *The Gospel according to St. Luke*, Edinburgh: Clark, 1922[5].

Taylor, V., *The Passion Narrative of St. Luke*. A Critical and Historical Investigation, Cambridge: U.P., 1972.

Tinsley, E. J., *The Gospel according to Luke*, New York:

CHAPTER FIVE

Blaiklock, E. M., *The Acts of the Apostles*, London: Tyndale Press, 1959.

Blunt, A. W. F., *The Acts of the Apostles* Oxford: U.P., 1934.

Bruce, F. F., *The Acts of the Apostles*, Grand Rapids: Eerdmans, 1960[2].

Clark, A. C., *The Acts of the Apostles* (1933), New York: O.U.P., 1970.

Conzelmann, H., *History of Primitive Christianity*, Nashville: Abingdon, 1973.

Davies, W. D., *Christian Origins and Judaism*, London: Darton, Longman and Todd, 1962.

Dupont, J., *The Sources of Acts*, New York: Herder & Herder, 1964.

Ehrhardt, A., *The Acts of the Apostles*, Manchester: U.P., 1969.

Filson, F. V., *A New Testament History*. The Story of the Emerging Church, New York: 1964.

Fitzmyer, J. A., *Jewish Christianity in Acts in the Light of the Qumran Scrolls*, London: Chapman, 1971,

Foakes-Jackson, F. J., *The Acts of the Apostles*, New York: Harper & Row, 1931.

Foakes-Jackson, F. J., Lake, K., *The Beginnings of Christianity* 1. London: Macmillan, 1933.

Goulder, M. D., *Type and History in Acts*, London: S.P.C.K., 1964.

Haenchen, E., *The Acts of the Apostles. A Commentary*, Philadelphia: Westminster, 1971.

Hunter, A. M., *The Gospel According to St. Paul*, London: SCM, 1966.

Knox, W. L., *The Acts of the Apostles*, New York: C.U.P., 1948.

Kürzinger, J., *The Acts of the Apostles*, 2 vols., N.Y.: Herder & Herder, 1969

Munck, J., *The Acts of the Apostles*, Garden City, N.J.: Double-day, 1967.

Neil, W., *The Truth About the Early Church*, London: Hodder & Stoughton, 1970.

_____ , *The Acts of the Apostles*, Greenwood, S.C.: Attic, 1973.

O'Neill, J. C., *The Theology of Acts in its Historical Setting*, London: S.P.C.K., 1970.

Ramsay, W. M., *St. Paul the Traveler and the Roman Citizen*, Grand Rapids: Baker, 1960.

Williams, C. S. C., *The Acts of the Apostles*, London: A. & C. Black, 1964².

CHAPTER SIX

Abbott, T. K., *The Epistles to the Ephesians and to the Colossians*, Naperville, Ill.: Allenson, 1956.

Amiot, F., *The Key Concepts of St. Paul*, New York: Herder & Herder, 1962.

Barrett, C. K., *The Epistle to the Romans*, New York: Harper & Row, 1959³.

_____ , *The First Epistle to the Corinthians; The Second Epistle to the Corinthians*, New York: Harper & Row, 1971², 1970.

_____ , *The Signs of an Apostle*, Philadelphia: Fortress, 1972.

_____ , *The Pastoral Epistles*, Oxford: Clarendon, 1963.

Beare, F. W., *A Commentary on the Epistle to the Philippians*, New York: Harper & Row, 1970³.

Blaiklock, E. M., *Romans*, Grand Rapids: Eerdmans, 1971.

—————, *The Pastoral Epistles*, Grand Rapids: Zondervan, 1972.

Bligh, J., *Galatians*. A Discussion of St. Paul's Epistle, London: 1968.

Bornkamm, G., *Paul*, New York: Harper & Row, 1971.

Bruce, F. F., *The Epistle to the Colossians*, Grand Rapids: Eerdmans, 1957.

—————, *The Epistle of Paul to the Romans*, London: Tyndale Press, 1971².

Buchanan, G. W., *To the Hebrews*, Garden City, N.Y.: Doubleday, 1972.

Cerfaux, L., *Christ in the Theology of St. Paul*; *The Church in the Theology of St. Paul*; *The Christian in the Theology of St. Paul*, New York: Herder & Herder, 1959, 1959, 1967.

Dibelius, M., Conzelmann, H., *A Commentary on the Pastoral Epistles*, Philadelphia: Fortress Press, 1972.

Dodd, C. H., *The Epistle of St. Paul to the Romans*, London: Collins, 1959².

Fitzmyer, J., *Pauline Theology*. A Brief Sketch, Englewood Cliffs, N.J.: Prentice-Hall, 1967.

Foulkes, F., *Epistle of Paul to the Ephesians*, London: Tyndale, 1971².

Gnilka, J., Mussner, F., *The Epistle to the Philippians; The Epistle to the Colossians*, New York: Herder & Herder, 1970.

Grayston, K., *The Letters of Paul to the Philippians and to the Thessalonians*, Cambridge: U.P., 1967.

Grossouw, W., *In Christ*. A Sketch of the Theology of St. Paul, Westminster, Md.: Newman Press, 1959.

Guthrie, D., *Pastoral Epistles*, London: Tyndale, 1971².

Hanson, A. T., *The Pastoral Letters*, New York: C.U.P., 1966.

—————, *Studies in the Pastoral Epistles, London: S.P.C.K.,* 1968.

Hunter, A. M., *The Epistle to the Romans* London: SCM, 1968.

Kelly, J. N. D., *The Pastoral Epistles*, New York: Harper & Row, 1963.

Kertelge, K., *The Epistle to the Romans*, New York: Herder & Herder, 1970.

Lock, W., *The Pastoral Epistles*, Naperville, Ill.: Allenson, 1959.

Lohse, E., *A Commentary on the Epistles to the Colossians and to Philemon* Philadelphia: Fortress, 1971.

Manson, W., *The Epistle to the Hebrews*, London: Hodder & Stoughton, 1951.

Martin, R. P., *The Epistle of Paul to the Philippians*, London: Tyndale Press, 1971[2].

Minear, P. S., *The Obedience of Faith*. The Purpose of Paul in the Epistle to the Romans, London: SCM, 1971.

Moffatt, J., *The Epistle to the Hebrews*, Naperville, Ill.: Allenson, 1963.

Montefiore, H. W., *The Epistle to the Hebrews*, New York: Harper & Row, 1964.

Morris, L., *Epistles of Paul to the Thessalonians*, London: Tyndale Press, 1971[2].

Moore, A. L., *I and II Thessalonians*, London: Nelson, 1969.

Moule, C. F. D., *The Epistles of St. Paul to the Colossians and to Philemon*, New York: Cambridge U.P., 1957.

Murphy-O'Connor, J. ed., *Paul and Qumran*, London: Chapman, 1968.

O'Neill, J. C., *The Recovery of Paul's Letter to the Galatians*, London: S.P.C.K., 1972.

Plummer, A., *A Commentary on St. Paul's First Epistle to the Thessalonians; A Commentary on St. Paul's Second Epistle to the Thessalonians; A Commentary on St. Paul's Epistle to the Philippians;* London: Scott, 1918, 1918, 1919.

———, *The Second Epistle of St. Paul to the Corinthians*, Edinburgh: Clark, 1925.

Ramsay, F. M., *A Historical Commentary on St. Paul's Epistles to the Corinthians* (1889), Grand Rapids: Eerdmans, 1966.

Reuss, J., *The Two Epistles to Timothy*, New York: Herder & Herder, 1969.

Reuss, J., Stöger, A., *The Epistle to Titus; The Epistle to Philemon*, New York, Herder & Herder, 1970.

Robertson, E. M., *The Epistles to the Corinthians*, New York: Macmillan, 1973.

Robertson, A., Plummer, A., *The First Epistle of St. Paul to the Corinthians*, Edinburgh: Clark, 1929[2].

Sanday, W., Headlam, A. C., *The Epistle to the Romans*, Edinburgh: Clark, 1905[5].

Schierse, F. J., *The Epistle to the Hebrews*, New York: Herder & Herder, 1969.

Schelkle, K., *The Second Epistle to the Corinthians*, New York: Herder & Herder, 1969.

Schnackenburg, R., *Baptism in the Thought of St. Paul*, A Study in Pauline Theology, N.Y.: Herder & Herder, 1964.

        , *The Church in the New Testament*, New York: Herder & Herder 1965.

Schürmann, H., Egenolf, H.-A., *The Epistles to the Thessalonians*, New York: Herder & Herder, 1969.

Scott, E. F., *The Pastoral Epistles*, New York: Harper & Row, 1948.

Tasker, R. V. G., *Second Epistle of St. Paul to the Corinthians*, London: Tyndale, 1971².

Walter, E., *The First Epistle to the Corinthians*, New York: Herder & Herder, 1971.

Westcott, B. F., *The Epistle to the Hebrews*, Grand Rapids: Eerdmans, 1950.

Wansbrough, H., *Theology in St. Paul,* Notre Dame, Ind.: Fides, 1968.

CHAPTER SEVEN

Beare, F. W., *The First Epistle of Peter*, Oxford: B. Blackwell, 1970³.

Best, E., *I. Peter*, London: Oliphants, 1971.

Bigg, C., *The Epistles of St. Peter and St. Jude*, Naperville, Ill.: Allenson, 1956.

Green, M., *Second Peter and Jude*, London: Tyndale Press, 1971².

Knoch, O., *The Epistle of St. James*, New York: Herder & Herder, 1969.

Moffatt, J., *The Catholic Epistles*, London: Hodder & Stoughton, 1928.

Reicke, B., *The Epistles of James, Peter, and Jude*, Garden City, N.Y.: Doubleday, 1964.

Schwank, B., Stöger, A., *The Two Epistles of St. Peter*, New York: Herder & Herder, 1969.

Selwyn, E. G., *The First Epistle of St. Peter*, London: Macmillan, 1946.

Stöger, A., *The Epistle of St. Jude*, New York: Herder & Herder, 1971.

CHAPTER EIGHT

Barrett, C. K., *The Gospel According to St. John*, New York: Seabury Press, 1955.

Beasley-Murray, G. R., *Highlights of the Book of Revelation*, Nashville: Broadman, 1972.

Bernard, J. H., McNeile, A. H., *The Gospel According to St. John*, 2 vols., Edinburgh; Clark, 1920.

Brooke, A. E., *The Johannine Epistles*, Naperville, Ill.: Allenson, 1957.

Brown, R. E., *The Gospel According to St. John*, 2 vols., Garden City, N.Y.: Doubleday, 1966, 1970.

Bruce, F. F., *The Epistles of John*, London: Old Tappan, 1971.

Bultmann, R., *The Gospel of John*, London: Blackwell, 1971.

Caird, G. B., *The Revelation of St. John the Divine*, New York: Harper & Row, 1966.

Charles, R. H., *The Revelation of St. John*, 2 vols., Edinburgh: Clark, 1920.

Dodd, C. H., *The Johannine Epistles*, New York: Harper & Row, 1946.

———, *The Interpretation of the Fourth Gospel*, New York: C.U.P., 1965.

———, *Historical Truth in the Fourth Gospel*, New York: Cambridge U.P., 1963.

Farrer, A., *The Revelation of St. John the Divine*, New York: Oxford U.P., 1964.

Feuillet, A., *Johannine Studies*, New York: Alba House, 1964.

———, *The Apocalypse*, New York: Alba House, 1965.

Fortna, R. T., *The Gospel of Signs*. A Reconstruction of the Narrative Source Underlying the Fourth Gospel, Cambridge: U.P., 1970.

Grossouw, W., *Revelation and Redemption*, London: Chapman, 1958.

Harrington, W. J., *Understanding the Apocalypse*, New York: Corpus, 1969.

Hoskyns, E. C., Davey, F. N., *The Fourth Gospel*, Naperville, Ill.: Allenson, 1956[2].

Hunter, A. M., ed., *The Gospel according to St. John*, New York: Oxford U.P., 1956.

Käsemann, E., *The Testament of Jesus*. A Study of the Gospel of John in the Light of Chapter 17, Philadelphia: Fortress, 1968.

Lightfoot, R. H., *St. John's Gospel: A Commentary*, New York: Oxford U.P., 1956.

Martyn, J. L., *History and Theology in the Fourth Gospel*, New York: Harper & Row, 1968.

Marsh, J., *The Gospel of St. John*, Baltimore: Penguin Books, 1968.

Minear, P. S., *I Saw a New Earth*, Introduction to the visions of the Apocalypse, Washington, D.C., Corpus Books, 1968.

Morris, L., *The Gospel According to John*, Grand Rapids: Eerdmans, 1971.

Richards, H., *What the Spirit Says to the Churches*, London: Chapman, 1967.

Richardson, A., *The Gospel according to St. John*, Naperville, Ill.: Allenson, 1959.

Rowley, H. H., *The Relevance of Apocalyptic*, New York: Association Press, 1964[3].

Schick, E., *The Revelation of St. John*, 2 vols., New York: Herder & Herder, 1970.

Schnackenburg, R., *The Gospel according to St. John* I, New York: Herder & Herder, 1968.

Stott, J. R. W., *Epistles of John*, London: Tyndale Press, 1971[2].

Swete, H. B., *The Apocalypse of St. John*, London: Macmillan, 1922[3].

Thüsing, W., *The Three Epistles of St. John*, New York: Herder & Herder, 1971.

Westcott, B. F., *The Gospel according to St. John*, London: Clarke, 1958[2].